NOT ALONE

1st SERGEANT
MICHAEL J. CONLEY

Not Alone
Published by Yawn's Publishing
198 North Street
Canton, GA 30114
www. yawnspublishing.com

Library of Congress Control Number: 2014958479

ISBN13: 978-1-940395-71-5 Hardcover
          978-1-940395-72-2 Paperback

Printed in the United States

EDITOR: MIMI FLYNT
Adviser: Ginger Polynipus
Technical Assistant: Noah Huggins

Dedication

After retiring from the military in 2008, I taught chemistry and physics in a small private school in Woodstock, Georgia, then took over the world history slot after Lt. Col. (Ret.) Joe Reinhardt passed on to Heaven's highest reward. The idea of writing this book started the day I stood alongside his hospice bed. My good friend Joe held my hand as he looked up at me very weakly. He told me I needed to tell my story while I had time to do so. I wondered to myself, "Did I hear him right? Is he talking to me?"

Another teacher from the school was also nearby, as well as his wife. Again, he spoke, this time with more insistence. "You need to tell your story before it's too late."

Col. Reinhardt had been writing a book entitled Iron Triangle, about his experiences in Vietnam, but it was not yet published. As I'd gotten to know him over the past year, we had discussed our similar experiences and reactions to events in Vietnam. Just three months before he'd told me, "I plan to be there for graduation, Michael." Yet, here we were together in his hospice room. He would pass on before noon the next day, during our actual graduation service. I had wanted to believe him those months before; on graduation day I believed he was present with us, in spirit. A few days later he was buried at the new Federal Veterans Cemetery in Canton, Georgia. He was one of the first to be buried there.

This book is dedicated to Lt. Col (Ret.) Joe Reinhardt, a Company Commander in the 25th Infantry in the Vietnam War.

Memorial and Honor

My book is in memory of Mr. Floyd Land, a veteran of World War II. While fighting in Italy, he was captured by the Italians and sent to a POW camp which was eventually overrun by the Germans. That Italian camp then became a German POW camp where he remained until he was liberated at the end of the war. Floyd became one of my best friends in life. He passed away the summer of 2008 and I miss him every day.

I also want to honor Mr. Willie Little, a Korean War veteran, who was wounded during the conflict and lost part of his left hand. For many years he has demonstrated daily courage. He has persevered in fighting Alzheimer's and Parkinson's diseases as they ravage his body, but not his spirit.

**Willie Little, Korean War veteran, on the left and
Floyd Land, World War II veteran and POW, on the right.
December 2003 at the home of Bill and Marie Little**

This book is also in memory of all those folks back home in southern Indiana, especially those in Lawrence County and the small neighborhood near Huron, who helped raise me. My mother was Laura Dumond; my stepfather was David Tolbert. Others influential in my life were Harold & Jean Tolbert, Jody & Norma Wade, Joe & Marsha Tolbert, my mother's Dumond cousins Everett, Pauline, Raymond & Francis Dumond; Grandma & Grandpa Byrd, Uncle Dutch &

Aunt Alice Carter, Uncle Archie & Aunt Annice Bex, Uncle Jesse & Aunt

Annie Chapman.

Tolbert and Dumond Reunion   October 12, 2013

Left to Right Bottom Row: Dylan Craig, dog Ellie, Jim Tolbert, and Patty Dumond Kidwell.

Row 2: Christopher Tolbert holding Gracie, his wife Danielle holding Faith, Martha Dumond.

Row 3: Alan Asbury, Sheila Waggoner McCormick, Roy Waggoner, Sue Tolbert Waggoner, Bertha Tolbert, Marcia Tolbert, Susan Dumond.

Row 4: Michael Joe Conley (author), Brad Tolbert, Jim Baxter, Karan Burton, Bradley Burton, Joe Tolbert.

Row 5: Becky's daughter Debbie Kinser, Becky Kern Kinser, Hollie Eugene Tolbert, Linda Walridge, Erika Robertson, Joyce Robertson & husband Donald, Roberta Kern Sherrill, Pam Tolbert, Mary Dumond, Randy Dumond.

Back Row: Bob Waggoner, William "Bill" Conley, Ben Robertson, Heather Robertson.

Picture made at annual reunion, descendants of Laurin & Helen Tolbert, Mary Frances & Raymond Dumond, Laura Ellen Dumond Conley Tolbert Boone at the Martin County Shelter.

To All Who Have Fought for Freedom

I dedicate this book to all who ever wore a pair of Silver Wings upon their chest or put on a CIB (Combat Infantry Badge). This book is for those Americans who never had a chance to tell their own stories because they gave the supreme sacrifice. Those of you who were able to return understand that it really hurts deep down to even think about those times. I will try to do my best to tell my story because I'm sure many of you have tried to tell the true story about your own life as a soldier and warrior, and know that it's very difficult to do.

My story begins in my childhood in rural Indiana. Events there shaped me as a person and developed in me the desire to join the U.S. Army in the first place. I became a Special Forces warrior as a very young man, and eventually an Army Ranger Instructor in later years. My road of life in the military spans across 42 years, from those early years in basic training, the 1967 race riots of Detroit, Michigan, Vietnam, the sands of Iraq, the mountains of Afghanistan. In each and every place I served as a soldier. I volunteered for it all.

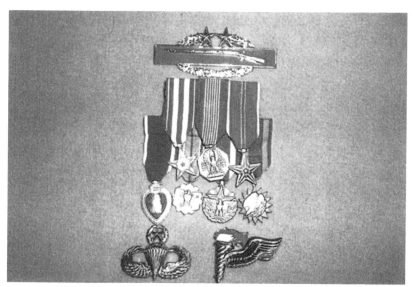

CIB (Combat Infantry Badge with Two Stars)

2 Silver Stars, 2 Soldier's Medals, 2 Bronze Stars, one With Valor

Purple Heart, Joint Services Achievement Medal, Meritorious Service Medal

Air Medal, Jump Master Wings, and Path Finder Badge

Time Line of My Life

1948 Born in Lawrence County, Indiana

1954 Began 1st Grade at Huron Community School

1958 Little brother Clifford killed

1959 Huron Community School burned to the ground

1960 Williams Community School

1962 Returned to the Rebuilt Huron Community School

1964 Mitchell Consolidated High School

1966 High School Graduation

1966 October: Joined the U. S. Army

1967 February: Graduated from Basic Training

1967 April: Graduated from AIT

1967 May: Graduated from Jump School

1967 August: Sent into the Detroit, Michigan, Race Riots

1967 September: Assigned: 101st Airborne Division

1967 November: Orders: Vietnam, 1st Tour

1968 Tet Offensive - Iron Triangle - Central Highlands - Hue

1968 Going Home Butch Dorsett KIA, I Got Married

1969 Reassigned: Special Forces, Fort Bragg, NC

1969 Assigned: Co. B, 3rd Bn., 11th Special Forces Group

1969 Orders: Hamburger Hill, Vietnam 2nd Tour

1972 Assigned: Co. D, Rangers, Indiana National Guard

1975 Assigned: 2nd Ranger Co., 75th Rangers - Instructor

1984 Assigned: Marine Corps Reserves Desert Phase Survival - Instructor

1996 Assigned: Co. H, LRSU, Georgia National Guard (Airborne)

1999 Assigned: RTI, Georgia National Guard – Instructor

2002 Assigned: Co. A, 1st Bn. (Mechanized), 121st Infantry, BCT

2004 Assigned: Republic of Georgia, NCOIC - American Embassy

2005 Assigned: C Co., 121st Infantry (Mechanized): Field 1st Sgt.

2006 Assigned: 2nd Mitt Team, Iraq, 48th BCT: Field 1st Sgt.

2007 Assigned: Army Active Reserve Unit, Fort Gillem, GA

2008 Assigned: Reserve Unit, Fort Gillem, GA - Retired

Contents

Foreword — 1

The Early Years — 5

Basic Training, 1966: Fort Knox, Kentucky — 31

March 1967: Aberdeen Proving Grounds — 41

Jump School: Fort Benning, Georgia — 46

The 82nd Airborne Div., Fort Bragg, North Carolina — 61

The Detroit Race Riots, 1967 — 65

Return to Fort Bragg: The 82nd Airborne — 68

Volunteers Needed,
The 101st Airborne Division, Fort Campbell, Kentucky — 50

November 1967, Heading for Vietnam — 75

Welcome to Vietnam! Digging in — 80

Angels Among Us — 95

Christmas Day, 1967 — 101

May, 1968: Iron Triangle and a Field Grade Promotion — 105

The Central Highlands — 122

Rock Monkeys — 126

The Purple Heart: 20th of August 1968 — 133

Getting Ready for the A Shau:
"PFC Dorsett Reporting, Sergeant" — 140

Into the A Shau Valley: 16th –17th September — 154

Along the Laotian Border: October 1968 — 167

Orders: Head for Home!   172

Company B, 3rd Battalion, 11th Special Forces Group,
Airborne, Special Forces Tab   181

Getting Ready to Take Hamburger Hill, 5th – 9th of May 191

Going Up Hamburger Hill, 8th – 24th of May, 1969   196

Indiana National Guard, Muncie, Indiana
Co. D Rangers, Det. 1, 151st Airborne Infantry   215

Ranger School: 21st of October 1973 –
10th of March 1974   222

Finishing Up Ranger School: Camp Rutter 1974   244

Jeffersonville & the Steamboat Days   267

Company B, 3rd Battalion, 11th Special Forces Group   271

United States Marine Corps (Reserve), 1984 – 1987   276

Company H LRSU, Georgia National Guard, 1997-1999 280

Going to the Republic of Georgia in 2004,
Bringing Spotty Home   292

My Last Overseas Mission   319

The Rest is History: Medevac to Baghdad   348

National Personnel Record Center:
US Decorations and Badges   375

Forward

I tried so hard to be a good father and husband, but the screams, the sounds of war, my dreams, wouldn't leave me alone. After Vietnam, I never slept well again. The best I can do is to tell about my life as a soldier and warrior.

I asked two special ladies to help me write this book. Ginger Polynipus published a book about her grandfather's experiences fighting in World War II; she provided advice about publishing. Mimi Flynt and I first became friends during school teaching days in Macon, Georgia at the alternative school; later we'd resume our friendship as teacher buddies in several small private schools in northeast Georgia. After a hiatus of several years, we resumed our teaching relationship at Chattahoochee Technical College, in the foothills of Georgia's Blue Ridge Mountains. We have been fast friends for nearly 20 years. She initially suggested that I write about my military experiences as a way to deal with my PTSD and invasive dreams. From that humble beginning, she edited my recollections into a cohesive, readable format, and made suggestions regarding the inclusion and placement of military memorabilia, my C-ration postcards and pictures. We've shared much laughter, somber moments and sometimes even tears as I've recounted these memories. Noah Huggins provided untold expertise regarding formatting, computer retrieval and technical assistance. Without his very capable abilities, time and dedication, this book would never have been produced.

I tried my best to tell my story the way it happened. This is about my life, the people who molded my life, and those who helped me become the man I am today. I truly believe that my early childhood days in southern Indiana, in the very small communities of Huron and Williams, shaped the direction my life would go. Those days influenced why I chose to become a warrior in the United States Army.

I spent 42 years serving my country from 1966 through 2008, as a paratrooper, a Senior Jump Master, and a Path Finder. I have served as a Green Beret, a Ranger, and a Ranger Instructor with the Army National Guard, in the Army Reserves and the Marines Corps Reserves.

My life as a soldier really began in Vietnam. I turned eighteen in October 1967, completed Basic Training and landed in Vietnam on the 8th of December 1967. I would eventually pull a second tour in Vietnam serving in Bravo Company, 3rd Battalion, going back in with the elite 11th Special Forces Group. Many years later, in 2004, I began to consider wrapping up my career. I went the Republic of Georgia as a Senior Operations NCO working for the Ministry of Defense and for the U.S. European Command Headquarters. My last tours were in 2006 in the deserts of Iraq and the mountains of Afghanistan. I served in LRRP (Long Range Recon Patrols) and LRSU (Long Range Surveillance Units) and in the U. S. Marine Corps as a stinger gunner and ammunition specialist. Finally, at the ripe age of 60 I retired. During all those conflicts I witnessed many disturbing events, as well as survived traumatic events in my personal life. I don't dream about any of that. I only dream about those awful days and nights from my tours in Vietnam.

Growing up was a long and lonely road for me, with trials and tribulations that would haunt anybody. Those early memories are overshadowed by moments in between, when my life was blessed by some wonderful people who somewhat eased my memories of horrific scenes I witnessed. However, my nightmares are still consumed with reoccurring memories of my tours in the Vietnam jungle, full of screams, mosquitoes, ants and leeches; and those heart-rending soldiers' pleas, "Help me, help me, please don't leave me here, Sarge!" that I hear every night, like a movie that was recorded for all to see. Unfortunately, it's one that can't be edited. It's set to automatically rewind in my mind, over and over again.

When I walked out of that Vietnamese jungle for the very last time, I promised myself and the boys I left behind: those rotting in fields, jungles, mountains passes and gaps, and yes, to those who did make it home, whether physically or in body bags. I made a promise to each and every one. I would do everything in my power to help any new guys going in, to give them a fighting chance of getting out alive to return back home to America and their loved ones.

I went into Vietnam with the famed 101st Airborne Division, 2nd Battalion, 506th Airborne Infantry. We were known as the "Currahee," an Indian word which means "those who stand alone." Training for the 101st Airborne initially began when America became involved in World War II and took place on Currahee Mountain in north Georgia, near Dahlonega, where gold was discovered in the late 1800's. The 101st Airborne became famous and were highly decorated after they fought the Germans at the Battle of the Bulge.

After Vietnam, I went on to serve with the elite Special Forces and the Army Rangers. I also served with the 82nd Airborne Division, Company D, Rangers, in Muncie, Indiana, as well as with Company H, LRSU, in Newnan, Georgia, in the Georgia National Guard. Other service was with both the U.S. Marine Corps Reserves and the U.S. Army Reserves. Tours of duty spanned from October 1966 to the end of my road in October

2008. I finished up as an instructor to Army National Guardsmen and Reservists, our "citizen soldiers," preparing them for their turn in Iraq or Afghanistan. These soldiers have been called to do something no other generation of American men had been asked to do: fight in the war on terrorism. They are called to fight in faraway countries and new environments, in the highlands and mountains of Afghanistan and the sands of Iraq. My last three years I instructed troops in small unit tactics, urban warfare and mountain training with the Army Reserves at Fort Gillem, Georgia.

The Early Years

Everyone's early childhood has an impact on the person they become. My early years were spent in small communities of southern Indiana, respectively, Huron and Williams, and later in the town of Mitchell. Collectively, experiences in each locale impacted my life. The effects of those early days constitute the reasons why I became a warrior. Most of what I now know about my youngest years has been told to me by family and friends.

My mother, Laura Ellen Dumond, was born in late summer 1928, right before the stock market crash. She was raised during the Great Depression near the Hoosier National Forest in a very small area called Huron. Her family was quite poor. In those days, school ended after the 11th grade. Consequently, when she finished Huron High School, she was just 16, but being industrious, she found a job in nearby Bedford cleaning houses. Then she was approached by the local mail carrier, Robert Conley, who enlisted her to help him care for his wife Ida.

Bob Conley was very highly respected in Bedford and had lived there for quite a number of years. He was born in late fall 1888 and raised near an Apache Indian reservation, close to present-day Fort Sill, Oklahoma. He served in World War I with the U. S. Navy aboard a submarine. After he returned home, he joined the local American Legion and was active with them. Although most of the men in his family built brick homes during and after the Depression, he became the local mailman. Soon after Laura began working for the Conleys, Ida was diagnosed with cancer and became seriously ill. Consequently, Bob asked Laura to work full time caring for her and to move into their home as his wife's live-in caretaker. She remained there for approximately two years, until Ida's death.

Robert Harrison Conley, astride Soap Suds   Fall 1948Crane, Indiana

Shortly afterwards, by the summer of 1946, Bob Conley and Laura were married. They took a trip out west to Wyoming, and then returned to live in Bedford. My father resumed his job as the mailman and my mother "kept house." Rather quickly, three children entered the picture. First was William Harrison called "Bill," born in July 1947; fifteen months later I arrived in October 1948. By this time my mother was 20 and my father, 56. Less than two years later, baby brother Clifford Dean arrived in May 1950. Shortly after Clifford's birth, our father left the home. Laura was left with three very young children: infant Clifford, me a rambunctious nearly two, and Bill, just barely three.

Basically, none of Laura's immediate relatives lived close enough to help her. She reasoned that Bill as "big brother" could be enticed to help her care for Baby Clifford; consequently, she arranged for me to go live with relatives back in Huron. Over the next few years, my father would periodically send Mother some money to help with bills; by 1952, they were divorced. Although my father remarried, he soon was hospitalized in the Veteran's Hospital in Indianapolis where he died in 1954. Most of this information I learned from Aunt Peggy Ritchison, one of my Conley aunts. Her father was my father's youngest brother, Uncle Pat. I'd returned to visit folks in Indiana in 2005 after a tour in Iraq. I became close to Uncle Pat's daughters after my second tour in Vietnam when I lived with him for a while.

On the left, Connie with her husband, Dr. Reid Crosby in front of her; Peggy Ritchison in the middle; Hallie with husband Buck Colter in front wearing the cowboy hat. Made at the Conley reunion in Mitchell, Indiana

After my father died, Mother saw that as her opportunity to move closer to family and friends in Williams and Huron. She sold our house and we moved to a small house we rented which is the first home I actually remember living in, five miles out of Huron, just a little past the Fairview Church of Christ on King's Ridge. Shortly after, Mother was able to purchase a 40-acre farm from her brother Franklin, whom we called Uncle "Dago." Mother was very industrious, periodically picking up paying jobs nearby. I remember one was in Orleans in an RCA television factory. She was also kept busy at home, canning food and making homemade quilts and blankets. Everyone in our community worked very hard.

Rather quickly after we moved back to Huron, Mother married David Tolbert, a returned Korean War veteran. After their marriage, her family thought, "They're a family, again," so I was at home living with my mother, my brothers Bill and Clifford, and David, our stepfather. I feel sure my mother expected that with David Tolbert in our household we would become an intact family, with traditional roles of mother, father and children. Perhaps David saw an opportunity, since my mother was young and well thought of there. He got a ready-made family with us boys as his three stepchildren. I truly believe David Tolbert loved us boys. He tried to be a father to all of us.

Physically, he was a large man, weighing approximately 230 pounds, and was quite strong. I will always believe with all my heart that David Tolbert loved us boys and intended to treat each one of us as his own children. I will give him credit for being a hard worker, and I believe he loved us in his own way, but life for all of us in those days was very hard. David tried to be a farmer, in addition to holding down a "day job" at Carpenter's Bodyworks in Mitchell. Every workday he would have worked a full shift, only to come home to more work needing to be done on the farm. Many's the day that it wasn't until after 9 or 10 in the evening before he'd be able to come inside to rest. This was our way of life for everyone who lived around there. Each person, including children, worked very hard daily with assigned chores. The good thing about our way of life is that every neighbor was a friend who would help anyone else out in time of need.

Each year as fall approached, days and nights began to get cooler, so mother would pile more quilts on top of us boys. My brothers and I all slept in one bed in an unheated bedroom, our only heat from a potbellied wood stove in the front room or the wood stove where Mother cooked in the kitchen. I remember we had a fire constantly going to some degree in the potbellied stove from late October to early March. Bill, as the oldest, was responsible for keeping all the firewood cut or busted up and my job was to split it into smaller pieces. My job was to carry this wood to the house and stack it up, bringing it in when needed. The only rooms where you could depend on being warm were the living room or the kitchen.

One winter it got so cold in our storeroom inside the house that some peaches Mother had canned the previous summer froze in their jars. We found busted and cracked jars in the storeroom, with juice oozing out everywhere. I must say, those peaches did not go to waste! We scraped them up into a very large bowl and ate them right up. I know that might sound silly now, but at that time, I do not believe anyone gave it a thought. I remember often looking out our bedroom window of a winter morning and seeing a line of frozen snow stacked up on our window panes.

Another regular job for all three of us boys was hauling or carrying water to the house from the spring down the hill from the house. Any water Mother needed for washing or cleaning had to be hauled by Bill, Clifford and me back to the house. Mother even helped us sometimes, trecking down the hill with us to help carry water back. One good result of Mother marrying David was he hired a company to come out and dig us a well. They chose a spot near the house, beneath our big old hickory tree. Having water closer by was good, but we still had to carry buckets into the house.

For us to take a bath once a week was another job in itself. As I've said before, we had to draw the water from the well, then carry it into the house. In winter, mother heated water up on our wood stove in the kitchen. She would set out a long aluminum tub which some people refer to as a "Saturday night special." As the water heated, we dipped it up with a pitcher or pot to carry over to our tub. We had to take care to not walk too fast, to keep from sloshing it out all over ourselves and on the floor. Filling that tub took a lot of water and for sure, was a whole lot of hard work. Now in summer, things were a lot easier. We would just draw up water from the well, then pour it into a bucket and haul it to a big cauldron set over an open fire Mother built outside. By full summer, Mother would simply place our washtub out on our back deck and we'd fill it half full with water. Then we let the sun do the work; instead of sun tea, we had sun bathwater! At dusk we'd all get our baths. To say the least, we got more baths in summertime, but of course, that's when we got the dirtiest. At least in winter, we did get bathed at least once a week. Bill, as the oldest brother, got in the washtub first. I was next, into that same bath water, and Clifford got in last.

We had plenty of chores around the farm to keep us all more than busy. Mother and David always had a garden going. If we ate it, we grew it. Lots of potatoes, corn, tomatoes and green beans. In early spring they'd plant a variety of lettuces, onions, and radishes. When the crops began coming in, Mother was kept super busy canning whatever was at its peak, fruits and vegetables, we also combed the country side for apples and in the fall we picked up persimmons to make persimmons puddings which was a real treat to all of us. As well as still having to prepare whatever we would eat for meals.

Our stepfather fixed up a shelter for us to store potatoes so we could eat them throughout our long winters. First, we covered a place on the ground with hay and then lay down the potatoes, being sure none touched each other. David would shovel more dirt on top of the potatoes, then we boys would lay in more hay, then more potatoes, and he'd add in a layer of dirt; we continued this until we ran out of potatoes. When we finished, he covered everything with a large tarpaulin and weighed it down with rocks.

Whatever needed to be done to keep our little farm running fell to each one of us to do our fair share. Life for us Conley boys did change considerably, in many ways – some good, others not so good - when David Tolbert entered our family. Quickly, we amassed much more on our farm. We acquired hogs and baby pigs, sheep, even goats. Of course we already had cows, which we all learned how to milk a cow in an early age.

I remember one time in particular, when Mother and David drove over to Williams in the pickup truck with a rack on it. They returned with a small Indian pony named Thunder in the back of it. I thought he looked like the one Little Joe Cartwright rode on Bonanza. It seems like I was the only one who ever rode him much, but I really loved that little horse. Many times I imagined I was back in the days of the Wild West. The picture below, made in May 1958, shows me on the left dressed like the ranch hand and cowboy I thought I was! Older brother Bill is in the middle and brother Clifford is on the right. The picture hanging on the wall behind me and to the upper left is of our Dad astride his favorite horse, Soap Suds.

David Tolbert bought some sheep and we loved feeding the little ones.

**Clifford and Joe feeding the lambs
May 1958 Bill is up on the back porch.**

Soon after this picture we moved from the house on 40 acres to a bigger farm near the Old William's, Brayntsville road next to Raymond Bex and the Port William's Church of Christ.

We boys were kept busy with daily chores centered on caring for the myriad animals on our farm, as well as doing everything that had to be done to keep the farm running. Each school day we boys rode the school bus to and from school. One specific day we'd ridden home from Huron School; Bill and I immediately set to doing chores. Clifford had always been a rather sickly child, so he went directly to the house. By the evening of April 2, 1959, our little brother Clifford was dead, from an accidental shooting while in our parents' bedroom. He was just one month shy of being 9 years old.

Understandably, family dynamics changed after Clifford's death. Now that the youngest child was gone, my place in the family moved from middle child to youngest, seriously altering other behaviors. Also, I missed my younger brother so much, but could not express my grief in words; I just knew I could not remain there, in the same house where my little brother had died.

Within just a few weeks I was gone. First, I went to my grandma's brother, Uncle Jesse and his wife, Annie Chapman. They were actually my great-uncle and aunt, quite up in years, but were instrumental in a lot of my upbringing. I think I told myself I was going there to help them out since Uncle Jesse had gotten hurt working up at Carpenter's in Mitchell. In reality, they helped me out much more. I especially loved living down at Uncle Jesse's; I even had my "own bed" to sleep in. Uncle Jesse and I hunted together in the woods and went to the White River to fish with our trot (our pronunciation of "trout") lines.

I stayed a few months there, and then moseyed on over to Grandma and Grandpa Byrd's house for the summer since

Grandma wanted me to help her with her garden. She would work in the garden and sing "While the Dew is Still on the roses" and she also sang the "Lilly of the Valley". One particular afternoon Grandpa was enjoying rocking in his favorite chair on the front porch. I sat nearby on the steps, just enjoying being near him, and at Grandmas.

I had been attending school in the Williams community, playing on their baseball and basketball teams after the Huron School had burned down. That summer before school started Mother and I had had a very long, heart-to-heart talk. She added, "The Huron Community School is being rebuilt and is almost finished," so I could go to school once again in my home community with my best friends. For the previous two years I'd had to go to school in Williams because our school in Huron had burnt down. Although I had made friends over in Williams, my best friends, the boys I liked best, lived at Huron. After listening to her reasoning, I agreed to go back to Huron and I would be entering 9th grade. Those years at Huron School were good ones as I began to mature into a young man. I had really missed being with friends I'd started school with, best friends such as Butch Dorsett, Bobby Tolbert, Robert Ritchison and Johnny Doan, and Lanny Williams.

I also claimed a couple of girls as friends, too. I thought Bonnie Miller was so pretty, no matter what she was doing; when we put up hay on her father's farm, she drove the tractor. Connie King and her sister were related to the Tolberts and sometimes came over to visit Jeane and Harold Tolbert. They were just easy to talk to. I claimed Tony Baker and her brother Mike as my friends; their daddy preached sometimes down at Port Williams. All those friends from Huron School would end up being some of the closest friends I would ever have for the rest of my life. Those schooldays remain in my heart as special days. I have never forgotten what it was like to be poor and cold, but I have always been able to find love from others wherever I've gone. Those good years at Huron Community School hold a very special place in my heart. As well, I have often thought the teachers there were some of the best in the whole world. I did not know it then, but I must have received a better education than I thought possible. Later in life, I would attend some very nice colleges and universities and was able to make pretty good grades, even excelling in some classes. Although I was not good with English and always had a difficult time spelling, somehow I learned how to compensate.

Although I returned home to begin 9th grade, my soul was restless. I sincerely tried to stay there with Mother and our family, but eventually I would feel constrained, like I was caught in a trap. I'd bolt off again, going back to Uncle Jesse's, Aunt Alice's or Grandma Byrd's. There was always someone willing for me to come do some work for them and they'd offer me a place to stay in return. I would continue to live in various households throughout my high school days until graduation, until I left to join the U.S. Army.

Although Uncle Jesse was already up in years when I went to live with him, nevertheless, he never missed a beat as far as I was concerned. He took me under his wing, teaching me how to shoot and set rabbit snares. He knew our woods like the back of his hand and how to live off the land, especially where to find the biggest mushrooms in our neck of the woods! I would go with him to plant corn down in the bottom land along the banks of Hopper Creek. Sometimes we would walk over to the river and put in a trot line (that's how we pronounced "trout") to fish for a day or two. I killed my first rabbit with Uncle Jesse Chapman. He taught me to be watchful, to listen for sounds that came from the environment. I learned to recognize what sounds specific animals make and how sounds can change, depending on weather conditions and seasons. These experiences taught me to observe, think and make predictions. During the summer months I would go on over to Grandma Byrd's to help her put in a garden and help Grandpa put in his trot lines. Often while I'd be there, my cousins Frankie and Jimmy Dumond might come to stay for two or three weeks. We were certainly growing boys and ate everything Grandma could cook! We were kept busy with plenty of chores and cutting wood. Grandma Byrd cooked down in a little house with wood in the summer time. She did a lot of canning and the little house would always have something good to eat in it if a small boy got hungry before dinner.

Aunt Alice, my mother's sister and her husband, Uncle Dutch Carter. They took me to Fairview Church of Christ down near Huron. Their home was one in which I stayed often.

Many's the time Frankie, Little Jimmy and I would go to the river with Grandpa to gather shells. We would get up before daylight, eat a good country breakfast with eggs, fried potatoes, sausage, homemade apple butter, and as many of Grandma's biscuits with "sawmill gravy" we could stuff in ourselves! Then we'd all make our way down to the White River and pile into Grandpa's boat. He'd get his motor running and away we would go. We might travel a mile or two and then it would be time for us to slip over the side of the boat into that cold river water. Of course we'd been barefoot when we left the house; it was summertime! No child in his right mind would put on shoes unless we were going to church! We'd begin to feel around in the mud and silt with our toes or even lean over into the river, trying to find mussels mired on the river bottom. Meanwhile, Grandpa arranged gunny sacks alongside the inner walls, as we chucked the shells into the boat. He was kept busy moving the sacks around as we filled them up. We'd work like this until the boat was so full the sides were barely above the water line. Then, as we held onto the sides of the boat, Grandpa would slowly maneuver us back to the bank. We all had to wrestle those gunny sacks of shells up a long steep bank, then dump them into a vat where they'd cook 'til they opened up, showing off all their beauty. We'd clean them out so Grandpa could take the shells down to Shoals and sell them. They'd be hauled to Japan to be made into buttons. We saved the "meat" from the shells for fish bait or we'd sell it to neighbors. I'd spend my whole summer doing whatever had to be done. When it was time to start school, I might go back home and then about Christmas time I would go over to Uncle Jesse's Sometimes, things would have maybe straightened themselves out at home, but I still wandered back and forth, from Mother's, to Uncle Jesse's, to Grandma Byrd's. In those early years I never ever really got over my little brother dyeing.

That first Christmas after Clifford died Uncle Jesse got me a 22-rifle made by Sears; he either traded something for it or bought it outright. It was a single shot rifle with a small roller block on top to kick out the shells. Another neighbor, Raymond Dumond, a first cousin to my mother, had some rabbit dogs, so Uncle Jesse and David and I often went to Raymond's place to run his dogs for rabbits. First, Raymond would turn the dogs loose; we'd follow them down through the corn fields and pastures, around brush piles where they had cut up trees into firewood. Finally, the dogs would hit a trail, circle back around and run a rabbit back where we waited. As soon as whatever was running, squirrels or rabbits, we'd shoot. At first, they "let" me shoot. But it wasn't long before I got good or so I thought, so I had as much a chance as they did of getting whatever was running. Over the next few years I learned how to shoot so well that I only needed one bullet to get whatever I was aiming for. After we had a mess of 'em, we'd clean and dress 'em, them take 'em up to the house and make stew, or fry 'em up for breakfast.

Many years later as a science teacher in a school for special students in Woodstock, Georgia, I would take my classes outside, into the woods behind the school, to teach them about nature. I taught them how to build fires with flint and steel, how to pitch tents and when it was necessary to boil water to make it safe to drink. We would collect leaves from different trees to identify them, as well as springtime flowers. One cold winter day, just for the fun of it, I took the students outside to show them what a rabbit track looked like in the snow. Just for fun, I told them I'd set a rabbit snare and if we were lucky, we might actually catch a rabbit! I baited it with a small piece of apple core. I knew if a rabbit tried to get the apple off, he would be caught. Later I went outside to check on it, but nothing was in the trap yet. I had told my students, "We'll leave it out for the night and check it when we get to school tomorrow."

As soon as I arrived the next morning, two students came running toward me in the parking lot. One of them was yelling at the top of her lungs, "You caught one! You caught one!"

I thought, "Oh, my God! I hope we didn't catch somebody's pet!"

Together we walked behind the school building. I was certainly wondering what exactly we would find. Immediately, I saw a rabbit hanging four feet off the ground, frozen solid. We returned to my classroom and I gathered what I'd need to "dress" him. I took all my students outside, explaining every step of what I had to do, what was necessary to clean and dress this rabbit, and why. Then, I herded all the students back inside. I arranged for someone to cover my class while I drove to the nearby Publix to get potatoes and carrots. I returned to make rabbit stew in my chemistry lab! While the stew simmered, we sat around that two-burner electric hotplate that I used and talked about how to survive in the wild, what one must do in a survival situation. All the students and teachers got to sample my rabbit stew and I got rave reviews!

I know some people might think "dressing a rabbit" at school to be a little strange, but I was brought up in hard times. Those life lessons have come in handy throughout my life. In Vietnam my ambush team would lay in wait for the enemy to come down a mountain trail or along a jungle trail, just like I used to lie in wait for a rabbit. Also, I knew I'd never go hungry, since I'd learned many lessons from Uncle Jesse about foraging for food and living off the land, wherever that land might be. I learned many lessons from so many good men. Everyone taught me something.

Some of my best experiences were over at Aunt Alice and Uncle Dutch Carter's home. I loved them both dearly. They showed me a lot of love and what it felt like to be in a good loving home. They also made sure I went to church. Many evenings we'd go over to the church and walk inside, just sit there, soaking up the spirit. They taught me about protective angels who would be instrumental in many life-altering experiences I'd have in years to come. It's on behalf of their love and their instruction to me about angels that I named my book Not Alone.

When it came to learning how to work, it was my Uncle Archie Bex who taught me many skills I've used all my life. He let me work with him and stay at their house. He taught me how to work in fields and put up hay, to drive a tractor, run a chain saw and dig post holes for a fence. I even worked alongside him in his raspberry patch; we picked many a raspberry to sell. I'm sure I ate a belly-full share of my own!

My grandparents were exceptional people. You would never have known that Grandpa Byrd was not my grandpa by blood. Grandma Byrd's first husband, my mother's father, died when Grandma was expecting my mother. By the time I came along, the man I knew as Grandpa had been married to my grandma for a long time. Every day both of them let me know they loved me, and loved me lots. They worked hard and taught me many lessons, especially lessons about the power of love.

Living in and growing up in southern Indiana provided great experiences for me. Grandpa was the one who really taught me how to fish. We would work for a night or two on getting our trot lines ready. Then, early of a morning while the fog was still hanging out on the river, we'd head out toward Chase Riffle. Grandpa always knew where the best places were to put our lines in. First, we'd pile everything in the boat, climb in ourselves, and head out. After we were out in the water good, he'd run the motor and let me take the fish off the trot lines. We'd catch catfish, what we called a "flathead" catfish, some perch, and one we called a "buffalo." Those boyhood days were like living in a dream. I have carried those memories of childhood throughout life. I know in my heart I had some hard years growing up, but my relatives filled my life with love. I matured into a young man who understood that hard work and love will overcome heartache.

My total existence wasn't taken up with work. I certainly had plenty of time for fishing and hunting! Also, many's the time I'd just look off into the distance and ponder about things far away. I had an itch that couldn't get scratched living in rural southern Indiana. I wanted to explore, see the world beyond my limited scope. Underneath my senior picture in the high school yearbook was the caption, "Most likely to wander." Boy, somebody accurately predicted my future!

I attended the Williams Community School (grades 1-12) during 7th and 8th grades, returning to the rebuilt Huron Community School as I began 9th grade and finished the 10th grade. I tried out for and played on both baseball and basketball teams. At the end of that year our school was closed because the county decided to close eight community schools and consolidate their students into two larger schools. My classmates and I were bussed to Mitchell for our last two years of high school. I tried out for their basketball team, but I didn't make the cut. Instead, I shifted gears and went out for track and cross country, where I excelled. I would race the mile and two-mile runs.

In summer I continued to run, just for the fun of it. It was very hilly where we lived and I enjoyed running up Pierce Hill, trying to see how fast I could run up it, even on Sunday mornings. Then, I'd run down the hill and on to Fairview Church. Since I generally lived at Grandma Byrd's in the summer, I would run up to the low gap, walk back down, turn around and just sprint back up the gap again. I might do this ten times or more in one afternoon. My lungs would hurt and my legs would get cramps, yet I loved the feeling running gave me. Later, when I saw the movie "Forest Gump" I laughed because that is how I felt. "Run, Forest, Run." Although I was good, I was certainly not the fastest runner on my track team and there were other runners across the entire state of Indiana much faster than I. For me, it was just a joy to run. It was also a time when I could talk to God or simply get off by myself mentally into my own little world. I never missed a track meet or a practice. I loved to feel the wind, the cool air against my face early in the morning or in the cool of a late afternoon.

I have many different feelings about my childhood days. Aunt Alice and Uncle Dutch took me to church at Fairview Church of Christ; they showed me love and a gentle way of life. Their daughter, Ida Rose Carter showed me friendship; she, her husband and children have always treated me just like I was part of their family. My mother's side of the family gave me places to live and later in life, I would attend their family reunions. The Tolberts, my stepfather's side of the family, were good, honest, hardworking people who loved their country. They helped me when I grew older, showing themselves to be another family I could also call my own. I guess, in a way, it took that whole neighborhood to help me grow up. In retrospect, I have come to realize I was more than a hand full when I was young; I needed the help of each and every one to get myself grown up.

High school was simply something I had to finish. I did alright and didn't fail anything. Most of my energy was spent doing lots of hard work on somebody's farm. I didn't really date, just hung out with friends, raced cars or went swimming. Often in

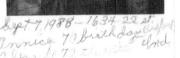

Sept. 7, 1988 — 1634 22 st.
Bonnie 70 birthday... and
...72 ...

Harold & Jean Talbert
and my mother 2001 Oct. 20

Joe & Marcia Talbert
Oct. 1999
Martin County ...

summer, after putting up hay or building a fence, we'd all go down to the quarries to swim. The quarry hole near Mitchell was near where my best friend, Butch Dorsett, lived. I dearly loved his grandmother. When I'd spend the night at his house, we'd go visit her. To me she was "my" Granny Carroll. I thought she was the Next-to-the-Best Granny in the whole world and I loved her almost as much as I loved my own. Granny Carroll taught Butch and me how to swim in the big pond. Then, when we got bigger, we moved on to swim in the quarry holes. The Mitchell quarry hole was surrounded by huge rocks. Every ten feet or so, they would back up about five feet and rise up another eight to ten feet. The first time I heard the word "chicken" in a derogatory way was when somebody yelled it to see who was brave enough, or stupid enough, to climb all the way up to the highest ledge, jump or dive off, out into the wild blue yonder, straight down into that cold, deep water.

One day in the 11th grade, while riding to high school on the county bus, we passed a small gas station. There sat the prettiest car I thought I had ever seen! Eventually, I bought it from Butch's dad, Sonny. It was a '56 Ford Crown Victoria with a 312 Thunderbird engine under the hood. This car was fast! I would drag race it up and down the highway, against '56 and '57 Chevy's, around some very curvy roads through the Martin County Forest, down to the ice cream shop in Shoals. Many times I listened to "Thunder Road" as it played on the radio while we raced from Tackett's Gas Station to Shoals and back.

During my senior year I was trying to figure out what I wanted to do with my life after graduation. The only place to really work would be at some nearby mills or at Carpenter's. I wanted something different for myself. I was just itching to get out of Mitchell and see the world. One night in late November 1965, while driving someplace, my car radio was tuned to a Louisville, Kentucky, station. The announcer began talking about American boys fighting in Vietnam, specifically those in the 1st Calvary Division in the Ia Drang Valley. Three days later our community received word that Paul Tolbert, my stepfather's brother, had been killed in Vietnam. I realized that he'd been right there in the Ia Drang Valley with the 1st Cavalry Division. I thought, "This is a small world. I heard them talking about that place on the radio just the other night."

Paul was the first man I'd known of who was killed in Vietnam. His body was accompanied home by soldiers who stood guard over his casket. I observed how those soldiers held themselves; I listened to them talk about him, as they told our family and friends, "He was brave." I also observed how neighbors reacted when they came to pay their respect to his family, telling his parents how proud they were that he'd served his country. After the funeral, I began to think seriously about joining the Army. Right before Christmas, coming home from a date with Sharon Davis, I was again listening to my car radio when "Green Beret" by Staff Sgt. Barry Saddler began to play. The lyrics, "Fighting soldiers from the sky …," really spoke to me. I think that's the moment I decided to become a paratrooper.

I began to dream that I could jump out of an airplane. I told myself, "I can be one of America's best. I can be good enough to put silver wings on my chest."

Then and there, I locked onto that dream. As soon as I graduated high school, I decided I would join the army and become a paratrooper. I would leave the hills I loved in southern Indiana, go out into the world and prove to everyone that I could do what it took to be a Green Beret paratrooper!

"Green Beret"
written by SSgt. Barry Saddler

Fighting soldiers from the sky
Fearless men who jump and die
Men who mean just what they say
The brave men of the Green Beret
Silver wings upon their chest
These are men, America's best
One hundred men we'll test today.

But only three win the Green Beret
Trained to live, off nature's land
Trained in combat, hand to hand
Men who fight by night and day
Courage deep, from the Green Beret
Silver wings upon their chest
These are men, America's best
One hundred men we'll test today
But only three win the Green Beret

Back at home a young wife waits
Her Green Beret has met his fate
He has died for those oppressed
leaving her this last request

Put silver wings on my son's chest
Make him one of America's best
He'll be a man they'll test one day
Have him win the Green Beret

All five of my stepfather's brothers had served either on active duty or with the Indiana National Guard. When Mother married David, everyone began to call me "Little Joe," since David's youngest brother was named Joe. That nickname has followed me my whole life, since many relatives still call me Little Joe or just Joe. I knew some of David Tolbert's military things were stored in the old smokehouse at my mother's house. After Paul's funeral I went out to look in the smokehouse, rambled around in the smokehouse until I found what I was hunting. I found a military handbook which I thumbed through, as well as picked up and handled a few pieces of small gear. Soon I be-came obsessed with anything to do with wars: the American Civil War, World Wars I and II, Korea. For some reason World War II especially fascinated me. I was driven to find every detail written about the D-Day Invasion. I found a book entitled A Bridge Too Far and read it over and over, from cover to cover. Any military handbooks I could locate, I read until I had them memorized. I learned how to dig a fox hole, how to put up concertina wire, how to walk with a compass. I was in World History class with Mr. Polson, so I picked the Battle of the Bulge for my end-of-year project. I read everything I could lay my hands and eyes on, about the 101st Airborne Division and how they fought the Germans, about their jump early on the morning of the 6th of June 1944, before D-Day. I learned about their heroic stand at the Bat-tle of the Bulge, how brave those men were, 'though surrounded by Germans.

I began to dream that I could prove myself as capable as they to the rest of the world. Before graduation, I had begun to talk to my brother Bill about going into the army together, on the "buddy plan." Bill agreed to wait for me to turn 18 in the middle of October; then we'd be off together to see the world through the eyes o the U.S. Ar-my. Graduation from Mitchell High School finally came in early June, 1966, but I had five months to wait to turn 18. After graduation I moved down onto the banks of the White River with a friend, Oscar Holt, from Shoals. He was also biding his time to go into the army, but he only had to wait a few weeks. Oscar and I camped alongside the river, living in a small tent and cooking on either a barbeque grill or a small one-burner Coleman gas stove. We laid out trot lines and built two catfish traps out of an old hollow sycamore tree, baiting them with soured cheese.

We found various ways to earn cash money. We dug freshwater shells from the bottom of the river. We'd cook them, just long enough to pop them open; after they cooled, we cleaned them and got the meat out. I knew from my experiences with Grandpa Byrd we could sell the meat as fish bait up and down the river. We dumped the shells in the back of Oscar's '53 Ford pickup; when we had a full load we'd drive to Shoals where we sold them there. Another way was by hiring ourselves out for farm chores, such as putting up hay or bringing in crops from a garden. We did a lot of work for Lauren Tolbert, David Tolbert's father; he always had a plenty of things for us to do. I also helped Grandma Byrd work in her garden.

Mother helped me get a really fun job working at M. Fines & Sons Sewing Mill in Bedford. I think Mother hoped that maybe

I'd stay and not go off to the army. About 200 girls and women worked there, so I certainly enjoyed helping them lift cloth up onto their sewing lines, but I only stayed about five weeks. My old restlessness re-turned, so I moved on; I just thought it had been a good place to work for cash. I was still determined to join the army and get out of Indiana.

Oscar and I often went squirrel hunting early in the morning, shucked some corn out of somebody's cornfield in the afternoon for supper, and then would ramble around to find other ways to amuse ourselves or simply waste time. I was still dating Vicky, just to pass the days. After Oscar left for his stint in the Army, I would go over to Grandma Byrd's, sit with her of an evening out on her front porch and listen to her sing "Lily of the Valley" while I dreamed of my future. I'd get up with Uncle Jesse and Bill Bridges to fish, hunt squirrels and do what they called "fox hunting." Sometimes Uncle "Dago" would show up and come along with us.

One of the last jobs I had as the weather began to cool was cutting firewood with Uncle Archie. We took two weeks to get as much wood as possible. We'd drive over to the old Sandstone Road and cut trees into manageable sizes, then haul the wood back to his home place and stack it in an old chicken house. Those cool days of fall made me realize I'd soon be gone from here. I had continued to date Vicky and although I wanted to be more than just friends with her, I still was determined to join the army. Most of all, I harbored dreams of becoming a paratrooper and a Screaming Eagle. I dreamed of faraway places and about the world outside southern Indiana. Many times my thoughts drifted to Gus Grissom, the astronaut. He'd also graduated from Mitchell High School and became a famous person. "Well," I thought, "one day I'm going to return to Mitchell as someone special, too!" I was determined to go out into the world, hold my head up high and not ever look back!

Biding my time, waiting for my 18th birthday, trying to enjoy every minute became my life as those summer days passed by ever so slowly. Vicky and I made quite a few trips in my '56 Ford down to Heltonville and to the movie theatre in Bedford. During my high school years, Mother had finally divorced David Tolbert; by the time I was a senior, she'd begun to date a nice man named Harold Boone. On quite a few evenings Vicky and I would drive to Mother's house to play cards with her and Harold. Those carefree days began to drag for me and I thought they would never end. Finally though, before I knew what was happening, the end of October arrived, bringing my birthday. It was time to clear out. Bill and I packed up and prepared for our journey to Fort Knox, Kentucky.

Basic Training, 1966:
Fort Knox, Kentucky

I don't know what I expected to find in Kentucky, but the ride down to Louisville, then further south to Fort Knox was a journey. I was extremely happy! Finally, the opportunity to stand on my own two legs, to show the world I could be somebody, was in my grasp! My thoughts turned back to home and my girlfriend, if that's who you could have called Vicky. I thought about the names people had called me. I had been called "Little Joe' by family, "bastard" by some in the community, while many others taunted me with "Hand-Me-Down Joe" because I wore clothes that had always been somebody else's first. Little did I know that years later, at my mother's funeral, Danny Terrell, then the Mayor of Mitchell, would ask me to come home to ride in the Mitchell Persimmon Festival Parade as the town's "Hometown Hero."

I didn't know where I was going, but I intended to enjoy it! Up to now, I had hardly been out of the state of Indiana. I don't remember closing my eyes that entire trip to Fort Knox. We crossed the Ohio River and continued further south. Only once before had I ever crossed the Ohio River. A year earlier Butch Dorsett and I had driven down to the state line of Indiana and Ohio, a distance of 100 miles; we thought then we'd gone a terribly long distance! Now, as I traveled south with my brother Bill, I looked out at the snow on the ground and wondered, "How long will it be before I see home and my girlfriend again?" Out of nowhere, it occurred to me. "I don't really care when I see home again because soon, I'll be in my new home, the U.S. Army!"

I knew that at times I might get sick, or feel lonely for Vicky and my other friends, but now, I was finally on my own. I was determined to enjoy every minute of this new journey. I was with my brother and we were on our way to begin a new chapter in our lives. Although many years have passed since those days of basic training, I thought then it was great.

A few days after our arrival, they issued each of us an M-14 rifle. We spent three days in class learning how to clean and operate that rifle. I had never in my life spent time taking one apart. All we had ever done to a weapon was to put some oil on the outside of it, on the metal, or clean the wooden part of the weapon. It was so exciting to find out what made guns work! We went into classrooms with our army instructors who taught us how to sight and fire our weapons. They would place a coin on the end of each rifle. Then we would practice pulling the trigger and try to keep the coin from falling off. They showed us how to handle our rifles. I thought all this was fun.

Well, a couple of days later, we were up very early, had a wonderful breakfast and prepared to go to the Zero Range. The night before, I was so excited about going to the range that I hardly slept. We marched out of Fort Knox with heads held high. We marched up Heartbreak Hill and another one called Agony on the way to the rifle ranges. I felt so fulfilled, full to the brim with joy and anticipation. As the sun rose over the hills of central Kentucky, the weather was cold and brisk. We marched about four miles, then I spent most of the morning either sitting on a bleacher or holding guard duty on the gate. I never heard so much carrying on or complaining from other people in my life. The soldiers griped and moaned about the cold; their hands and feet were cold, their bodies were cold all over. But me, I thoroughly enjoyed the day.

Finally, they let my squad, with my brother beside me, go to the firing line.

I zeroed in nine rounds and thought I'd be able to hit a target. We looked out over the firing range where berms were set out at 300 meters. I could already see where the targets would be because the ground in front was so shot up that the snow was gone. I waited in our fox hole as I heard orders coming up the line. Finally, I heard, "All clear on the firing line. Commence firing!"

I watched, waiting for the first target to jump out of the ground 25 meters in front of me. I shot it down. Then, just like shooting a squirrel off a limb of an old hickory tree back home, I watched. As more targets popped up, I shot and another and another! Pow! Pow! Pow! Oh my! I had free ammunition! All I had to do was just point and shoot! Point and shoot! Targets kept on popping up and I ran out of ammo. Finally I heard, "Remove your magazine from your weapons! Get out of the fox hole!"

We cleared our weapons. As I climbed out, I noticed seven or eight drill instructors quickly approaching us, coming up directly behind me. Immediately, I was on alert. I thought, "Uh, oh! Have I done something wrong?" I was not sure what was going on, although I thought something bad had happened.

One instructor stepped around in front of me, turned towards me and stretched out his arms and turned his arms over, with his hands facing up. I laid my M-14 into his hands. He just looked down at it. Then he looked directly at me and asked, "Have you ever shot a rifle before?"

I almost laughed out loud! I thought, "Who do you think you're kidding? Everybody's shot a rifle, Buddy!" But I was smart enough to keep my mouth shut. I simply answered, "A few times."

Out of the corner of my eye I saw a young private, probably about my own age, come running toward us. Quickly, he blurted out, "Thirty-eight, Sergeant!"

Everyone began talking at once. Finally, I realized what I had done and why they were so excited. I had hit thirty-eight out of the forty targets! My instructor told me I did a good job. The Sergeant added, "Mighty fine shooting, son!"

We made formation and began our march back to Fort Knox. As we marched along, one of the songs that day was "Hey, hey, Capt'n Jack"

Hey, hey, Captain Jack,
Meet me down by the railroad track.
With my rifle in my hand,
I want to be a fighting man.

Hey, hey, Captain Jack,
Meet me down by the railroad track.
With my suitcase in my hand,
I wanna be a traveling man.

Hey, hey, Captain Jack,
Meet me down by the railroad track,
With that K-Bar in my hand,
I wanna be a jackin' man.

Hey, hey, Captain Jack,
Meet me down by the rail road track.

With my bayonet in my hand,
I wanna be a stabbing man.

Hey, hey, Captain Jack,
Meet me down by the rail road track.
With that woman in my hand,
I want to be a loving man.

Hey, hey, Captain Jack,
Meet me down on the rail road track.
With a rifle in my hand,
I want to be a fighting man.

Oh, I was so happy! I knew I had done something right. I didn't realize it at the time, but my life had shifted. From that day on, every day, people came to watch me as I worked on the rifle range. My company commander, a captain, would come to watch, as well. Toward the end of basic training, we were given leave for Christmas break. Bill and I put on our uniforms and headed back home to Indiana. Bill had done well in basic, but out on the rifle range he struggled. Sometimes, if he was in a fox hole next to me, I could help him out. I never told anyone, but at night we helped each other; he was very good at polishing boots and I was good at ironing. We had come to Basic Training as buddies and in the process, had become pretty good as brothers. Those winter days at Fort Knox were good days for us. Little did I know that soon I would be in Vietnam. On the way home, Bill talked constantly about Joyce Baker, the girl he had been dating before we'd left for Kentucky. He said he couldn't wait to get back to see her. Although I wanted to see Vicky again, I also was just as excited about being able to drive my '56 Ford!

Mother was very pleased to see us both. Immediately upon arriving home, Bill and I went our separate ways. I took off my uniform, hung it up, and then put on my "regular" clothes. As I looked at myself in a full-length mirror, I could tell something was different. I had gained at least ten pounds, had begun to fill out and didn't look so much like a kid any more. I looked taller and now my hair was cut short. Home on leave that first time was the best home leave I ever had. I did spend a lot of time alone. I'd wanted to contact Vicky, but by the time I actually got home, she was already dating another man. Consequently, I had time to think, to be quiet and just let my mind wander. I kept asking myself, "What is ahead for me? Are we going to make it to Jump School? What's after that?"

Asking myself so many questions wore me out. I would drive my '56 Ford out onto Kings Ridge, park someplace and think how my new life was unfolding before me in the U.S. Army. I'd sit there, as I looked off into the distance. If I saw another car coming, I'd start my car up again and drive away. Sometimes I'd drive over some of those sandstone roads where Uncle Archie and I used to work or I'd drive to the quarries, get out and climb up on the big blocks to look off into the distance. One day right before we returned to Fort Knox, while looking off over those hills of southern Indiana, I realized the picture I saw was a very blue sky with spots of green where the cedar trees stood out on Pierce Hill. I wondered how this place would look in another year, and I wondered where I would be.

Everyone I saw asked lots of questions about the army and what life was like there for us. Bill and I didn't have a lot of answers for them since all we had done was to go to basic training. All the family gathered at Uncle Archie's for Christmas. Everyone was glad to see us. Many family members were there: Aunt Alice and Uncle Dutch, Grandma Byrd, all of Uncle Archie's children. It seemed to me that everyone talked to us all at once and at the same time. They told Bill and me how good we looked; some said we had filled out and looked stronger. I finally stood on the scales and weighed in at 130 pounds.

We went to a service over at Fairview Church of Christ. Everyone there also asked lots of questions and remarked on how we were doing. This church holds a very special place in my memory bank. The building sits up on a long ridge line. From the churchyard you look out over smaller hills and valleys. Through the thick and thin of all my years, I had relatives at this church that helped me over rough spots. People from this church have prayed for me whenever I was on a battlefield. I truly believe that God has worked miracles through the many fine people at Fairview Church of Christ. A year later, I would be home again, this time getting ready to go to Vietnam.

Mother wanted me to go with her to a big family reunion being held down at the Martin County Forest. While there, I saw a good friend, Fred Harrell, a veteran of World War II. He asked me, "Have you had any hand to hand combat training?"

I replied, "A little bit, but not much."

Quickly he grabbed for me, but I countered, bracing against him with my left arm and then stepped in and under him. I grabbed one of his wrists with my right hand, bent forward and threw him over my right hip onto the ground. He lay there, looking up. Then he laughed and said, "I think you can take care of yourself!"

"I hope no one gets that close to me, in any war!" was my reply.

To this day, Fred is still a very good friend. He lives on the Old Williams Road, between Huron and Williams, overlooking the White River. Whenever I go back to Mitchell, I stop by and visit.

Both of us sit outside his house, laughing and talking about those good old days.

I had been so glad to get home, but eventually the nights ran out and it was time to go back. Bill and I had not seen much of each other while at home, as he went his own way, spending the majority of his time with Joyce. Mother was still dating Harold. Before I left, Harold and I had a serious talk when he told me about some of his experiences in World War II. I liked Harold; it seemed like he thought a lot of Mother. I felt glad because I thought she was settled and content and I believed she was happy with him in her life.

Bill and I said our goodbyes to friends and family, then climbed aboard a Greyhound bus down at Shoals, to head back to Fort Knox. Bill and I raced through those last days of training. I competed for Best Rifleman for our company, and against others from our battalion, finishing second out of ten riflemen. I fired at Expert level on the rifle range, highest in our company and second in the battalion.

Quick as a wink, my brother and I were on our way to our next assignment, the Aberdeen Proving Grounds in Maryland. I was getting closer to what I had been trying to find most of my life. I was determined to be somebody and to become a paratrooper. I wasn't going to let anything stand in my way! Little did I know that I would be in Vietnam by next Christmas with my thoughts on those back home.

18yrs old trained with an M-14 Rifle and finished 2nd in the Battalion

Graduation from Fort Knox, Ky. Graduation from Fort Knox, Ky.

PFC E-3 William H. Conley   **PVT E-2 Michael J. Conley**

Michael J. Conley

March 1967:
Aberdeen Proving Grounds

Bill and I boarded a train bound for Baltimore, Maryland. From there we transferred to a bus headed to the Aberdeen Proving Grounds. When we stepped off the bus in Maryland there was snow on the ground. Over the next three months I would very seldom ever see ground. By early March it was still snowing; one night we received more than 14 inches! Nevertheless, our classes continued. I had never in my life seen so much snow. On more than one morning the temperature was well below zero. Wind howled all the time. I wondered what would make people want to live here.

A three-day leave gave me the opportunity to go to Gettysburg. I walked over the land and fields that had been the scene of a great Civil War battle. For two days I walked in warm sunshine as it shone across those old battlefields. I bought a book for tourists, so I could walk the trails and roads. My book had copies of maps that were used during the Battle of Gettysburg. My thoughts went to those men who fought and died in that four-day battle. I had read and studied about the Civil War when I'd still been in high school. I touched what I thought of as hallowed ground, as I looked out at the lay of the land. I remembered that Pickett's Charge took place there. As I closed my eyes, I could almost see and hear that battle taking place. I imagined how much noise there must have been. I mentally asked myself, "What happened, right here?"

I began to think about going to war myself. On a daily basis I was reading and hearing about the war in Vietnam. As I pondered those thoughts, my mind conjured up more questions.

"What will it be like there? Will I be scared?" The biggest question I had for myself was, "Can I be a soldier? A warrior?" I knew I wanted to go to jump school, but I was beginning to think a lot about actually going to war.

While at Aberdeen, Bill and I each received a letter from Mother telling us that she and Harold had been married. They would continue to live on the 40-acre farm and would wait for us there whenever we could return from the military. Bill and I talked about that farm. We knew it had been paid for by money Mother had received from our father and from settlement money when he died. I told Bill he could have the front half of the property with the house; I would prefer to build myself a house on the back, along the Old Sandstone Road. I loved that part best because there weren't any neighbors close by. Bill didn't really have a lot to say about it at all. He just stared off into space. But I felt really happy for Mother. I remember I said to him, "You wait and see. This will be the best for Mother."

Pvt-E2 Michael Conley   **PFC William H. Conley**

Springtime finally came to Maryland and the world around us began to thaw out. We began to see ducks and geese returned to swim in the Chesapeake Bay. One day I saw a couple out on the water in a small sailing craft; I could hear them laughing and music playing. I thought they must be very happy "living in paradise." The last few weeks began to fly by, as we prepared for the final exam. I had learned a lot about heavy equipment and how to be a mechanic on wheeled and tracked vehicles. Bill also did very well at Aberdeen and helped me prepare for our final tests to qualify for Jump School. We still wanted to go there together. We thought the training we'd received so far was okay, but I couldn't help but think about being a "real" soldier, a paratrooper. I wanted to be in the infantry, not be a mechanic or a driver. I was very happy when we passed our final exams. Now we were qualified for Jump School. We received a specialty as MOS (Military Occupational Specialty) and given 63HA, wheeled and tracked vehicle mechanics. Bill was promoted to Private 1st Class; now he could sew on his first stripe. I made Private 2nd Class. Next for us was Jump School! Now, we would find out if we could jump out of an airplane.

DEPARTMENT OF THE ARMY

POSTAGE AND FEES PAID

Headquarters, 4th Student Battalion (Airborne)
The Student Brigade, USAIS
Fort Benning, Georgia 31905

OFFICIAL BUSINESS

Mother Bill and I have arrived
at 1st Runway Co. 7 June 1967
Going to Airborne School.
    We will make it! Don't worry

Michael J. Conley

HEADQUARTERS 4TH STUDENT BATTALION (AIRBORNE)
THE STUDENT BRIGADE, USAIS
Fort Benning, Georgia 31905

(Date)
22 June 1967

A soldier, in whom you have a great interest, has arrived at USAIS, Fort Benning and will begin three weeks of very arduous airborne training.

The discipline and training which he will undergo as an airborne volunteer will be strict, but fair. He will be instructed by expert commissioned and noncommissioned officers who have already proven themselves capable in the field of parachuting. These military personnel are highly dedicated individuals, and because of their outstanding abilities, form a group of elite instructors, rendering training that is the envy of the Armed Forces. They will insure that he is more than qualified to become a member of the U. S. Army's proudest group, the Airborne Fraternity.

While he is here, please address his mail as follows:

_____
(Rank)   (Name)   (Service Number)

_____7_____ Company, Class #_____
4th Stu Bn (Abn,) TSB USAIS, Fort Benning, Georgia 31905

Due to the large number of students in training here, it is extremely difficult for the orderly room to receive telephone calls and to locate students for phone calls. Therefore, under normal conditions, if you need to contact him, please send a telegram and he will call you. However, if an emergency exists at home, a phone call will be accepted, or contact the Red Cross and they will immediately notify him through Unit Command Channels.

When sending money, please send a money order. It is extremely difficult to cash personal checks here.

Your cooperation in adhering to the above policies will be greatly appreciated and will assist materially in providing prompt service for the airborne students.

Very truly yours,

COMMANDING

FB (TSB) FL 75
13 JUN 66   PREVIOUS EDITIONS ARE OBSOLETE

Jump School:
Fort Benning, GA

Parachute training began on the 4th of May 1967. Our class started like many others before us, each one of us full of "piss and vinegar and raring to jump!" It didn't take long for the Jump Instructors and the Black Hats to let it be known that this was "not" basic training. Jump School turned out to be downright hard labor. We were up early at 0500 hours. Every day. The instructors acted like they thought we were out of condition, so their job was to get us "into condition." Over the next few years I would hear a lot of this same type of talk. For the first few days and nights all we would hear was the mantra of the Instructors, "Once more," which was repeated over and over. If one instructor grew tired of us, there was always another ready to step up and take his place. This was professionalism at its highest grade. The moment any instructor told us to take a rest, we headed straight for the water bags, trying to replace all the water that we had just sweated out.

It was an endless cycle. We would drink water; take salt tablets, run, do pushups or parachute landing falls, sweat. They would finally get around to letting us get a drink and then the cycle would start all over again. Over and over and over again. Had I looked up the words "swing land training," Bill and I would have been a little better prepared and known what to expect. We walked in there thinking, "This will just be another military school. Stay awake and you'll pass."

Boy, were we wrong! This course had some real thrills in store for us! To take a break from the monotony of exercising we were hung in a horse harness, similar to those found on a parachute.

Then the harness would slip and turn to prepare us for landing. With a stroke of one finger an instructor could crash us into the ground. Over and over again. How many times my body hit, rolled and struck the ground during those three weeks is anybody's guess. My whole body hurt. I got worn out, with torn knees and hurt elbows; even my ribs hurt. When I tried to sit down, that even hurt, much less try to lie down.

When you begin to feel like you are finally just about to get the hang of what's been thrown at you, then the training changes. We had to climb up stairs onto a platform a few feet off the ground. They told us the platform was only three feet off the ground. To this day, I still think they must have measured it in metrics. It was more like two or three meters off the ground. The pit we jumped into had been packed down by twenty-some years of paratroopers pounding into that pit, crushing their bodies into this pile of sand and sawdust. Even with a few good rains, pretty soon that ground felt more like solid concrete. We were told, "This will strengthen your arms and backs, along with your legs."

I'll give it to you straight. Every four or five minutes we were climbing the stairs, jumping off the platform into the pit, climbing and pulling ourselves out, then climbing back up the stairs to the platform. We continued this for five or six hours. Sure enough, I built up my leg muscles, but the rest of me was beyond sore, stiff and sore all over. Many nights no one was capable of talking to anyone else because we were so exhausted. Every muscle we thought had been ours now belonged to Airborne School! They hung us out to dry like clothes on a line, then screamed, "Slip, turn and prepare for landing!"

Some jerk would pull a rope and you'd fall. Your feet, then your knees and finally your chin would slam into the ground. You could see the humor of the situation when it wasn't happening to you. We would stand in line and laugh at each other as we watched each of us get what we knew we'd soon be getting ourselves. We just cussed when we had to do it because we knew the others would watch us do it and laugh. From a fuselage on the ground called a "mock-up" we were taught to leap into space. When that began to go well, they put us in groups for mass jumps. Now, you have to imagine all these soldiers trying to jump out of a mock-up airplane, but the plane isn't really flying at all. We all ended up in one big pile of human legs and arms. Sometimes, you'd just have to laugh, as we rolled around on the ground, trying to get out of each other's way.

Week Two finally came around. We were all busted up, bruised and bloodied, but ready for more. We sang louder and we ran faster and farther than the previous week. We'd go over to the 34-foot towers strung with a trolley line. Today, we would call this a zip line, where you are hung in a suspension harness prior to sliding down an incline. At the end of the line someone waits to catch you, pull you back and help you unhook off from the line. Most of the time, we ended up eating sawdust and dirt, with lots of sand thrown in, before we finally stopped.

On one particular morning we found they had changes in store for us. The wind was blowing pretty well. They hooked us up to real parachutes, attached us to harnesses, and allowed the wind to catch us. We were dragged across sandy ground. This was designed to get us used to being dragged after a landing. They also used these exercises to teach us how to collapse our parachute in a strong breeze. Similar physical training and teaching techniques went on forever. I woke myself up one morning from a dream; I thought I was falling and yelling. I knew then I was getting apprehensive, I had to admit it to myself. I talked to Bill about my fears, but he didn't seem afraid at all.

Doubt was setting in for me, but I was determined that I would face my fears and that I would be able to jump. I knew that we were going to the towers the next day and they would drop us over 250 feet to the ground. I thought, "Why am I doing this? Why am I here? Who said any one could live through this?" I knew the answer. "I am becoming a paratrooper."

Our first day on the towers was actually fun. Three men at a time rode a chairlift to the very top, with a very pleasant ride back to the bottom. On the second run came the controlled chute. Here you got your first real taste of what parachuting would be about, for over your head hung a real parachute and underneath your feet was nothing, … nothing but air. I looked out over Fort Benning. I could see the company barracks, other towers, and people below running around, hear songs. I was rising up, going higher and higher. Then I came to a short stop. Far below, the landing mat looked as small as a postage stamp. Then I felt a tug. My chute had been released and I was floating out over Fort Benning. I thought, "What do I do now?"

What could I do? I knew where I was going…. Down! I could hear my chute overhead as it made a slapping sound, kind of like a wet flag flapping in a breeze. I was still looking straight down when I realized people were yelling up to me, calling out my number, yelling for me to move away from the tower so I could drift with the wind. As if on autopilot, I responded. I prepared for landing. It seemed like it was going to be so easy! To my amazement, I felt like someone had pulled me up on a swing and then dropped me or cut the ropes. Before I knew what had happened, I crashed! What I hadn't realized is that air currents may change quickly as a jumper approaches the ground. Unexpected mishaps do occur. I felt like I had been in a very bad car wreck, minus the noise. I tried to get up. I couldn't move. I took a deep breath and pleasantly surprised, found out I could actually breathe. Nothing was broken.

That evening I took a very hot shower. Every muscle in my body finally began to feel a little better. Later, I realized that in three days I would be in a real airplane. Heck, I was just a young kid from southern Indiana who had never ever ridden in any kind of an airplane. In three days I was going to jump out of one! It was funny to realize that on my first airplane ride, I would also jump out of that airplane.

During this phase of Jump School I began to have sleep problems. Over the next three nights I didn't get much sleep. Every day we practiced, jumping off the 34-foot towers, sliding down the zip line, making more parachute landing falls. On

the last night before our novice jump, Bill and I talked. For so long we both had looked forward to this day and repeatedly talked about it since joining the army, way back in October 1966. Bill told me the scuttlebutt he'd overheard, about what happened to refusals, how they got kicked out the door or even picked up and thrown out the jump door. That was beyond my wildest dream! The reality is that never, in all of my years of service, did I see a Jump Master or anyone else touch any soldier on a jump or threaten him in any way.

The night before our novice jump I slept very little. I thought the night would never end. Finally, they blew a whistle. We all jumped out of bed and prepared for that first jump. We jogged to the airport and sang all the way as the sun came up. On the runway sat six C-119's, known in airman's terms as the Flying Boxcar. Their engines were warming up as we lined up for inspection. Jump Masters walked down the line. With a pat on our butt and, "You're ready," we walked toward the airplanes and climbed aboard. We actually walked up the back door ramp. There are seats that have already been pulled down in four rows, two inboard rows of seats and two outboard rows. We loaded into the plane, going all the way back to the pilot and co-pilot's cabin in the front of the plane before we began to sit down. The last man sat down next to the door and the Jump Master stood right in front of him, with three assistant jump masters sitting or standing in the rows between the jumpers to check them during the ride and immediately after they all stand up. After a ride, usually less than 20 minutes, things begin to happen outside the plane. A pathfinder had been hidden out on the drop zone and had been there, sometimes for days or at least hours, to make sure the drop zone was secure and there's no danger from an enemy, wandering cows or farmers on tractors out there when the paratroopers will begin to fall.

The pilot calls the Jump Master on his radio and yells the words, "Execute! Execute! Execute!" He watches until he can see the first paratrooper leave the plane. The Jump Master can stop the flow of paratroopers by yelling, "Stop Flow! Stop Flow!"

At this time the pilot measures the plane's flight path to put as many paratroopers onto the Drop Zone as possible. A field can hold 200 paratroopers from one end to the far end of the field. The airplane will only be over the field for less than 30 seconds, so if two airplanes come through the same flight plan, 400 troopers can be put down onto a field in less than a minute. A loud shout is passed along from the men, from the back of the plane to the front. "Stand up!" All stand up, or the inboard group stands up, then the outboard group. The last man who jumps out is the first one on board, so you load, in reverse order. The first man out sits next to the door and was the last man to load into the plane. From the moment the first paratrooper "hits the silk," to the last man, might be less than 30 seconds.

The airplane slowly turns and leaves the area. After the last man jumps, the Jump Master leans out to check to see that all of the troops are gone, being sure that no one is hung up, on the outside of the plane. Then, he jumps out and turns immediately toward the last parachute behind him.

Our pilot taxied out to the takeoff runway. We sat there for only a few minutes, but to us it seemed like hours. The pilots revved their engines and picked up their RPM's a couple of times, then made their last minute checks. We felt a small bump as the plane began to roll forward. Suddenly, Lawson Field was rushing past us! Some men gasped. I heard the wheels come up and I knew we were airborne! We climbed into that early morning sky, over Lawson Field and the Chattahoochee River. Down below I could see what I knew was Fort Benning, home of the Airborne. Just like me, I knew that some others had never before been in an airplane, much less been about to parachute out of one. I thought, "Although I'm riding on an airplane, I won't land on this plane."

I was making my first flight and first jump on the same day. We banked to the left. After just a few minutes, our Jump Master yelled, "Number One Man, stand up!"

The first man stood. Jump Master checked him over very carefully, and then commanded, "Hook Up!"

Number One Man snapped the static line from his parachute onto the steel anchor cable running the length of the plane. Next voice command: "Stand in the Door!"

Number One Man obeyed. For a few tense moments he just stood there as Jump Master looked out. The Number One Man took one step forward onto the jump platform, then Jump Master yelled, "Go!"

He jumped out, on his trip towards Mother Earth. The rest of us watched as he gradually lost altitude and finally disappeared, far to the rear of the plane. The pilot made another big slow circle. We lined up. This time each of us obeyed the jump commands. We stood up, and then hooked up. Every time Jump Master yelled, we obeyed. Not one person refused to stand up. We sounded off, "OK!" to the one standing in front. My brother Bill was standing in front of me. In later years, I had to admit it; he jumped before I did!

Our line began to move forward. I was part of a team of men being sucked out into the universe. I hardly touched the side of the aircraft as my hands reacted automatically, rising up to my reserve and I was out the door. The plane's prop wash pushed me from head to foot as I loudly counted, "One-thousand, two-thousand, thr...."

Before I could finish "three-thousand," I felt the jerk on my shoulder risers and a tightness across my chest. I knew my chute had opened! I could breathe again! I looked all around. I had a pain in my chest like I'd been hit with a two-by-four, but I was airborne. In spite of myself, I yelled at the top of my lungs, "Airborne!"

It no longer mattered how many bumps and bruises I'd had to take or how much pain I'd suffered! I felt exquisite joy and happiness as that first parachute opened. That joy knew no bounds. Later, when my children were being born, I also felt a similar exquisite joy and happiness, but deep in my heart, I knew it was not the same as when my first parachute opened.

I had plenty of time to gaze around. A slight breeze blew me away from the drop zone. I grabbed my risers which ran from my shoulders to the lines which run down from the parachute and pulled myself back up toward the chute. I turned so I was headed back toward the drop zone. All the jumpers on the ground were yelling and looking up, so I looked down. I realized Mother Earth was coming toward me really fast! My approaching speed had increased. For the very first time I realized I was about to land, on the ground! I instinctively held onto the risers as I prepared for landing. Both boots hit the ground at the same time and then I rolled back in a somersault and rolled up laughing. The grassy field underfoot seemed solid.

I was safe! I had really done it! I had jumped without hesitation and somehow, landed without breaking anything. I looked around and saw others rolling up their parachutes and stuffing them in the bag. I looked around and saw trucks nearby, waiting on us. I realized that since I had been nearly the last one down, I'd had the farthest to go. I spotted Bill. He was already up and heading toward the turn-in point. I forgot everything else, began to put my chute away and made my way across the drop zone.

What a day it had been! As we loaded up onto trucks, I noticed many soldiers were already konked out. It also didn't take me long to fall asleep on that ride back either. Tomorrow, I would do it all again. That night I went to bed early. I only remember that I closed my eyes, dreaming. As a boy I had played cowboys and Indians with my friends and cousins. We built forts with hay bales and created tunnels. I enjoyed hunting and things that went boom. In high school I had begun to dream about being a paratrooper. I knew I was destined to see this kind of action; I wanted to take that ultimate risk. I felt compelled to volunteer for the Army Airborne. Frankly, that day, my first jump, provided me with more excitement than I ever imagined I would experience. In my dream that night I was falling and yelling. I woke myself up; my heart was pounding in my chest. I had been scared that I would fail, but I knew I was not scared of falling. I knew I would jump another day and find out how much better I could be.

My second jump was practically the same as the first, except this time we jumped out of a C-130. We flew faster that time and the opening shock was much stronger. For this jump I worked my way towards the front of the line, so I was not so near the end. Bill was still in front of me and doing well. After we were out, he dropped faster than I did because he outweighed me. On the way down we shouted back and forth to one another about the wind or which way we were going to turn. I knew he would beat me to the ground, so I tried to see how close I could land to him. I didn't really land very close, but I did much better on that second jump, thinking I had used the PLF (Parachute Landing Fall) Technique. It was much easier if you did it right. Already, I was looking forward to Jump Number Three.

After that second jump I slept much better. I began to look forward to our next jump the following day. We lined up for chow call with the wind blowing against our face. I thought I felt a chill in the air. Our run in the morning over to the airfield was quieter than the morning before. I noticed that the wind had seemed to pick up. Intuitively I felt anxious. One thing paratroopers are scared of is wind. As we lined up, here came the Jump Masters. All of us got our chutes on and passed inspection. Then we were told, "Sit down!"

Minutes started to eat up an hour; again, we heard, "Line up!"

We all helped each other to our feet and lined up, went through our Jump Master Checks, then more waiting. After standing for 20-25 minutes we heard again, "Sit!"

Time dragged by. Men on my left and right drifted off to sleep. I noticed Bill dozing off, but then he jerked awake, smiled at me and said, "Well, Little Brother, it looks like we're going to make it."

I laughed out loud. To this day I remember my response. "Bill, I never had a thought about not making it. I just knew I could."

The Jump Masters finally began yelling at us again, so we stood up. I hoped that this third time would be the charm. Finally, we loaded into a C-130 whose engines were already jumping to life. This third jump was different because our line was much shorter by now. Jumpers had begun to get hurt, with sprained ankles or twisted knees. What mattered to me was that Bill and I were still jumping. I made sure he got in line in front of me. This time only a couple of men separated us from the door. The C-130 began rolling down the runway. Just as we rose off the ground, Jump Master stood up and hooked himself in. He turned around and yelled, "Five minutes!"

I thought, "Boy, we are really going fast on this one!"

We banked left as our Jump Master went through his commands rather quickly. I heard, "Stand in the door!" Then those big motors outside made their beautiful noises as the plane straightened and slowed down to jump speed. I was only four or five from the door when I heard the yell, "Go!"

I stepped forward, right behind Bill. Neither of us faltered as we hit the door. Then, it was open sky! Our chutes opened. Oh, what a beautiful sight! I turned slowly, looking for my brother. I saw he was much closer to the ground than I. Immediately, I thought, "Is the wind blowing harder down there?"

I watched as Bill approached the ground. Then, I realized, "I better pay attention to my own business!"

I went through my risers, pulling my chute down so it would slow me down. I hit the ground hard. It took me a couple of minutes to get up, get my chute packed. Then, I began to look around for Bill, but I couldn't locate him. I began to walk off the Drop Zone, and finally saw him sitting off in the distance. I wondered, "Why he wasn't up, tending to business. Doesn't he know he's got things to do? Why isn't he packing up that chute?"

I ran over, since he still wasn't getting up. He looked really worried. I could see he was visibly in pain and sweating a lot. As soon as I was within hearing distance, he yelled, "Joe, I think I've sprained my ankle!"

I looked down at his left ankle. It didn't look right to me, but what did I know? I helped him pull his parachute around, and folded it to store in his parachute bag. I helped him get up and put one arm around him to help him as we walked very slowly together off the Drop Zone. He didn't say much. He was really having a hard time trying to walk. I asked if he wanted me to get a medic.

He replied, "I can make it! I don' need no' medic!"

He was tough. Together we made it to the busses. We both thought he only had sprained the ankle. I helped him get aboard the bus. I don't remember Bill going into lunch as he usually did. I do know it wasn't until long after dinner, after I was back in the barracks, that Bill told me his ankle was now hurting really bad. He had already gone to the showers two times to run cold water on it; he had tried to keep it elevated. When I looked at his ankle, I knew it was bad. I felt apprehensive as I remarked to him, "Bill, it doesn't look good."

That was probably the last thing I said to him before they took out him of the barracks. I wouldn't see him again for the next year and half. The next time I would see my brother was the winter of 1968, when I returned from my first tour in Vietnam. My brother, my Army buddy and my jump buddy, now had a broken ankle. I would have to go on without him. I believe that was the closest my brother and I ever were. Yes, our young lives had been hard, but we had made a pretty good team in the army and in jump school.

Graduation day at Fort Benning was very special for me, but I missed having Bill there with me. Two days later, I stood on the first floor in the long barracks as they called out names for new assignments. Bill was assigned out west to Fort Carson, Colorado. I had orders for the 82nd Airborne Division and would be stationed at Fort Bragg, North Carolina, home of the Airborne Division and the Army's Special Forces. I felt such pride; I had worked hard and achieved my goal. I had become a paratrooper!

Although our lives had merged for a while in basic training and paratrooper school, Airborne School was the first real "bigtime" school my brother and I had gone to together. It was the most exciting school experience I ever had in the U.S. military. Years later, I looked back and thought about what doors were opened for me by my becoming a paratrooper. From this point on, Bill and I would each follow our own path; we would go our own way. I was on my way to Fort Bragg, NC

Headquarters 4th Student Battalion (Airborne)
The Student Brigade, USAAIS Fort Benning Georgia
Pvt. E-2 Michael J. Conley 4th Student Bn. Airborne Student #41

82nd Airborne Division
Fort Bragg, North Carolina

Some research on the 82nd Airborne Division yielded some noteworthy information. The 82nd is the largest formation of the United States Army. They are completely qualified to parachute into combat. The 82nd together with the 101st Airborne Division, often work together using parachute jumps or air assault via helicopter, but they can also attack across intercontinental distances or be deployed around the continental United States, to Alaska or Hawaii. The Air Force usesaircraft to transport the C-130 Hercules. In my days in the 82nd, there were 4 Infantry Brigade Combat Teams, 1 Aviation Brigade and many Division Support Groups, including the 12th Support Brigade. Each brigade's lineage or colors derive from a specific parachute regiment. The 1st Brigade Combat Team is in line with the 504th Parachute Infantry Regiment. The 2nd Brigade Combat Team colors come from the 325th Parachute Infantry Regiment, while the 3rd Brigade Combat Team colors are from the 505th Parachute Regiment. The 4th Brigade Combat Team colors come from the 508th Parachute Infantry Regiment.

My first morning at Fort Bragg I realized I was now a replacement in a company up on Smoke Bomb Hill. I could hear voices off in the distance, singing,

Stand up,
Hook Up,
And shuffle to the door,
Jump right out and count to four!

"Oh, my," I thought, "Yes! I am finally in the right place." I heard another new song through the early morning fog. I was already a paratrooper, but here I would become a qualified parachutist. This picture was taken shortly after I arrived in Vietnam, in December 1967. Notice the Airborne tab 2/506 above the Screaming Eagle patch.

I didn't want to be anywhere else in this world. I learned to love Fort Bragg, North Carolina, and in turn, I found love at Fort Bragg, both in the military and in my personal life. It would be my "most visited station" over the next 40 years. Eventually, I would marry a woman from nearby Aberdeen and raise two sons on the doorsteps of Fort Bragg.

After my first tour in Vietnam, I returned to Fort Bragg. One day I drove out to the Pine Bluff Golf Course where I met a soldier who invited me to play a round with him. Although he beat me, he asked if I would like to join the Special Forces. He was an instructor at Camp McCall, west of Fort Bragg, and worked on an operation called "Gobbler Woods." Later in the book I'll talk more about how I was introduced to golf and to the Special Forces at the same time.

Now, in the summer of 1967, I was assigned to 782nd Maintenance Battalion, 82nd Airborne Division, Headquarters Company, as a battalion mechanic. But, I did not like that job! When I woke up every morning, I could hear the infantry units already up and running, chanting their songs. I loved those songs! Yes, we in Headquarters Company ran, too. Hey, we ran a lot, not as much as in Jump School, but our superiors worked very hard at keeping us slim and trim. Then it was off to the motor pool. I learned to hate the smell of diesel fuel and oil on my hands. I kept thinking, "There has to be more to the army than this."

One day I was driving past the drop zones. Out of the early morning fog I heard some C-130's coming through. I continued on to the next road, got out and watched as nine huge planes made a small turn before heading out. I saw their doors open and parachutes fall everywhere. I watched as men floated across their jump zone for as far as I could see. They were fully loaded and were supposed to be the best fighting men in the world. And, I wanted to be one of them! I wanted to get out of that maintenance battalion and into the airborne infantry! Now, how crazy does that sound?

In preparation for field exercises, we were given a few days to pack up our trucks. This was to be a very big FTX (field training exercise.) We headed west, following a different map than I had ever seen up to that time. The terrain changed to sand hills and sandy roads. Out here we would live in tents. Everyone had a great time, working on equipment, keeping trucks, jeeps and even the armor running. It was one of my most exciting times in the Army up to this time.

Late July found me counting down days for my first long leave. Three friends and I drove in my '56 Ford to the Atlantic Ocean. I can't tell you how it felt to see the ocean for the very first time! I sat in the sand and looked eastward, as far as I could see. I walked to the ocean's edge and watched as waves reached towards me. I dipped my hand in the saltwater and licked my fingers. I thought, "This is the ocean!"

I was completely overwhelmed. One day I would return back home and tell the folks there that I had seen the ocean, tasted it and walked in it! That day, the world shrank a little bit more. I looked forward to completing my first year in the U.S. Army. Looking back, I reminisced about my brother and the time we'd spent together. Although I had become a paratrooper in the 82nd Airborne Division, I still wanted to be assigned to an airborne unit and more than anything I wanted to be in the Infantry. I do not know why but I had this strange feeling about being in a fighting unit. I did not want to be a mechanic where it was safe. I wanted to see action.

The Detroit Race Riots, 1967

Shortly after our return from leave, a special formation was called. "We are on alert! Be ready to move out in 24 hours!"

Rumors were rampant and flew around like crazy! Many men with family nearby drove over to see them in Aberdeen, Pine Bluff or Fayetteville. Fort Bragg became a beehive with everyone in panic mode. Maintenance battalions loaded boxes into Conexus and equipment onto huge trucks. Supply companies were very busy with their own preparations I wondered, "Where are we going?"

No one told us anything until later that evening when another formation was called. Now we heard new words. "We are going into Detroit, Michigan."

The following morning we headed for Pope Air Force Base. The entire 82nd Airborne Division was on the move. The Detroit riots of 1967 resulted from a botched raid on a small, after-hours drinking club called The Blind Pig, located downtown on the corner of 12th Street and Clairmont Avenue. Two Detroit native sons, now Vietnam veterans, had just returned home that day. Army buddies had brought them to the club to celebrate. Of course, everyone inside was enjoying themselves. As more people crowded into the club, the manager called the police for help with crowd control. Just one police car initially responded to what they supposed were a few drunks who needed to be corralled. Instead, they discovered over 80 people crammed inside a bar which could only accommodate 40 at most.

All across America young people had begun to demonstrate against our involvement in the Vietnam War, questioning how our country was being run. Attitudes were changing. Questions were being raised about sending Americans to Southeast Asia into conflicts that certainly seemed like war. Yet a war involving America had not actually been declared. Many people no longer shared their parents' attitudes towards America rescuing other nations. Vietnam was not their fathers' war. The Vietnam issue would drag America down over the next ten years.

When the police first entered, the drunk and disorderly naturally began to protest. Initially, the police tried to arrest a few, including the two veterans. That act sparked the volatile undercurrent regarding anti-Vietnam sentiment, adding fuel to an already volatile environment. Quickly the police realized they needed more help and radioed for a Cleanup Crew. More and more cruisers arrived on the scene as crowds began to congregate outside. Some bar patrons who had managed to escape outside were intoxicated; others simply tried to avoid being arrested. Many who got out were duly agitated because the only place they had to go to drink was now shut down.

Who knows what the specific spark that signaled the riots? Crowds grew into gangs, gangs morphed into mobs. Windows were broken, wholesale looting and riots began. All night long vandals looted the whole north side of Detroit. People threw anything they could lay their hands on. Fires were set. The riots spread over to the east side, across the railroad tracks, escalating, gathering more steam. After 48 hours, the Michigan Governor activated the Michigan National Guard. By the riot's fourth day, we in the 82nd Airborne Division came in as reinforcements to the National Guard. By the fifth day, 43 people were dead, 1189 had been injured and over 7,000 had been arrested.

I remember being there, seeing things that no 18 year old should ever have seen: people throwing rocks and bricks into shop windows, lobbing bottles filled with gasoline and a burning rag stuffed into the end, what later became known as a Molotov cocktail. Mob mentality ruled. Rioters grabbed anything they could get their hands on. I saw lots of buildings burning. Gang behavior ran the night, people breaking and entering, wholesale looting, yelling and screaming. The night sky glowed from the fires.

The world watched them and us on the evening news. The 82nd Airborne Division and the Michigan National Guard marched and did the echelon, left and right. We were dressed in full riot gear. We would back up the mobs until they'd regain courage, throwing rocks or bottles as they approached us again. It was a constant dance for us: back them up, duck, weave in and out, move in close, control, back them up, duck, and then weave again. As soon as we arrived on site, we were taught how to handle prisoners, if it should come to that. However, I never knew anyone who actually took any prisoners. We each held our batons as we marched up and down the streets, while the city burned all around us.

Finally, after eight days it was over! Maybe the mobs just wore themselves out or enough were dragged off to jail. I don't know why, nor did I care. All I do know is that, to this day, I have never ever wanted to go back to Detroit. I knew then that never, ever again, did I want to face my own people, fellow Americans, in the streets of the United States. I never wanted to see my country torn apart like I had seen there. It had taken the joint efforts by troops from the Detroit police, the Michigan National Guard and the 82nd Airborne to regain control of Detroit.

Return to Fort Bragg:
The 82nd Airborne

We loaded everything back in our airplanes and head back to Ford Bragg. I, for one, was sure glad to get back to the sand hills of North Carolina, specifically, to Fort Bragg. The following week I began preparations for my first jump since graduation from Jump School. I thought to myself, "Oh, Boy! I am going to be a 'real' paratrooper, now!"

They called it "busting your cherry" and I was certainly ready to jump! Our drop zone was over a place called the Holland Drop Zone. Everyone behaved so professionally. I saw more parachutes that fall day of 1967 than I ever again saw in my entire life. I think the whole 82nd Airborne Division jumped that day!

My first jump after jump school.
Fort Bragg, North Carolina

The sky was full of T-10 parachutes. The stands on the northeastern side of the drop zone were full of civilians who came to watch as we fell from the early morning sky. Fog was light that morning as we dropped with much precision. It was one of the most beautiful sights I ever saw. As soon as I hit the ground, I looked up. I saw the sky full of parachutes and thanked God for this opportunity and for the wonderful feeling it gave me. I was a long way from Fairview Church of Christ, but I believed that those people back home had certainly had a hand in bringing me here. I was no longer "Little Joe" or the boy who got picked on. I knew I would never again be bullied. I lay there and watched as men fell from the sky. I knew who I was now: Michael Joe Conley, PFC, U.S. Army! I finally believed that I was a man. I knew for certain that I was a paratrooper!

I had never done any of those things they say makes a man "a man." I had not "been with" a woman, nor had I killed a man, but I felt like a man. I had people praying for me, who'd had the faith that I would make it here and here I was. I felt gratitude towards all the people back home in my little community who helped me realize that my dream had come true. I didn't have a real camera in my hand that day, but in my mind's eye I would never ever forget that sight.

Volunteers Needed
101st Airborne Division,
Fort Campbell, Kentucky

Three days later we were standing in formation when the call came down. "We need volunteers for the 101st Airborne Division. They are preparing for Vietnam."

My best friend stepped forward and I followed right alongside him. Steve Hodgeman and I had been through Jump School together and we had discussed remaining together for further training and missions. We both wanted to go on to Fort Campbell, Kentucky, to join the Screaming Eagles. I already wore the famous 82nd Airborne patch and had become part of the best known airborne division in the U. S. Army. Now, it was time to continue on to Fort Campbell, Kentucky, home of the 101st Airborne Division and get their Screaming Eagle patch.

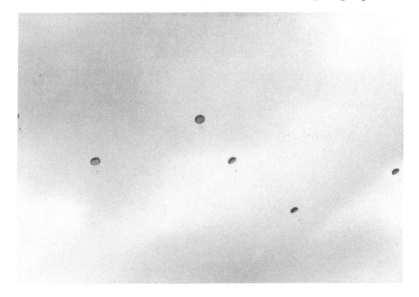

Just a week after that call came down, I was on my way, driving along roads north of Nashville, Tennessee, on through Tennessee until I crossed into Kentucky. As soon as I saw the sign, "Welcome you Bastards of Bastogne!" I knew I was close to the 101st Airborne Division, home of the Screaming Eagles and the 5th Special Forces Group. At Fort Campbell I was assigned to Headquarters Company, 2nd Battalion, 506th Airborne Infantry, 3rd Brigade, 101st Airborne Division.

Later, during the summer of 1998, I served in a very special company of the Georgia National Guard, Company H, LRSU (Long Range Surveillance Unit.) While at Fort Bragg, we made three jumps. That time, I did take a lot of pictures. I visited with my two sons and we all went out to eat before I left to return to Georgia. Little did I know then that those would be my last jumps. The sky looked so beautiful as our planes moved off into the distance and our men floated down. Oh, what a sight! It took me back to my first summer at Fort Bragg in 1967, when I knew then that I would never forget how beautiful that sky looked. I believe I had approximately 280 jumps by the end of my career, but I have no idea how many times I functioned as a jump master. I knew I was one of the few America had to offer. I was proud to be called a paratrooper. What a wonderful sight to jump out of an airplane, under a parachute!

Two days after our arrival in Kentucky, without even having time to unload our equipment, we were sent home on leave. I headed west in my '56 Ford for Indiana. As soon as I arrived, I traded in that car for a '57 two door Chevrolet with black and white stripes on the tail fins. I also purchased a set of brand new tires. What a day that first day of leave was! It was the best day of all five of those days. All of my Conley and Dumond relatives were having a family reunion down at the Martin County Forest, so I headed on over there. I knew there would also be other friends of the family there, as well, so I knew I was in for a wonderful time. Mother had wanted me to go down there with her, since I hadn't been to many family reunions.

Fred Harold, my veteran friend who'd fought in World War II, was also there and got to horsing around with me. He must have forgotten about the first time he'd asked me about hand to hand combat. This time, I knew what he planned to do to me, so I was not caught unawares. I just laughed when he asked if I had any experience. Once again, he grabbed for me. I was able to jerk him over my left hip before he was aware of what I'd done. I laid him down gently on the ground in just half a second. He laughed as he remembered the first time this had happened. He drawled, "Yah, Joe, I still think you're able to take care of yourself!"

We sat together and talked for quite some time, but eventually our remarks became serious. He asked me how I really felt about fighting in a war and he talked frankly with me about how it felt to be scared. It was a relief to be able to talk to a man who understood my feelings. Fred had served in Gen. George Patton's 3rd Armored Division and had been with men who broke through enemy lines in Bastogne, Germany, to help rescue the 101st Airborne trapped by the Germans. He told me more about the reality of war than anyone else had ever told me. Fred told me, "Be careful! I promise to write often." He certainly kept his word about writing, since I got more letters from him than from anyone else during my tour in Vietnam. Every time I am in Indiana I stop by his house and visit him and his wife.

My former stepfather, David Tolbert, still lived in the community. Although a veteran of the Korean War, I never had the feeling that he'd actually seen much fighting. Even though David had gone out of his way to make some of my childhood hell, his being nearby didn't bother me. I had moved beyond anything he could do to me, mentally or physically. Besides, he was no longer my stepfather, now that Mother and Harold Boone were married. Everyone at the reunion was real nice and told me to stay safe. It has been many a year since that family reunion, but the Tolberts and Dumonds still ask me to come to their family meetings each fall. I always enjoy going and talking with them about our growing up days in southern Indiana. They've always treated me like I was family; to this day, I appreciate that.

I had changed a lot over this year. I had grown another inch taller, almost to 5'11" and weighed about 135 pounds. I was filled out with muscle, but had changed other ways. My thoughts were now about the war in Vietnam. Previously, I'd known nothing about any war, only that I wanted to train "for war." The term war had not had a specific meaning for me. Now that I had become a paratrooper and had been preparing to go to war, I felt ready for whatever might come my way. I knew the reality of Vietnam loomed on my horizon. This leave seemed to morph as days, evenings and nights seemed to go on forever. I was getting antsy, ready to get on with my business and see what this war in Vietnam was all about. However, I didn't breathe a word to anyone as to where I was headed with the military. As far as anyone there knew, I was just home on leave.

Every family wanted me to come over and eat a meal at their house. As well, many of my relatives and friends of the family came by Mother's house to visit with me. I just acted like I was home on leave before beginning my next assignment with the Screaming Eagles. I "omitted" telling anyone, especially Mother and Harold, that Vietnam loomed heavy on my horizon. In retrospect, I expect many of them realized the inevitable, because before I left, they said, "Be careful, and keep your head down!"

Grandma Byrd's words were reassuring. "I'll be here when you get home." I had been to see Aunt Alice, Uncle Dutch and Grandma Byrd once and I told them I'd come back for one more visit before I returned to Fort Campbell, but I didn't get to do so. That would bother me later on, since I would never see any of them alive again. On the way to Vietnam I did write them postcards, mailing them from Wake Island as we flew to Viet Nam. Many years later while going through some of my mother's effects after her death, I found all the cards I'd sent Mother and Harold, as well as some others. They were in a shoebox, along with the telegram that told my parents I'd been wounded in Viet Nam, but that I was going to be all right. Early on the morning I had to leave, before the sun came up, Mother and Harold drove me down to Shoals, where I caught a Greyhound bus back to Fort Campbell. I left that '57 Chevy I'd bought, telling Harold, "When Bill comes home on leave, he can drive my car." Harold told me not to worry; he'd take good care of my car and keep the battery from going dead. I boarded the bus and headed back for Fort Campbell.

Michael J. Conley

November 1967:
Heading for Vietnam

At the "request" of Gen. Westmoreland and some U.S. politicians, 10,000 American males, myself included, most of us young 19 and 20 year olds, reported to various military installations to answer that call that would involve America even further in the Vietnam conflict. Much later I learned that ten times that many served in uniform during the entire time America was involved in Vietnam. Yet, only one out of every 58 actually served in the bush, down in the jungle, in the bamboo thickets or up on the Central Highlands. My stories are about what happened in specific places in Vietnam like Cu Chi, the Hobo Woods, the Iron Triangle and Peaceful Valley. Many people have read or heard about well-known places such as Hamburger Hill or the Rocket Belt, but many more places were known to those of us there.

Mother and Harold who had been married less than a year when I shipped out. I had visited and seen everyone I wanted to see, but I was restless on that leave, anxious to begin the next leg of my journey. When I got back to Kentucky, I became even more restless. The night before we were to deploy, the 4th of December 1967, I could not seem to go to sleep. My mind simply would not shut off. All night long, I tossed and turned. I had been in the Army just over one year and thoughts kept up a steady stream. "I'm only 19 years old; tomorrow, my buddies and I are heading for Vietnam." I realized I was scared. I didn't know what we would find there and I expected my team and squad members were just as worried as I. Late into that night, even after lights out, we all just sat around in the dark and talked. We were ready to go; our rucks were packed, as well as a sea bag which we called a duffel. Weapons had been cleaned and we were carrying the brand new M-16 rifle off to war.

Finally, at 0300 Sgt. Marvin L Gearheart, our squad leader, entered our barracks and turned on the lights. I, for one, was glad we were getting going. By 0430 we were all standing outside in formation with wind blowing our jungle fatigues and our boney hats. We silently marched off to the chow hall. I have no idea what we ate, but my thoughts turned to Jesus and His Last Supper. After so many years I still remember my thoughts that morning. I thought it strange that 12 men sat there at our meal just like those 12 men who sat at the Lord's last meal, our last one before we headed for Vietnam. Our squad was made up of two teams of six men and we were a 12-man squad, marching off to war.

After breakfast, the sky began to turn grey on the eastern horizon as we started our march to the airfield. Along the way snow began blew at us as the wind picked up. We were really cold since we were dressed in jungle fatigues for Vietnam, not jackets for Kentucky. In less than 56 hours we would be in Vietnam, but here at Fort Campbell, Kentucky, it was still very cold. Snow billowed around our faces as we marched off. The C-141 Star Lifters were waiting for us, with engines already running. It only took a few minutes before everything was loaded: us, three mule vehicles and two small jeeps. We sat down, hooked up our seatbelts and waited. Lights were turned down low.

I thought, "This time, I am going to land while in an aircraft." Although I had nine airborne jumps under my belt, I had never yet landed in a plane. To this day, I still hate landing, but I love taking off. I felt detached, almost an out-of-body experience. Soon after taking off, each of us began to look around to try to find a place to sleep. I climbed atop one of the mules, a small, four-wheeled motorized vehicle which is used to carry men and supplies. Ammunition boxes were stacked on top of it. I tried to make myself comfortable amidst these, stretching out as best I could. I probably slept about four hours, then woke us hearing the pilot announce, "Prepare for landing!"

We were coming in at Travis Air Force Base, California, to refuel. As I woke up, my mind went in a thousand different directions, toward home, family and friends. I had volunteered for this, since I didn't want to be drafted. Now, I asked myself, "What have I gotten into?"

When we were airborne again, I prayed as our plane headed west. If my memories serve me well, I felt revived after my short prayer to God. The thought never entered my mind that I would not make it. I felt at peace and believed that I had angels who were traveling alongside me. I thought we'd only been flying a few hours when I felt the plane slow down, then bank into a large circle. I looked out the windows and there, below me, appearing beneath the clouds, was Mother Earth and a large city. Slowly I could make out an airfield as I heard wheels descend. I realized, "Oh, my God! We are landing, again!"

With a small bump, I felt the forward thrust as the engines shifted into reverse. We had landed, for the second time. That wasn't so bad! I don't really remember much about our stay there since we were only allowed to get off the plane and go into the hangar while they refueled our C-141. Soon enough, we were back on board where I found a real seat. Now we were headed for Hawaii.

As I tell you about flying toward Vietnam, I also have to write about being scared. It was a deep kind of feeling scared. I didn't think about dying, but rather, whether or not I would be a fighter, a quitter or maybe, even a coward. I wondered, "Could I actually kill another man? Would I be able to save a friend if I had to? How will I react in the heat of battle?" My worries were so intense that my mind wouldn't allow my body to rest. Thousands more questions chased each other round and round in my mind. Once in a while, I thought about home and those I'd left behind. I looked out a window as we flew over the ocean. Slowly land underneath us disappeared, until nothing remained but a deep, blue sea. It took hours to fly to Hawaii and then we landed again.

Outside I saw all kinds of activities going on, and I thought, "Wow! They're having a parade for us!" Quickly, I found out that the Annual 7th of December Celebration was not on our behalf. The place was crawling with old soldiers, sailors and airmen. This parade was the commemoration of America's entrance into World War II, when the Japanese attacked Pearl Harbor in 1941. It was a celebration for those who'd survived, as well as a memorial to all those who died that day. As I looked on, I thought, "Who were those men here in 1941? I know those men were brave and they won the war, but what was the cost?"

Yet, what a night we spent in Hawaii! Trying to sleep in an airplane hangar would not allow sleep to occur! Constant sounds of jet airplanes coming in and taking off every few minutes kept most of us from getting any semblance of sleep. It was a very long night, as I watched the hours slip away. I didn't know it then, but there were many long nights ahead for me in which I'd get little sleep. Thoughts about being scared and lonely crept back into my mind; those same questions I'd asked myself before kept up a running pace. Again, my thoughts returned to friends and family back home. I almost wished now that on that last trip home I had told someone that I was slated to go to Vietnam.

By morning's light I found a small shop and bought post cards to send home, but ended up instead, holding onto them. Our next flight took us far out across the Pacific. As the pilots prepared to land on Wake Island, I saw small white dots down on the island. As we got closer in, I realized they were white crosses set in those black lava fields. The reality of a war hit me squarely between both eyes. "World War II was fought right here!"

We did not remain on Wake Island for long, but it was long enough for me to drop my cards in a mailbox. I had written Mother, Grandma and Aunt Alice. I told each one that I sent love and also, that I was on my way to Vietnam. I knew they'd get the cards before Christmas and I hoped in return, somebody would send me a care package. I hoped I'd get some good things to eat in a Christmas box. I sent out a prayer with my cards, "God, keep those fine ladies safe, if it be Your will and return me home to see their beautiful faces once again."

Not long after midnight we made formations. Each of us somberly walked out to reboard our plane. We now realized that our next stop would be Vietnam.

Welcome to Vietnam!
Digging In

On the 8th of December 1967 we arrived in Vietnam airspace. Even from a high altitude I could see the green of the fields below, and the patchwork of the crops. We were told we'd land at Bien Hoa Air Base, about 35 kilometers north of Saigon. I could see a huge military base as we flew over the town and nearby rice paddies. After landing, we loaded onto trucks which drove down one long road, then down many smaller roads to Long Bien. We finally arrived at a small tent city which had showers and a mess hall. We actually stayed there for about four days before receiving orders: "Load up!"

It's very hard to explain how a young man from southern Indiana felt those first few days in South Vietnam. Everything was strange. The people were much smaller than most Americans I'd ever seen. The place smelled moldy. Everything I touched felt damp, even soggy. Totally foreign smells emanated from the jungle along with unfamiliar sounds that I had never heard before. The heat and humidity were beyond anything I'd ever experienced. I thought, "There's no way we can do our best in this place! I can barely breathe here!"

No matter what we had to do, it was done in extremely hot and humid conditions. Our first job was to build a base camp near a small village called Phuc Vinh, just northwest of the Iron Triangle. We filled sandbags, carried timbers and using anything we could find to build a bunker. We found empty ammo boxes and mortar boxes, taking them apart and reusing them to build our bunker. Inside, the bunker was crowded. After our second week, the Seabees came in and helped us build squad barracks. We stacked sandbags up two deep and at least four feet high.

We lived like this about a month when we first came in country. I belonged to a platoon which was broken down into four squads. Two squads stayed in one tent which had sandbags stacked up waist high. When we laid down on our cots, we were below the tops of the sandbags. Later on I thought that we were like little moles there, living and sleeping below ground.

I don't know what the average person thinks life was like in the infantry, but digging became our way of life. We dug everywhere: in rice paddies, along jungle trails, high up on mountains. Always digging, no matter the weather! When we'd dig in the rain, we watched our holes fill up with water. Even if we'd begun digging before the rains began, those holes'd still fill up. Many times, just as we'd start to dig a hole, we'd have to pull some cover over our heads. Rain, more rain; water ran into our holes.

I thought I knew about digging from digging gardens back home. Digging a garden was easy! Digging in Vietnam was very hard work, sometimes virtually impossible. All we had to dig with were our entrenching tools, which, in reality, were just miniature shovels. We fussed over these shovels because they were all we had and their handles were prone to break off. We did what we could with them; some men would even figure out how to weld them together with another piece of metal, but that just made them a lot heavier. Consequently, we'd use anything else we could find to dig holes.

Besides the physical act of digging, we had to contend with rocks and roots. Rocks were a constant; I thought somehow we'd been transported to New England and those rocky landscapes. Rocks were every size and shape you could imagine.

Then, we'd find roots entwined with the rocks and of course, the ever-present mud, because of the rain and constant humidity. We had to deal with that gluey mud, mud with rocks, gluey mud and rocks and roots … and always, more rocks.

No one can truly understand what a monsoon is actually like unless you've experienced one. In the Central Highlands, it rained every day, sometimes 24 hours a day. It was normal to receive 14 - 15 inches in a day. Sometimes it came down so hard that we could not even see our own buddies who were standing practically in front of us. It never just rained for only one day; instead, it would rain a month, constantly. That mud turned to glue, almost as strong as horsehide glue! It attached itself to our jungle boots, making every step we took heavier. Even our feet were never dry once the monsoons set in. Not long after arriving in Vietnam I began to think about wars between nations.

I came to the conclusion that often war moves beyond a conflict between nations, to one on a personal level, a conflict between people who have their own sense of pride, deep feelings about their home and country, and an intense frustration at not being able to make the other side see the situation from their point of view. What it all gets boiled down to, at a very basic level, is that everyone experiences hunger, thirst, sore shoulders, legs that ache for days. Conflict makes you stronger if you survive the bullets. You develop a strength tempered through survival, experience, time in field. Nevertheless, the noises, screams, bright lights from explosions, fear, running for your life, just trying to stay alive, are all events which extract a cost. Mostly, resolving conflict for me just boiled down to the basics of, "You're not going to kill me, just so you can stay alive!"

Although it has been many a year since I walked out of Vietnam, the war is as close as last night's dreams. I still hear sounds from those nights, screams and cries for help. What I dream is real to me. I don't know if life will ever be any different. I do think, as I've tried to write this book and as I have talked to others about it, my thoughts, reminiscences and the actual act of writing have helped me begin to cope. I can see mistakes I made in the past and have a better idea now why I made those mistakes. One weekend when I first began writing my book, my cousin Connie and her husband Dr. Reid Crosby came from Indiana to visit me and my wife. We talked a lot about my early years and what I was like after my first tour in Vietnam. I think the more I've reflected on who I am now, the better idea I have of how Vietnam impacted me. Those everyday places and everyday men who fought alongside me are in this book. It has been my intention to tell the stories of those who are no longer around to tell them. I'm simply the storyteller for so many who were there. Together we walked down the streets of Hue, fought together across rice paddies in the Mekong Delta or on the outskirts of Bien Hoa. So many of us, men and women, went there.

I served in a line infantry company and we wore our Screaming Eagles patches for everyone to see. We wanted the burden of the fighting on us, on our backs, because we were unafraid of this enemy. Our job was to find the yellow man, draw him out into battle and beat him. Yes, we were very naive and also, so unforgiving. Little did I know that one day I would approach a dead NVA, open his breast pocket to find a picture of what I thought might have been him with his wife and two daughters? I sat down right beside him on the trail and cried like a baby. He, too, was just a young man, maybe in his early twenties. It hit me that this man also had a family who cared about him: a wife, children, a mother and a father, siblings. What were we doing? Why?

This war touched many of us, yet left untold peers, even some out here in Vietnam in uniform, untouched. We were all grunts, carrying 60 to 70 pounds in rucksacks, sleeping in that stinking mud or near that foul-smelling jungle, but we certainly got to experience life as it was. We developed a bond among us that became stronger than blood, stronger than anything I had ever known. Each day for us was a blessing; each evening brought a beautiful end to the day, but one which signaled the beginning of many long nights. Any grunt who walked and crawled through Vietnam can tell you how much it meant to receive mail or packages. Letters from home from anyone, especially from loved ones, meant so much. If we got some socks and presweetened Kool-Aid, we thought we'd gotten a perfect gift!

Most civilians think we dug fox holes to prepare for battle. The reality is we usually only had enough time to scrape out a shallow trench, just barely deep enough for somebody to lie prone in. A lot of time neither we nor the NVA actually knew a firefight was coming; we would just stumble on to each other in a chance meeting. When we met each other, a fight would start and we certainly didn't have time to dig in!

It's not like you have all the time in the world when you're in a war, to dig a fox hole. We were in a war zone, for God's sake, and who knew where the VC were! We knew we needed fox holes to stay alive; time was not a commodity we had too much of. Time was precious! We'd grab anything we could lay our hands on - limbs, leaves or even weeds to pull over on ourselves as camouflage. You'd also have to consider how long you'd be lying prone because camouflage would "give you away" if you lay any place too long. You had only about a 1 - 2 hour timeframe for any weed cover to protect you. Also, if you remained in one place too long, the enemy could easily spot you from a distance of 50 meters. In addition, some holes needed to be large enough for one or more people, as well as whatever munitions they were carrying. If you were a machine gunner, the hole had to be big enough and deep enough for two men to lie in it, as well as wide enough for the two of you to work side by side, while in the hole.

Only at night would we actually have time to dig what could be classified as real foxholes. My initial memories of Vietnam are digging, always digging. We dug dirt to fill sandbags. We dug bunkers and made tops for them with sandbags. We dug fox holes for fighting positions. Hell, I dug all over Vietnam - in the low grounds soaked with water, in the mountains full of roots and rocks! Instead of being called the infantry, we should have been called "the dirt diggers."

If we didn't have time to dig a hole, or couldn't get the hole big enough, we'd simply push our rucksacks out in front of ourselves, then, hunker down behind them as we lobbed our hand grenades out in front. We would build an NDP (nighttime defensive position) around a whole company of about 120 men, maybe more, if the headquarters platoon and a weapons platoon were also attached to the company. On any such night, the company commander would usually order one of the platoons to send out an ambush team made up of one or two squads. These men would move about 200 meters away, then set up for an ambush. Also, the company commander might want to send out LP's (listening posts) of three men together; we'd have two or three LP's out at a time. The next day those men didn't get any extra rest to make up for having to stay awake most of the previous night. They simply came back to their unit and began doing whatever the unit was doing. Daily we moved forward, what we called "humped" forward another 1500 meters or 3000 meters, right along on sore and tired backs and legs. That became the life of the grunt.

Oh, yes! They called us "the light" infantry. Well, my ruck sack weighed anywhere between 70 - 75 lbs. You never wanted it out of your sight because anything you might need was in that ruck, 24 hours a day, every day. Everything we needed to survive was in there: extra ammo, 300 - 400 rounds per man, M-16 ammo, ammo pouches. We also carried claymore mines, bags filled with full magazines. At least 10, if not 15 magazines, full. Each magazine had a least three tracers of rounds in them, placed toward the end of the magazine so we would know when the magazines were about to be done. Most of the time I would put the first two rounds in as tracer rounds, then again at about round 10 or 11, I'd add in another tracer.

We also learned to carry our own first aid provisions, because in a life or death situation or in a firefight, you might not be alive if you had to wait for the medic to get to you. Don't get me wrong; medics sure saved their fair share of us! But we knew we'd better be good scouts and go in prepared. Any soldier carries all kinds of medical equipment including bandages, band aids, cloth, and tourniquets, anything you might need to help yourself or a buddy survive.

We'd created some special types of bandages where needles were placed in tubes, then wrapped up in cloth; in case we needed to do a blood transfusion, we could do it right there. Something that the average person doesn't even think about was that we were also paired up with a buddy who had the same blood type, so in case of serious injuries or if one of us was bleeding profusely, we would do what's called a "left arm transfusion" to your buddy's right arm, right at his elbow. We'd do what we had to do, to help save a buddy's life. I know I carried all kinds of stuff for blisters, bites and stings. Everyone had a variety of medications to combat infections. Vietnam was a damp, mildew-infested place which created all sorts of rashes. Something would sting and bite you every day.

Furthermore, we all had to carry whatever food we intended to eat, which became problematic in itself. Yes, we all carried the same amount of C-rations, but every person does not eat the same quantity of food. Our second problem was how to carry C-ration cans which came in many different sizes. Although we often were told we ate like horses, we sure didn't gain very much weight. I went in-country weighing about 140 pounds and came out weighing considerably less. Both tours. C-rations are not the most appetizing foods around, so we were always looking for a way to make food taste better. Many folks would trade C-rations with each other to get cans of whatever was their favorite meal. I loved pound cake and blackberry jelly, so I would trade off my little packs of cigarettes for pound cake. Those C-rations certainly had a unique taste of their own, to say the least!

An interesting thing that happened during my first tour was we had two men in our company from "Lower Louisiana," somewhere down south they told us. It became a game with us as to whose family back home would send the most Kool-Aid or various foods to us. One day one of these Louisiana men told the rest of us that they could get us some hot sauce from Louisiana. We all thought, "That's such a joke!" We all just laughed and carried on for a week or two. Then, lo and behold, one day here came a whole caseload of Louisiana hot sauce being humped out to us in the field! God's Truth! We put hot sauce on our ham and green eggs, even to our cans of Vienna sausages and beans! We added hot sauce on our ham and beans, even though I had told myself they were butter beans in that can. Everyone sure did made a lot of noise around the patrol base that night! Needless to say, that Louisiana hot sauce really did keep us a happy for quite a few days. We certainly enjoyed our opportunity to eat like those Louisiana boys. We loved these men for helping us out the way they did.

Another thing, we'd come up on gardens out in the jungle and wild fruit trees. We didn't think we were stealing someone's food, sometimes we just wanted something to eat something that actually had some real flavor. Whenever we could get back to base camp, we'd get excited if we found some Seabees there. They always had great food and would trade with us or even give us food outright, like bacon or steaks when we were in the rear.

In addition to food, each C-ration package contained a small pack of four cigarettes. Since many of us didn't smoke, we were able to trade our cigarettes with those who did so we could often create a pretty good meal. After my first tour I heard about soldiers smoking pot in Vietnam. If anyone in my unit would have lit up a Mary Jane out in the field, they would have probably either been shot or got their throats cut! Lighting up in the field would have endangered everyone.

The other thing that people seldom thought about was that getting water out to the troops became a real problem. There is the monsoon season and then there is the hot season. When it would finally quit raining, we'd be sent north into a very hot and dry climate where there were very steep hills. The heat there assaulted us relentlessly; we felt like the humidity literally burned into our very souls. We could never carry enough water with us. Often we went without water while we were fighting a battle. They'd send out ammo, shells and medics, even replacements and take out our wounded, but they never sent us any water!

Water did not seem to be a big issue to those people who had it. We were in at least three or four different battles that lasted a long time. Men were so thirsty that they crawled around under live fire and during mortar attacks to get their other buddies' canteens, literally consumed by an intense thirst and the need to search for a drop of water. Three gallons a day was supposed to be issued, but normally we carried at least a gallon and a half at time on our person.

When there was a lull in the fighting, I'd often try to write home. I'd find me a C-ration box and whack off a piece with my Marine Corps K-bar. After I'd whacked off a box flap, I'd rustle around in my shirt pocket to find something to write with, a pen or pencil. On one side of the flap I'd just write wherever there was space, even in between the printed words and then flip it over to write down the address. Up in the top right corner I'd draw a box and write in, "FREE" so it would go through the mail system, like a regular postcard.

At first I'd carried a 10-inch buck knife that my half-brother sent me from Kansas City, Missouri, but I'd lost it on a helicopter ride. Later on, I'd bought myself that K-bar; I finished off my tour with it still in my possession. To this day, I still have that K-bar and another one I purchased. Every once in a while I'll go outside and throw one at a large pine tree 12 to 15 feet away. I can score most every time, to at least twelve out of fifteen "sticks" into a pine tree.

A friend of mine whom I worked with for a time is Ken Freeman. I came to know him through my church and we bonded early on. He has visited me on the farm; I taught him how to throw this K-bar knife and make it stick in the pine tree. One day I gave him a coffee cup from Iraq and the special knife they issued me there. I was proud that he'd learned to throw this knife so well. I think a lot of him as a friend and even as an adopted brother. He and I worked together for a time as fellow electricians.

In evening hours, before last light we would put out trip flares and booby traps. We'd also rig up small explosives. Sometimes, we'd use claymore mines or just hand grenades. We seldom slept much at night since we knew that was when "Charlie" preferred to travel. We knew the enemy wanted us out in the open, so our lives were a constant game of cat and mouse. Charlie was a very good enemy and fought a very smart war against us. Anyway, our time in country, in that Vietnamese heat, made us stronger so we started to run some night ambushes. We would send a squad out beyond the wire. We called it the FFU (friendly forward unit.) We spent a lot of time outside the wire.

I had originally been in Headquarters Company, but soon I was transferred to Alpha Company, 1st Platoon, and assigned to the 1st Squad as a M-60 machine gunner. I carried at least 400 rounds draped over the outside of my ruck. I liked the belts to cross my shoulders and hang around my body where I could get my hands on them quick, if need be, which happened many times. I practiced hooking my rounds onto the belts so they wouldn't kink up and stop the gun from firing.

Almost all the time I was actually carrying at least 800 rounds of ammo for the machine gun. Our fire team together was carrying almost 2,000 rounds of ammo when we went out on patrol; in defensive positions we might have as many as 3000 rounds. I took really good care of the gun and took pains to keep it dry and clean if at all possible. I also humped at least a couple of ammo cans of 7.62 mm cans that had not been opened; each ammo can carried 200 rounds.

I was a Private 1st Class with two men on my team: the ammo bearer carried at least 600 rounds of ammunition; the assistant gunner could also carry the gun, set it up and make it work as good as me. He also carried at least 500 rounds and an extra barrel for the gun. We often traded jobs during a hump though the day. When one of us would get so tired we could hardly walk, another would step in and trade places.

On the 16th of December our squad was given the task of going out on our first combat patrol for an ambush. Sgt. Marvin L. Gear was our squad leader and that afternoon we began our preparations. We all gathered together and received the warning order. I was to carry an M-60 machine gun and be third in the line. We began to get ready. Weapons were cleaned again and ammo was drawn. A terrain model was built on the ground with toy soldiers in place. Your buddy was beside you as lots of questions had to be asked, answered and then discussed. Our flank security was told how far away they would be to watch for the enemy. We practiced moving into the NRP (Nearside Rally Point) in case we were hit or discovered and would have to make a run for it.

Another thing we had to be able to do was find our own rucksack in the dark. We practiced taking them off and lining them up. We had to be able to lay our hands on our own ruck in the dark and know it was our own. We went through the actions of the objective, practicing going across the kill zone to search for bodies. On the night of the ambush we were almost 300 meters beyond the rubber plantation. We were the first squad to go through the wire. This was dangerous because if you get caught between friendly fire and the enemy, both sides are firing over you or at you. Sgt. Gear stood up in the dark and actually tapped each of us on the head as we came up alongside him. Each man whispered his number to him; in this way, Sarge could be sure that the 12 men going out were the same 12 who returned.

We walked, stopped and listened. We learned this was the way to survive: Walk, stop, listen; then move on. It would take us a long time to get to the NRP (nighttime rally point,) but we'd get there alive. We whispered as we set our rucks out in line, leaving a two-man team with them, one of whom was our squad medic. We moved forward into place; we were scattered out along a well-beaten road just as the moon set. Mosquitoes flew around our faces and bugs crawled along our arms. No one could see the night sky because the undergrowth and trees were too thick. Slowly minutes ticked by.

Soon I realized I was getting very sleepy. Another soldier from southern Indiana lay beside me, Garry Snyder, who was my assistant gunner. At first, he seemed to squirm around, but finally he got still. Night sounds penetrated through the darkness. My mind began playing games with me because I thought I saw trees move! I knew some of our men were moving around, but it still looked like the trees were moving, too! We tried hard to listen, straining to hear something, but we heard nothing. The hours went by so slowly. Each of us pulled two hours at a time on guard duty, while others were supposed to be sleeping. Well, on that first patrol, I do not really believe anyone slept at all. We whispered and talked very low and listened to others around us, also making noise. The hours and the bugs were all in the game to keep us from sleeping. It was not in our cards for us to get any sleep.

At 0400 I heard Sgt. Gearheart on the radio, ordering the flank guards back in. We got back to our rucks; each man reached out and grabbed his own and then shouldered it up on his back. I was really disgusted! I couldn't believe that we'd done everything for an ambush, and it had been a total bust! We just got totally eaten up by mosquitoes. I was really disappointed.

"Coming through the wire" we were met by another sergeant who stopped us. He asked lots of questions about the terrain and what we had seen. Later, I began to understand why things were done the way they were, but on that first patrol, I thought we had just wasted a lot of our time! As time passed I would learn what we did wrong that night and I would find out more about just how lucky we were that the enemy didn't show up that night! Eventually, I would take all I learned about that first botched ambush and train others to do things a lot differently. Later, I found out how amazing it was that all of us returned from our first patrol, intact and alive. Every one of us had been on edge all night.

Out beyond the wire, Garry and I had been out further than anyone, except for the flank guards. I'd had my M-60 machine gun at the ready. If an ambush had occurred, it would have been our job to stop them from getting in reinforcements or coming on down that trail while we were in the KZ. Later, I would change a lot of things about how an ambush should take place, but that first night we were "right in the door," so to speak.

I'm going to digress here to explain about my dreams. Some nights, out of the blue, without rhyme or reason, they occur. I have no idea why they come into my mind or when they'll come, but I do know this: they are as real to me as if they only happened that night. One night not long ago, I dreamed that Garry Snyder was walking into a tent in Vietnam carrying an Orange Fanta bottle. Someone else I didn't recognize was also was carrying a bottle of soda pop, like Wild Cherry. Both of those bottles were so cold they were dripping water! Now, I don't know if that really happened, but I saw it in my dream. I feel like I'm having trouble breathing. I think I'm in jungles which rise up 100 feet high; some trees rise up even higher. In my nightmares I feel scared, yet then I'll shift to some beautiful place firmly planted in my brain. I feel myself sweat, then I fall. I feel my heart pounding loudly in my chest, even up inside my neck; I jolt awake. Immediately, I taste something acrid, like gunpowder smoke, and smell that rotten-egg smell that rockets and shells give off. I think I'm feeling jungle leeches crawling on my body. I smell fear. Then I'm yelling and screaming. I wake up, look around and realize I'm in a room, in my own house, my own bedroom, not in a tent in Vietnam. The quiet slowly settles back into the room, but I seldom return to sleep. I have come to realize: This is my life, now.

Cpl. Michael Conley, Bullet, and Larry Berry. Larry will be killed two days after this picture is taken in the Iron Triangle.

Angels Among Us

Garry John Snyder lay next to me out on that first patrol in Vietnam. Whispering, he asked if I was scared. I whisper back, "Of course I'm scared, and I know you are scared! Hell, 'Hill Billy,' we're all scared! But see, there's some angels out here with us. We don't have to worry."

My Aunt Alice Carter talked to me about angels when I was little, when she took me to Fairview Church of Christ. I have never felt like I was ever alone in any situation because I was taught that angels always accompany me wherever I might go in life. Although Garry never seemed to have a care in the world, I knew that night that he was scared. Over the next 20 months I might ask myself this same question hundreds of times, yet I knew in my heart, I should not worry.

Some 40 years later I found myself serving in the Republic of Georgia. Even though I was older and "knew the drill" as a serviceman, I still felt lonely. One day at mail call I received a large brown envelope containing 12 cards and letters, addressed to "Any Soldier" from a little church on Sugar Pike in Cherokee County, Georgia. Little children from a Sunday School Class had written to me as a soldier and drawn pictures for me. Right then and there, I knew these children were "my little angels," and they were letting me know that I was not alone in this world. I knew then that everything was going to be all right for me.

Fast forward to present day: I now attend this same church on Sugar Pike in Cherokee County, the Antioch Christian Church. One week my buddy, Ken Freeman, asked me to teach a Sunday school class of young people at our church for his wife who was their teacher. He and she were planning a trip out of town and would be gone for a few weeks. I replied, "Sure, I could do that. It would be an honor to do so."

The following Sunday I ran a roll call and later, I got to thinking about some of the names on that roll. Some sounded familiar, tickling my memory bank, making me ask myself, "Why do these sound like names I've read before? Where have I read these names?"

As soon as I returned home, I went to my desk and rummaged around in a couple of drawers, then moved to some nearby boxes. Finally, I found an old brown envelope with cards and pictures inside. I opened up the cards and read the names written on those cards. I thought, "Holy Moses!" There I found names of six of the children in that Sunday School Class, children who had written to me, who had sent me cards while I was off fighting in a war zone. Peggy Freeman had been their Sunday school teacher then, when I served in the Republic of Georgia and when I later went to Iraq. That following Sunday I again planned to teach the Young People's Sunday School Class. This time I took the letters and pictures these youngsters had sent my way in the Republic of Georgia. I passed them out among these youngsters. They did remember making those cards and sending them, but they hadn't realized I was the man they sent them to! Small world! I certainly let them know how much their cards had meant to me then. Now that I knew them as individuals, those cards and pictures were even more precious. Right then and there, I said a prayer over these teenagers, thanking God for them and asking Him to look after them and keep them far away from war.

From my early days as a little boy and as I grew to be a man, I have always believed in angels. Angels are the reason I named this book Not Alone. Over all the years I've been in war zones, church members from many churches have prayed for me. I received prayers from the Fairview Church of Christ in southern Indiana when I first went to war, to Vietnam, and prayers from the Antioch Christian Church in Canton, Georgia, when I experienced war for the last time, as well as from many other churches in between.

Let me relate to you a special circumstance regarding the Antioch Christian Church, when they sent up specific prayers for church members during World War II. They prayed for Floyd Land who was first in an Italian Prisoner of War camp that was later overrun by the Germans! He survived to be liberated. They prayed for W. A. Presley who survived fierce fighting on Iwo Jima. Mr. Presley told me that 17 other World War II veterans left from this church to fight and each one returned home safely. Just before I was deployed to Iraq, Louise Sims, another member of this church, told me and my wife, "Don't you worry, no one from this church has ever been killed in battle." That was reassurance I carried in my heart while I went to war, again, and I felt courageous every day.

Out on that battlefield in Vietnam, I explained to Garry, as best I could, about angels being with us. I told him I believed there were different types of angels: killer angels lift a person away from this earth, very fast, so there's no suffering; death angels remain beside you if you are hurt bad, but you'll remain on earth. Maybe you have to live in pain, sometimes for a long time, but they'll be right there with us every step of the way. They'll look out for us, just like people who know us. There are also other good angels who'll help lead us away from danger. Sometimes other people, who don't really believe in angels or a higher power, might say, "My intuition told me to do that," but I knew different. I prayed with Garry that night in the jungle, asking

God, "Please help us get through this night and help us live to see daylight."

No ambush happened. After a few hours, we all got up and worked our way back to camp where we discussed what happened. Finally, after being awake for more than 27 hours, we were allowed to get some sleep. However, just four hours later, we got orders to go to the Battalion Ammo Dump. Help load helicopters! Never in my life had I felt so tired! Every one of us grumbled as we pulled our jungle boots back onto our feet and then headed out for the ammo dump.

It was hot and dusty as helicopters flew in and descended down. We quickly stripped down to T-shirts and jungle fatigues, loading ammo boxes of 5.56 for M-16's and 7.67 for M-60's as fast as we could. Just as fast as a helicopter landed, we'd rush forward to load it with claymore mines, star clusters and smoke grenades. Everything that a line company could use out in the field. Three helicopters were coming in when I heard the explosion. Immediately, I looked up. About 200 meters to the north, I saw a helicopter smoking as it fell from the sky. The

---

JANUARY 21, 1968

Mitchell Airman Is Cited

MITCHELL — A United States Army paratrooper from Mitchell, has been nominated for the Soldier's Medal for saving the life of a helicopter gunner.

Sp4 Michael J. Conley, son of Mr. and Mrs. Harold Boone, R. 1 Williams, has been in Vietnam since Dec. 9, with the 2/506th Infantry, 3rd Brigade serving with the 101st Airborne Div.

A week and a half after he arrived at Phuc Vinh, he was working in an ammo dump watching five helicopters fly over.

One of the choppers' engines sputtered and then failed. The copter crashed and burst into flame. Moments later Conley began to move.

He ran around a bunker and jumped a barbed wire fence and came into the opening where the burning helicopter's ammunition and rockets were beginning to explode with shrapnel flying past him.

Some of his buddies, running with him to aide the downed crew, hit the dirt but Conley saw the machine gunner stumbling out of the wreckage and crying for help. Conley crawled to the youth and drug him to safety.

Conley was recommended for the citation, the highest non-combatant medal a soldier can earn, by his unit commander. It will be presented later this month.

3. LOST AND FOUND BLOOMINGTON

NEWSBOY LOST WALLET

citation and write-up in the Mitchell paper explains what happened:

Citation: In the Republic of Vietnam on 19 December 1967. For Heroism, the Soldiers Medal was awarded to Private First Class (E-3) Michael J. Conley, United States Army: While working in the battalion ammunition supply point, Private 1st Class Conley heard an RPG round go off and watched in horror as it struck a helicopter in the tail section. PFC Conley observed the helicopter losing altitude 200 meters from his position. The tail section struck a tree and the craft crashed to the earth. PFC Conley ran to the flaming aircraft and saw a door gunner strapped inside the helicopter. But Private First Class Conley was first knocked down by exploding ammunition. Disregarding the flames and exploding ammunition, Conley ran to his comrade and carried him to safety. He then ran back a second time towards the craft, but this time the intense heat and flying debris drove him back.

I was able to get the door gunner out of the helicopter and carry him to safety. When I returned to the helicopter, the flames were too intense. I could only stand and watch in horror as the pilot and the co-pilot struggled to get out, clawing desperately at the Plexiglas windshield. I watched as they were both engulfed by flames and disappeared from view. This scene plays itself over and over and over in my dreams. Even though I could not actually hear the pilot or co-pilot, in my dreams I hear them screaming.

THE UNITED STATES OF AMERICA

TO ALL WHO SHALL SEE THESE PRESENTS, GREETING:

THIS IS TO CERTIFY THAT
THE PRESIDENT OF THE UNITED STATES OF AMERICA
AUTHORIZED BY ACT OF CONGRESS JULY 2, 1926
HAS AWARDED

THE SOLDIERS MEDAL

TO

PRIVATE FIRST CLASS (E-3) MICHAEL J. CONLEY, RA 16 946 808 UNITED STATES ARMY

FOR
HEROISM

IN THE REPUBLIC OF VIETNAM ON 19 DECEMBER 1967

GIVEN UNDER MY HAND IN THE CITY OF WASHINGTON
THIS   EIGHTEENTH   DAY OF   JULY   19 68

O. M. BARSANTI
Major General, USA
Commanding

SECRETARY OF THE ARMY

Christmas Day, 1967

Several weeks later Christmas season was upon us, but it was not a joyous one for us. On Christmas Day we'd had mail call after breakfast and I was grateful that I received two letters from home. The night before, on Christmas Eve, we'd been out on a line in a bunker. It was just "business as usual" in Vietnam. We'd returned to our tent set up in the middle of a rubber plantation, what we referred to as our "hooch." Inside, mosquito nets hung around our bunks. Outside the tent we'd built showers. Also, around the tent's edges we had dug bunkers into the ground so when mortars came in, we could make a run for it, into those bunkers. Then, of course, those proverbial sandbags were stacked up, maybe three feet high. As per usual, if we weren't digging, we were filling sandbags. Out total existence, anytime, anywhere, was digging holes or filling sandbags, if we weren't fighting.

Later on in life, I thought a lot about that Christmas. I did not know then, that within a few days, I would be in a firefight where I would be forced to kill a soldier, another human being. I had often thought I was brave and a good soldier, but I did not really have a clue about what "being scared" really entailed. Much of my life would change over the next year. Before Vietnam, while I was still back at Fort Bragg, North Carolina, a friend and I had stopped in to visit a palm reader, what some people call a "future teller." She predicted, "You will face a thousand deaths before you are twenty years old."

Now that I was in Vietnam, sometimes I thought about what she had said and I had the distinct feeling that my future was about to catch up with me, that soon I would see things that no one would want to see in any lifetime. This Christmas Day in 1967, my thoughts turned back to the Christmas of just a year ago, back when I was at Uncle Archie and Aunt Annice's house. I remembered how happy I'd felt that I was finally in the U.S. Army. I had realized my dream to be "somebody," and had become a paratrooper and a light infantry soldier in the 101st Airborne Division. There was no way for me to know that within one more year, only a few of those men around me would still be alive in 1968.

Our commanding officer, Sgt. Gearheart, sat nearby, listening to a tape recording sent from his family back home. He often shared information with us about his wife and very small daughter and it was obvious he missed them very much. I looked over at another trooper named Johnny sitting on his bunk, with a puzzled look on his face. I could see he was holding a letter in his hand, but he had a strange look on his face. I walked over to talk to him and found out he'd gotten a letter from his longtime girlfriend, Sharon. She had written, "I have some living to do so don't expect me to be here when you get home."

My thoughts were, "Dear God, please help him this Christmas Day." I waved to some other buddies to come over and help me try to cheer him up. One soldier remarked, "At least she was truthful with you."

Someone else added, "Now, Johnny, when you get back home, you'll be able to find somebody who'll really and truly care about you."

Johnny simply sat there in his bunk. For a while he was tearful; we could hear him sniffling off and on. The overall mood in our little tent had turned very somber. Every one of us felt that Sharon might not have been the woman of his dreams, but we all thought, at this time in his life, she could have been more considerate of his feelings.

I had stayed nearby while this was playing itself out. Finally, I walked over to Johnny and sat down beside him on his bunk. I tried to get him to talk to me, just have a conversation with me. We talked about where we each had grown up. He was from a beach near Bakersfield, California. I told him I had no idea what life there was like because I expected southern Indiana was a very different sort of place. Johnny finally told me that for a long time he'd had a premonition that he wouldn't make it to his 20th birthday. He was right about that; by that following February he would be dead, three days before his birthday.

Time has its own way of moving forward. For us, the hours of that day just continued moving. Finally we walked to the mess hall to eat our Christmas dinner, but everyone one of us was quiet. We knew we were a long way from whatever place any of us could call "home." Later that evening I sat on my bunk inside the mosquito net. I thought about where home really was for me, what my life had been so far. I wondered what my brother Bill, now at Fort Carson, Colorado, was doing. I knew he was already married to Joyce.

In my soul I felt my life was getting ready to change. Here in Vietnam the law was, "Kill or be killed," so I felt that this next year would be a hard one. I had no way of knowing that very soon I would have to kill a man. Eventually, I lay down on my bed and wondered if I would still be alive by the New Year, just a few weeks away.

I thought about home and the people I loved back there, but they sure seemed a long way away. I decided to write Mother and Grandma Byrd a "Merry Christmas" card on the back of a C-ration box flap. If I couldn't be with them physically, at least I could be with them in my mind. Thoughts intruded. "Here I am in the rice paddies of Vietnam, on a rubber plantation, in a place they call the Iron Triangle, on Christmas Day, 1967. I sure have gotten myself a long way from Huron, Mitchell and Williams. I couldn't get much farther away if I tried!" I wrote my cards and then I said a prayer for Johnny Johnson, Garry John Snyder, Sgt. Gearheart, Ray Irragang and all the other men in our platoon. I asked God to look after us all and my angels to protect us, hoping one day I'd get home, sometime in my future. Then I simply stretched out and prepared to go to sleep. I trusted that my life was in God's hands.

May 1968: The Iron Triangle and a Field Grade Promotion

The next year found us still fighting. During the Tet Offensive of 1968 the 101st Airborne Division moved us into the Iron Triangle, north of Bien Hoa. Here we encountered a lot of fighting. We got used to hearing mortar rounds falling at night; then having to go out on ambush patrols by day. Slowly we were becoming a pretty good fighting unit. On the 8th of May I went out with the 1st Platoon on an ambush patrol, but things didn't go well. We began to find all kinds of signs of the enemy along the banks of the Song Be River as well as paths that went down to the river. We realized many people had gone down those paths; in some places the trail was wide enough for three men to walk abreast.

Let me divert here for a story about the M-60 machine gun. Before we left to go out on this patrol, I had witnessed another M-60 gunner get himself killed when he lifted the butt end of his gun up to shoot at the enemy below him. This trooper had had to physically pick up his gun, point it down to shoot the enemy within 20 feet of him. As this gunner stood up, he was completely oblivious that a war was unfolding all around him; it was as though he no longer realized he was vulnerable. I watched in total horror as a round came in and hit him square in the head. His skull, the whole backside of his head, exploded. My assistant gunner was inexperienced, and the sight and smell of blood made him violently nauseated. He also witnessed this soldier's violent death and immediately began to retch repeatedly, rendering him completely incapacitated for the rest of the day. Over the next week this assistant gunner began to see more "signs of war." He began to see wounded men who had lost arms or legs, but the worst to witness were stomach wounds where a person's internal organs would spill out or burns from napalm.

Even though we were out on patrol, we sure did not want to walk into a company of NVA or a whole bunch of Viet Cong. Twice we made radio contact with our company and reported what we had seen. We felt like we were in the middle of something big that was about to happen. As evening came on, we were told to set up an ambush along the trail and wait. We were a platoon of 28 men. We had three M-60 machine guns and our M-49's which we could use to lob small grenades. Each of us also had our M-16's, but we had begun to experience a lot of trouble with them firing. Right before dark Lt. White found a place where two trails met. He told us to prepare for ambush. We set out an observation post (OPS) and listening post (LP) on both sides of the platoon, with three men in each position. The rest of the platoon lined themselves along the trail for about 50 meters. This type of ambush was known as a linear ambush.

I know we were very quiet. Each of us got early warning devices put out in front of our positions. Then we set claymore mines down so that they would overlap each other. It was really quiet as night came on. Lt. White called back to the mortar section, for us to close off both ends of the ambush with mortar rounds in case we needed it. We ate our C-rations and watched as the sun set to our west.

Only eight men would be alive when morning came. Of course, none of us had any way of knowing that then. We could feel that something was in the air. I remember that the men around me spoke softly. We were wary; we had already been through a lot of fighting, but we had a bad feeling here because we were more than two clicks (2,000 meters) out from our company. There were things that just didn't seem right. My sixth sense kicked in. We had seen signs that the enemy was close and had found well-worn paths in our area. As night came down on us, most of us felt that we should have gone back with our company and not stayed out there by ourselves.

We felt very vulnerable, very exposed, since we'd not been able to dig ourselves in because of the noise discipline. We were lying on top of the ground or were hunkered down behind anything we thought might offer a little protection. The night was warm, but being so near the river, the mosquitoes were just awful. I thought they were going to eat us alive. The last rays of light left the sky as our early warning team sent a message out to the listening post, asking if we were going to be in that spot very long. On our right, the listening post called on the platoon radio; the platoon leader's RTO sent this message on down to our squad's radio: "Enemy in the open, moving in your direction! Enemy in a line, moving in your direction, lots of 'em, maybe a company." Pause. The next thing I heard was almost a whisper. "Lots of movement on the trail, so get ready!"

We were petrified! We could hear the enemy talking not very far from where we waited. All at once they materialized right before our eyes! Everywhere we looked, we saw them. Worse yet, they knew we were there, too! We realized they were the hardcore NVA because they were wearing pith helmets on their heads, and were dressed in black camouflage fatigues. The last thing I heard, before Hell found us, was our radio sending out a message. I managed, "Thank you, Lord!" as I heard the RTO call in mortar rounds to help us out.

Enemy fire opened up on my right. All Hell broke loose! They hit us with RPG's and mortar rounds, followed by automatic weapons fire. I heard something I'd never ever heard before…a whistle! Immediately I saw them rise up like a mosquito swarm, materializing out of bamboo thickets and tall grass, with guns and weapons a'blazing! The noise was unbelievably intense and just kept getting worse. Everything imaginable flew through the air. Split-second flashes! Rounds crisscrossed each other! Mortar rounds shot out, RPG came in. We knew we were surrounded! They were all over us! Every gun in our platoon was firing as we received shots from every direction. I reached over to my clacker, blew my claymore mine and saw three or four bodies fly by as the explosion flashed! "At least I'm helping to even the score," I thought.

Trip flares went off; we threw hand grenades. "God! We're in a fight for our lives!"

In just a few seconds, our war was right on top of us. All around me I heard screaming. The three-man team next to us took a direct hit from a RPG; all three were killed instantly. I was firing my M-60 as fast as the bullets would fly. Spc-4 Larry Barry and PFC Kevin Shaughnessy, our ammo bearer, were right there with me and by working together, we were able to hold off the first attack. We'd had claymores out front, but had saved one for their final rush, so we'd be able to blast a hole down in front of our position.

I realized I only had one box of 100 rounds of ammo left. I decided, before they hit us again, "We need to move our position!"

I backed up and crawled, maybe 15 meters to our left, deeper off the trail; they followed my lead. Although I knew we were surrounded, my survival instinct was working overtime! I was able to locate a small depression in the ground and we three squirmed over into it. I got my M-60 set back up and loaded, ready for bear! I did not attach those front legs.

After witnessing that incident with the M-60, I had taken the legs off of my M-60. I stuffed them in my ruck sack, so I could use them for limiting stakes when we set up for a defensive position. I knew that without those legs attached, I had a lot more flexibility. I could roll over without it getting caught up in vines or tangled up in any brush and grass that might be around us. Most of our fighting took place out on the ground because that's where we usually found our enemy. Up until this firefight I had never seen the enemy stand up and run at us. Experience had taught me, if enemy troops were 20-30 feet in front of us, they would crawl or squirm slowly toward us on the ground, so as not to draw attention to themselves.

I realized that now our whole platoon was cut off from each other, as well as surrounded by the enemy. Our squad radio wasn't working again, so we had no way of knowing where anybody was. Within five minutes, those woods and jungle exploded again with another human wave of men materializing up out of the bamboo. "Here we go, again!" I thought.

AK-47's and SK's were blazing, their green tracers flying off in every direction. Larry and I fastened two 100 rounds of 7.62 mm rounds together for our M-60 and we opened fire! Immediately, I realized mortar rounds were coming in overhead. "Thank you, sweet Jesus!"

They helped us tremendously! Parachute flares helped us see the enemy so we could see where to concentrate our fire. It was much better that time around. We remained where we were and survived one more attack. The enemy seemed to back off so I decided we'd better take advantage of the lull and take stock fo what we had left. We'd used all our hand grenades and our M-60 ammo'd run out. We were also out of water, but that was the least of my worries. We crawled back around to our first position and found some ammo in an ammo can and two M-16 rifles, with ammo in 'em! We didn't have the wherewithal to process that we were picking up ammo and rifles that just a few minutes ago had been in our friends' hands. Those friends were now dead.

We slithered back to our depression, but this time to the other end of it. We pulled anything we could lay our hands on - grasses, brush, weeds - on top of ourselves, praying we were sufficiently camouflaged. Three more times that night the enemy came back at us. We didn't dare to think that we might be the only ones still fighting against this enemy. After the third attack, we lay still and totally quiet, and each of us said our own personal prayer. We sensed that enemy troops were so near we could literally have "reached out and touched them." We were acutely aware of our dilemma and how vulnerable we really were. Once in a while we'd hear a shot fired. We expected the enemy were hunting for wounded and executing whoever they found. Our angels were right there with us as the enemy walked right past us. And they moved on out beyond our hearing. Each of us thought, "We're still alive!"

Early on, Larry Berry had been wounded in one thigh. Our medic Kevin had done a superb job of quickly getting him bandaged up, so Larry'd survived all of this. Slowly, Kevin and I helped Larry maneuver as we moved away from where the rest of our platoon had been. That night we had probably traveled more than a hundred meters. Finally we located a small ditch, thick with vegetation. I decided it was a good place to wait for daylight. We hoped, no, we really prayed, they'd send a chopper to get us out.

Slowly, what few remaining sounds of enemy fire gradually faded and we were left with an eerie quiet. After a very long night, we realized the sun was slowly rising. Grey streaks on the eastern horizon appeared, what we called EMNT for early morning nautical twilight. Gradually we realized the jungle was wakening to yet another day. Again, we realized, "We're still alive!" Then we began to hear such beautiful sounds: choppers headed our way!

We were all stiff, but slowly Kevin and I managed to get up and then we were able to get Larry up. We positioned him between us as we made our way towards those glorious sounds! We hoped we'd find someone from Company B, 2nd Battalion, 506th Infantry, 101st Airborne Division, come to get us.

I thought I was looking into angels' faces when I saw Sgt. E-5 Chris Beckman and Sgt. E-5 "Teddy Bear" Tilson. They were equally surprised when they saw we'd survived. They helped get us aboard a chopper. We saw five other men also climbing aboard. As we became airborne, I realized we were the only survivors of the original platoon. Only eight of us were still alive.

I received a **Field Grade Promotion from E-4 to E-5** from Lt. Col. Kessling for my efforts to keep men alive that day, 17 May 1968.

Paperwork for this promotion would not actualize itself for another year! By 1969 I was again at Fort Bragg, North Carolina. I had told everyone that I was promoted in-field, but had no papers to substantiate my claim. At Fort Bragg, I was serving under Capt. J. Suydam, then Commanding Officer of Company A, 47th Engineer Battalion. On just an ordinary day, he called me in and handed me my long-awaited promotion paper. Finally, proof of my claims! I was again pinned in front of the company; that same day, I was given and pinned with a Bronze Star with a V, a Purple Heart and my Sergeant's rank.

111

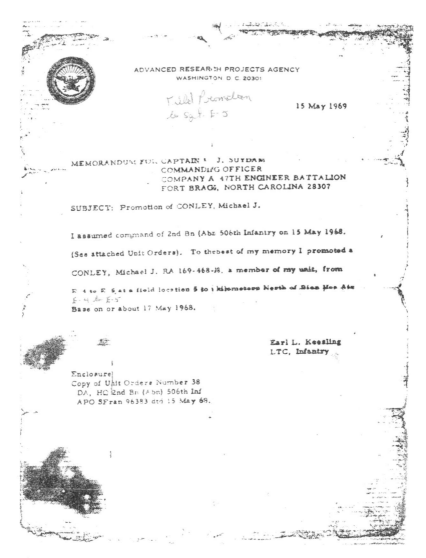

ADVANCED RESEARCH PROJECTS AGENCY
WASHINGTON D C. 20301

Filld Promoton
to Sgt. E-5

15 May 1969

MEMORANDUM FOR CAPTAIN ' J. SUYDAM
COMMANDING OFFICER
COMPANY A 47TH ENGINEER BATTALION
FORT BRAGG, NORTH CAROLINA 28307

SUBJECT: Promotion of CONLEY, Michael J.

I assumed command of 2nd Bn (Abz 506th Infantry on 15 May 1968.

(See attached Unit Orders). To the best of my memory I promoted a

CONLEY, Michael J. RA 169-468-J8, a member of my unit, from

E-4 to E-5 at a field location 5 to 1 kilometers North of Dien Hoa Air

E-4 to E-5

Base on or about 17 May 1968.

Earl L. Keesling
LTC, Infantry

Enclosure
Copy of Unit Orders Number 38
DA, HQ 2nd Bn (Abn) 506th Inf
APO SFran 96383 dtd 15 May 69.

Since the Army had taken its own sweet time about getting me my promotion, I had quite a bit of money due me. I promptly hitched a ride into town, to Southern Pines, and quickly located the Chevrolet dealership. I paid cash for a light blue 1970 Chevy Impala. Afterwards, as I wore my sergeant's stripes, I thought about what had happened to me in the Iron Triangle. Those memories have never left me.

Two events repeat in my dreams to this day. I remember the men in the helicopter that crashed and burned in the ammo dump right before Christmas 1967. And, I remember the night of 9 May 1968 in the Iron Triangle. I suppose these days will remain in my mind until my dying days. The eight of us from that fight in the Iron Triangle went on to live another day. I have often wondered where Kevin and Larry might be, those two men who moved about in the jungle that day with me. I've often wondered if they're still alive, if they'll get a chance to hear about this book or even read it.

Within just three days I had become a 19-year-old Platoon Sergeant. New men were coming into Vietnam daily. I now knew I could lead. I felt the weight of responsibility to train new men as them came in and to take care of them. I would feel responsible until the day I finally left to return home. I would lead more men into the A Shau Valley, staying with them until the middle of November 1968. We survived heavy fighting in the Central Highlands as well as farther north, close to the A Shau Valley, the Ia Drang River and its valley. Almost always we would find ourselves deep in a jungle, daily drenched by rain. Some days as much as five to ten inches of rain might fall. The terrain was steep and because of the rain, very slippery. There were few actual roads; even if we found a road, we were apprehensive about traveling on it. Mostly we used paths made by wild hogs. Soldiers farther down the line learned to step directly into the footprints left by the person walking in front of them.

I wanted to be the Point Man. Building on the boyhood training by Uncle Jesse, I had applied those skills in Vietnam, listening to sounds that came from the jungle, trying to learn the ways of our enemy. We were now traveling, if you could call it that, in a heavily forested mountainous region. We literally crawled and clung to vines, tree roots, and rocks, anything we could put our hands on, just to hold on, to keep from falling or sliding back down those mountains. Vines hung down all around us. Every place we put our hands and feet was mucky, slippery ground. As well, we still had to always be alert for any sign of the enemy. Even if we might come out onto a level spot where the sun shined on the ground, we could not let our guard down.

Our clothes became saturated from the torrential rains and would literally rot on our bodies as we wore them. We virtually lived in our clothes. As a result our bodies suffered; we always had some type of terrible infestation on our skin, often diagnosed as skin fungus. Later in my life I would return from yet another war, from the sands of Iraq where there, too, we experienced similar skin problems. Heat under our body armor and the resultant filth that we lived in created yeast infections on our skin. Soldiers seldom removed that armor unless back at rear or base camp. Out in the field, we would only take it off for, at most, one hour in a day. Temperatures there might rise as high as 130 degrees!

In Vietnam, wear and tear on our uniforms was unbelievable. Boots would literally rot off our feet. Our feet swelled from constantly walking while wearing wet socks, resulting in trench foot, just like soldiers in both World Wars. When we got a chance to remove our boots and socks off, skin came off as well! The skin of our feet became glued to our socks. After my second tour in Vietnam, it took nearly six months to heal my feet and rucksack calluses on my shoulders. Thick calluses formed on our shoulders, so thick that they were visible through our shirts. We would place towels under the ruck straps, in an attempt to protect our shoulders.

We learned that spiders and snakes could be just as deadly as the VC. The deadly bamboo viper lived in the bamboo forests. It looks similar to the green snake in North America. It's known as the "three stepper," because after you're bitten, you will only take three steps before you die. It was very hard to see until it actually fell on someone.

We might get stung from just one bee or a whole hive of them. Mosquitoes bit any exposed skin. After stream crossings we had to check our bodies and our buddies' for leeches. Ants were pervasive, everywhere in the jungle; when a point man chopped bamboo or attempted to cut through vines with a machete, ants would drop down by the hundreds. In just a second, you'd be blinded by them. Their stings were worse than fire ants in the southern U.S. Any part of our body was fair game for scrapes and scratches from rocks, briars and vines constantly tearing at us.

Out in the deepest part of the jungle a phosphorescent fungus grew on the trees. Many times during night movement phases, men would simply stand and look at this stuff growing on a tree. It was not unusual to see troopers mesmerized by it. They might even get left behind if their patrol moved forward, and they were still standing and staring at it.

Some of us said that at night the phosphorescent fungus looked like the Ranger eyes we wore on our wide-brimmed jungle hats, also called "boney" hats. We always kept our hats in good order so we could be easily located by our own troops during night maneuvers. These hats might get caked with mud and/or blood, so we'd have to wash them. We'd often use our helmets as wash basins since it was not unusual to go weeks without a chance to take a shower or a bath. Our helmets would get rusty, but we could get a new cover for it. When often wrote funny things on those covers, such as how many days or months were left on our tour, draw pictures or write funny sayings, sort of like how the soldiers decorated their airplanes during World War II.

As we moved farther north we threw away the ground sheets we'd been issued to sleep on; instead, we just used our ponchos to help keep the rain off or slept uncovered. If you got tired enough, you could even sleep exposed to the elements. As I've said before, each one of us carried 40-60 pound rucks. Loads could be even heavier if we added trip flares, parachute flares and smoke grenades to signal helicopters.

Also in those rucks was our food: the all mighty C-ration! I actually enjoyed those old fashioned C-rations and learned to create some pretty good meals. Of course, I loved the chocolate, and also, the pound cake. I would tear off a small piece of C-4 from the back of a claymore mine and light it, then put it in a can with holes punched in the top. I'd spear a C-ration pound cake and hold it over the heat. Next, I'd add water to the sugar and cream from the coffee package and then pour it over the top of my pound cake. I thought it was the best meal in the field! We would make scrambled eggs in a can. They came out green, but we'd eat them anyway! I liked to mix up different kinds of rations and see if I could make them taste good.

We had to cross streams and rushing water with our rucks on our backs. It was always dangerous to attempt to cross a stream, no matter whether it was narrow or wide. First, we had to tie off a 120-foot repelling rope near where we were. Next we'd pick a very good swimmer. Those who were small were the best since they were least likely to be seen by the enemy. We called him the "Far Side Lifeguard." His job: Swim across a fast-moving stream with one end of a rope tied around his waist and head for the other shore.

When he got across, he'd find a strong tree, but not one too close to the shore. Then he'd untie the rope from his waist and retie it around that tree. Then the Far Side Lifeguard tugged three times, the signal for us to use our transport tightening system where six to eight men pulled the rope as tight as possible. Then we'd tie it off, so now the men had something to hang onto while crossing the stream. The patrol or platoon would line up; one man at a time would move across until only the last man remained. His job was to untie the rope, retie it around his waist or use a snap link to attach it to himself. Those of us on the other side had the task to make sure he got across. Then, he'd untie the rope, roll it back up in a mountain coil and put it into a sandbag for the next time. These maneuvers were very dangerous up in the highlands because if the enemy could catch us on both sides of the stream, they could split the platoon apart. Consequently, our primary objectives became:

Get across as fast as you can!

Reunite the platoon or get the teams back together, as quickly as possible. Get 'er done, so we can "Charlie Mike" (Continue the Mission.)

Problems developed when men dropped stuff or their rucksacks got caught in brush or vines along a trail. Sometimes one could not believe how long it might take to get a man out of such a mess. It was like a wild animal tangled up in a barbed wire fence. Sometimes we had to cut the straps or strings holding things onto the ruck just to get it untangled. Then, things fell off or out, such as ammo or some other important piece of equipment might fall out of the rucks and be lost forever.

Although our lives out there were miserable, very few men ever complained or talked about it. We just wanted to do our job and go home. It was not about our country or the president, but about us as a team. Staying alive was a team thing and your buddy became your closest friend for life. That's the way it was then and that's the way still is. I never ever felt as close to my brother Bill or any other group of men as with those brothers who fought alongside me in war, any war. There was a very special bond I felt with the men who served with me in Vietnam. Over the years I served in Company B, 3rd Battalion, 11th Special Forces Group, in a Ranger Company as an instructor and with the second Mitt team in Iraq. Yet, I would never again feel as close to anyone as I did to those men in Vietnam.

I continued to pray and ask God to be with us, especially before we started a mission. I always asked the angels to walk with us and to especially be beside us during the night. I truly believe they were. I prayed for strength to see another day, for protection from harm and prevention from capture. I don't think I was nearly as afraid of getting killed as of getting captured.

I know from my experiences that no one wants to feel alone at the end. I've heard men whisper, call out God's name as they grow weaker, pleading, "Please, don't leave me," or call for their mothers, down to their last breath. I don't remember any soldier ever asking or calling for a Dad or a father. All these many years later, in my dreams I still hear men begging me to help them. "Please, help me, help me!" When I go to the nursing home to visit my father-in-law, I hear a lady saying, "Please, help me," as I walk past her. Those words so remind me of Vietnam. In my mind I hear the sounds of men whispering for their mothers and loved ones. Others whispered, "I don't want to go like this."

Sometimes as we moved about, there would be a break in contact with the rest of the platoon or a company would get stretched out. Questions would haunt me as I did the platoon head count. "Had someone just fallen down? Has someone broken a leg or tripped? Is somebody impaled on a limb or something even worse? Are they simply lost? Where is the rest of the platoon?" My first reaction would be to send a message back. I might send, "Hurry up, catch up with us." If we were the ones lagging behind, I'd send the message forward, "We'll catch up to you." That's all well and good, except that we were also out there surrounded by an enemy. Also, unless its daylight, you can't actually see footprints or a trail left as men (hopefully your own) move on ahead of you.

Additionally, we had terrible experiences with radios over there. The PRC-125 was a piece of shit. You never knew whether it would work or not. Maybe the battery was dead, just when you needed it. Batteries were always getting corroded because of the moisture. You just never knew when it would happen. Then again, it might not have been the battery, but who knew? It seemed strange to me that when I was last in Iraq, we still had a terrible time with our military radios. A man from America walked on the moon more than 40 years ago and we have cell phones in our own hands today, but batteries for military radios cannot last more than few hours. Is this for real, or not? The radios we carried in Iraq were not much better than the ones we carried in Vietnam. I do know, as the Georgia National Guard went to Iraq and when I worked with a Mitt team, we had awful communication experiences, such as trying to talk from one Bradley to another, or with a Humvee, for that matter. We could see each other over there in the Sunni desert, since everything was in a straight line, or as we called it "a line of sight," but sometimes we could not talk directly to each another.

One trick I did learn in Vietnam was this. I would call an artillery unit. I'd give them a pre-arranged target on my map and have them send an air burst over that target reference point. Knowing from what direction the artillery came and the point where it landed or where it went off up in the sky helped me triangulate and get me back on course. Sometimes I would use two different target references drawn on a map. Where the lines crossed is where we would be. These types of procedures didn't seem that hard for me to use. I could analyze and make calculations relative to known points, draw them on my map and close in the two sides to determine where I was located. Often, we would set up rally points at a stream junction or on a hilltop; in this way, we could find each other.

In my mind I can still see the C-130, "Puff, the magic dragon", or the C-24 we called "Snoopy" with mini-guns stuck out his windows. Those planes carried 500 pounds of bombs. I'd see them coming in on a dive run, then realize, "Oh, no, not here!" I watch as they pull up too soon, bombs falling to earth. I realize they are coming down on us and it's Napalm! I watch in total horror as barrels are released, realizing they are going to hit right in the middle of my men! There's nothing I can do! I hug Mother Earth and pray, "Oh, God, help us!" I watch the short, friendly fire of our own artillery as I call and scream to that voice in the radio, "Shift fire! Shift fire!" I still hear screams of men as they are carried off by killer angels, their voices fading, fading as they are carried away.

In my mind, there are two types of angels during a battle. Death angels and killer angels. Death angels grab you immediately, maybe even before you hit the ground. Killer angels are slower about taking you to Heaven; they are the ones who hang around, sometimes for years. I think I witnessed fights between these different angels, those there to protect me, yet death angels showed up to take me away. I was always glad my protecting angels won!

I have been told I have chronic PTSD, Prolonged Post Traumatic Stress disorder as a result of so much exposure to war. Supposedly, that's why I'm wound so tight. I can talk about war to anyone who asks about it. I can't explain to a blind man what the color of red is, but I sure can tell anyone who has never been in battle what war is like. I know what it's like to be scared. Really scared! Really, scared stiff. I have seen men who could not fire a signal round or squeeze a trigger because they were so scared.

I also recognize the face of courage when I see it because I have seen it so many times. I know courage is present when I hear the sounds a man makes as he struggles for his last breath, struggles through a sucking chest wound. I see faces of young men who begged for their mothers or called out to their wives as they gasped that last breath. I hear the wounded groan where they fell. For me, a sort of quietness takes over, like I'm in a time warp. The battle stops and I realize, "I'm alive. I'm not hurt. I'm still here."

The Central Highlands: May 1968

Off in the distance I could see a big mountain. My map said it was Dong Ap Bia Mountain. By May 1969 the 101st Airborne Division would be in one of the biggest battles of the war on that mountain, but not this time around. Since our 3rd Platoon was already at the front, they began to move forward. We soon came to a small creek. The Platoon Leader had them move to the left and set up a position over top of some termite hills, while three machine gunners with riflemen watched the other side. I was following the 3rd Platoon with 28 men from the 1st Platoon and one officer. We walked across the creek and ran a cloverleaf on the other side. Maybe it took us 20 minutes. We saw where the enemy had been, but we didn't draw any fire, so we motioned the rest of the company to come on over. It was very steep getting down into the creek and up the other side. By then it was nearly 1130 hours. It was rough going; men had to hold onto small trees and vines, while some even turned backward to slide down into the creek. We had to help each other get up the other side by pulling each other up. As more men tried to climb up, the slope became almost impassable. Gradually, our perimeter was pushed up the mountain. Finally, the whole platoon got across the stream and back up the other side. As we'd crossed that stream, we'd gotten chilly in cold knee-deep in the water. It only took a few minutes back into the high heat of the jungle before we were gasping for breath.

I began by walking point while Garry John Snyder walked behind, carrying a 12-gauge pump shotgun. We had four M-60s in our platoon and one in each squad. After about 500 meters we had to stop and set up our perimeter. We were facing the mountain. Lt. Whiteside sent up word for us to stop and eat. The whole company had stopped for lunch; men began to break out C-rations and started talking. We had not yet sent out an observation post or anyone a few meters on up ahead to see what was close to us. We just came to a stop and men began eating. Big Mistake! Suddenly, a man stepped out from the jungle, holding an AK-47 in his hand. He pointed it straight toward the middle of the platoon and let loose a whole magazine of bullets straight into us! Before anyone could get a round off, wounded men lay everywhere ...many in groups of two or three, wounded and dead! No one got off even one round before he disappeared back into the jungle where he'd come from. I felt overwhelmed. Jesus Christ! How did this happen to us? Where did he come from? How was he able to just step out from the jungle and shoot us and get away so quickly? I realized, "He's just killed four of our men and wounded more without even one shot being fired at him!" I felt I was to blame myself for this mess up and took it to heart. I made the conscious decision, then and there, "This will never happen again as long as I am alive. Maybe a 2nd Lieutenant doesn't know what he's doing, but by God, I do."

I vowed to never let this happen again. I realized a battle had begun for us, now. Quickly, I instructed the men to move forward, while crouching behind logs and fallen trees. We turned our M- 60's loose and fired straight up that hill. As if waiting for us as a signal, 10 to 15 NVA appeared, materializing out of the jungle and from small bunkers nearby. They had been down in their "spider holes." Everywhere we looked we saw them: standing beside trees, lying alongside huge logs. They would fire at us, then literally disappear. They caught us in a crossfire, hitting us from the side or off at an angle, rather than from straight ahead. As we moved farther up the hill, they materialized behind us. They hit us with RPG's; shrapnel was flying everywhere, all up and down the line.

We hit back with hand grenades, M-60's and M-49's. Everyone was fully engaged! Yet, in less than just a minute, the attack was over. Wounded lay everywhere! The Captain was calling on the radio, wanting to know what had happened to us. The Company Commander called higher and then we heard, "Prepare for a bombing raid!"

The lieutenant told me they were calling for 500 pound bombs to destroy the enemy bunkers and spider holes. Bombs came in and the entire hillside lit up for 20 minutes; then they came back and dropped napalm with hundreds of artillery rounds on that small mountain. Our boys hit them back again and again. I thought, "Thank you very much!" While our bombs were falling, I was so very grateful that the U.S. Air Force and artillery were there for us. "We have the Air Force and better artillery, and you have the mountain, so I guess that about makes it even."

Over the next 24 hours our helicopter pilots saw enemy fleeing westward, back over into Laos. I did not know it then, but we were preparing that mountain for another battle on another day which would become well-known to the world in May 1969 as the "Battle of Hamburger Hill." By the fourth morning we began to pull companies out, one at a time. We'd survived this time, but we sure got our hands dirty and our noses bloodied. They'd hit us hard and taught us some things about fighting in the mountains. Lest we forget, these mountains didn't belong to us. We finally realized the enemy'd been busy preparing for a battle they knew was would take place. They intended to fight it on their terms, not ours.

Four days after flying into the A Shau valley we were finally on our way out. It had been costly for us and for the Special Forces troops. I later found out they were a part of a LRRP (Long Range Recon) team which I'd seen earlier when we were been briefed by the 1st Sergeant. Twelve of them had gone in as three teams. They'd been across the border and up high on the mountains. They'd found paths and roads leading into Laos, straight off the Ho Chi Minh trail.

Rock Monkeys

On a recent visit with my good friend Ken Freeman, I reminisced with him about the rock monkeys we encountered up in the Central Highlands. Ken is also a veteran and close as a brother to me. After I related this story to him, he remarked, "You must tell this story in your book."

Late in June 1968 things had cooled off a bit in the Iron Triangle and the Rocket Belt. Many NVA regiments were almost completely wiped out, so they'd pulled back across the border. The higher ups, such as Mac-V and Gen. Westmoreland, had decided it was time to move the 3rd Brigade to the Central Highlands using helicopters and small C-124's, affectionately called "the caribou." We also drove truck convoys as we began our big move north. At first, many of us were apprehensive about going up to the Central Highlands. We'd all heard many a tale about the 173rd Airborne Division and the battles they'd fought there during late fall 1966, as well as stories about the Special Forces Camp overrun along the Cambodian border. I thought, "Let's just get it together and buckle down our helmets."

We headed north. It was a beautiful day it was as we flew up, landing on a very small airstrip at a place called Dak To. This airstrip was on atop a mountain and was, maybe, three football fields long. We literally fell out of the sky as our planes came in, with engines in reverse and wheels and brakes locked down; the pilots brought us to a stop, very different from our first plane ride into the Bien Hoa Air Base.

The Dak To airstrip was absolutely beautiful. We felt like we were sitting atop the whole world. Green jungles surrounded us and a small village at the eastern end of the air field. In 1967 a

Special Forces Camp had been wiped out west of here, which the jungle had long since taken obliterated. Later, I found out that more than 300 Special Forces plus an entire village of the Mountain 'Yard had been killed. Here we were, a year later, with more men and equipment, in the same location, where they'd all died.

We set up a small rifle range with some of our new men who had come in since the Tet Offensive. They had new M-16's they'd brought in. We made them zero their weapons by putting the hindsight directly in the middle, and their forward sight stick three clicks up. We collected up a bunch of case tops from boxes of C-rations and together with the LRRP's team, we all went over to the rifle range. After we'd shot a couple of rounds, I found out that only a few of my new men could shoot. They'd been taught a lot of things, but certainly not how to shoot. Mostly, all they'd ever heard was "Spray and pray!" God himself knows how long and how hard I worked with these new men. I'd lay beside them as I talked them through various firing techniques. I showed them how to breathe, how to properly hold their stock handle, how close to put their face to the rifle to be correctly aligned with their weapon. I myself had been carrying an M-16 because they'd put another gunner in my squad. Now I was the Platoon Sergeant and enjoying my new status. After a few days we began going out on short range patrols. We went into the nearby village with the LRRP's (Long Range Recon Patrols) for a "look around." We also got to meet some of the men they'd been training.

We'd had a lull in our activities so I took the opportunity to write Mother and Harold a C-ration box flap postcard. I tried to interject some local "color" in my writing, telling them where we were and about the Mountain 'Yards. I'd learned to dash off a card whenever I had a chance, drop it in the mailbag to go on its way. I'd learned through experience that if I held onto any type of correspondence, intending to wait until we got back to base camp, the jungle rot would get to it, just like everything else in our possession or it might get dropped in the mud, trampled or even get left behind.

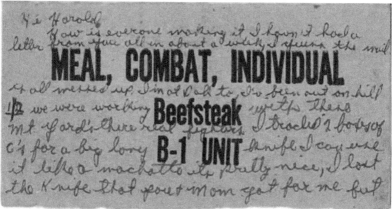

After being around those mountain folk I realized they often talked about something they called "rock" monkeys. Since the mountain folk thought these monkeys were really dangerous, I asked them to elaborate. They explained that these monkeys lived way out in the deepest valleys, not up in the trees, but on the ground, under rocks or in small caves under rock overhangs. They told us stories about how they'd seen the rock monkeys chase anybody or anything that tried to hunt them. They'd been seen chasing, even killing other types of monkeys, who tried to prey on their young. Some of the 'Yards had seen rock monkeys even chase tigers! I still didn't understand why the 'Yards thought those monkeys were dangerous. My feelings were, "Hey, monkeys are just monkeys!" Of course, the only experience I'd ever had with a monkey had been at a zoo where they were in cages.

Finally, an interpreter stepped in to relate the rest of this story, since we seemed to be having difficulty understanding the concerns the 'Yards were trying to express to us. He began explained that the key factor regarding these monkeys was their solidarity and teamwork, stressing, "… they fight as a group and use their long sharp teeth, their strength and small size to their advantage."

The more stories he told, the more we sat right there laughing about those monkeys. We still thought, "Hey, we 'ain' got nothing to worry about! He thinks we're s'posed to be concerned about a bunch of monkeys on the loose? Well, he can think again, 'cause we don' think they're anything to worry about!"

That night our entire platoon spent an uneventful night out. We never saw any sign of our enemy or any monkeys, nor did we hear anything. Not long after daybreak, we moved on out, heading west, continuing up and across the mountain range through an early morning fog. Eventually our point man sent back a report that he thought he saw or heard enemy ahead. Slowly, I made my way up to him, knelt beside him and looked toward where he pointed, further ahead, on up the mountain. I remained beside him three or four minutes. This was a man I trusted; I'd often put my life in his hands. I'd learned from experience to take his concerns seriously. I concentrated on listening, concurring with him that something indeed was up ahead, but I thought, "… maybe whatever we're hearing is higher up on the mountain, higher up than we can see."

Slowly I moved back to the platoon, intending to talk with both our platoon sergeant and the platoon leader. They asked me what I'd seen, but I had to tell them, "I didn't really see anything."

It did cross my mind that maybe what we heard were some of the "Yards" moving through the gap or just moving about the area in general. I thought we should be cautious. Soon we heard familiar words, "Move out!"

Slowly, one squad at a time, we moved forward. After about 20 meters the fog began to lift. Up ahead we all thought we heard something that sounded like a yell or a scream. Everyone froze. We stopped in our tracks, on alert, listening intently. Nothing but quiet, so we began to move again, but this time, very cautiously. Then we heard those same screeches again. I was certainly convinced that something was definitely happening up ahead, I just had no idea what it was. Without me saying anything, nor giving any hand or arm signals for "Enemy up ahead!" half our men began to move quickly into position. Then I heard M-16 shots! First, three rounds, "Tap, Tap, Tap!" Then, two more. I hoped somebody'd actually seen something to shoot at. Again, "Pow, Pow!" Then I thought I heard a child yelling, no, "It's screaming!" I could hardly believe what I thought I was hearing! I really wondered if the stress of battle was getting to me!

Then, right before my eyes I saw my first rock monkey! He was almost close enough for me to touch him! He was crouched down, on the very edge of a rock. His mouth was wide open and I could see very long teeth inside! I shifted my eyes; everywhere I looked, in every direction, I saw monkeys oozing up out of the ground. Right before my eyes! Everywhere I looked, monkeys ready to attack! I thought, "Oh, my God! Those 'Yards weren't fooling, after all!" There must have been 25 or so, all sizes and shapes, materializing before us, swarming out from rocks, up onto logs and other rocks, anywhere and everywhere any of us looked.

What we found out later was that one of their small youngsters had been shot and the adults were coming to rescue him. Also, unknown to us, a local VC unit had moving down the mountain to ambush us. Whoever wounding that young rock monkey messed up the VC's timing because those monkeys grabbed everyone's attention. Those rock monkeys charged directly into us. It was a "no holds barred" attack, with heads reared back and mouths wide open. A few of my men opened fire directly at whichever ones were closest. Into the midst of this chaos, the VC opened fire with their AK-47's! More monkeys screamed from higher up the mountain. The VC, those monkeys and us were all mixed in together, with less than a hundred meters between us. The rock monkeys had charged both us and the VC at the same time.

Now, as I'm writing this, I'm almost laughing. Talk about a time for divide and conquer! Monkeys would get to within 10-15 feet of us and pick up a pretty big rock. With a winding motion, sort of like a baseball pitcher, they'd circle their arms around, then let the rock fly. They were good pitchers because they hit us most every time. These monkeys chased us down the mountains, back down the same paths we'd just come up. They were also chasing the Viet Cong back up the mountain, and they were running, too! Later on that day, I began to understand a little better what had actually happened there. As we moved up the mountain, the VC moved down the same mountain. This put the squeeze on the rock monkeys who were caught in the middle. Anyway, I've always thought those rock monkeys saved a lot of lives that day, ours especially. I always wondered if any more monkeys were killed. After less than a two-minute battle, the rock monkeys won!

We had three or four men wounded with knocks and scrapes, some with really deep cuts that needed sewing up, others with shoulder wounds, a few with head wounds. One of those monkeys had bounced a rock off my chest, so for a week it hurt to breathe. I felt like somebody had whacked me across the chest with a 2 x 4, but at least none of us was dead. The rock monkeys went their way, the VC another, and we left that side of the mountain to them both. I never saw another rock monkey again.

After-Action Report: Rock Monkeys win: 1 to 0.

Change route and continue with mission.

We left those Central Highlands and moved farther north. I actually missed the 'Yards, those mountain people we had gotten to know. I felt they were loyal and trustworthy as fighters. I have never forgotten the time I spent with them, as well as the beautiful sights there, pretty streams full of rushing water as they headed down, out of those jungles.

Michael J. Conley

The Purple Heart:
20th of August 1968

We had been in the Ia Drang Valley for about two weeks on a
company-size operation with approximately 100 men. Some of
our men had gone on R&R; others were out sick or in a hospital,
so I don't know how many were actually present that eventful
day. Things had been hot in our zone for some time. Earlier, the
night before, on the 19th of August, I told three of my best
friends, "Today is my mother's birthday." These friends and I
had all been together since leaving Fort Campbell, Kentucky,
back in December 1967. By dark the next day, all three friends
would be dead.

We had kept on the move since we were on a search and destroy
mission. We had seen lots of signs that the enemy was close. It
was around 1400 hours when things begin to go wrong. First, we
started to getting hit by small arms snipers. They were not very
good shots because they kept shooting too high. I knew they
were up in the trees because shooting down is very hard to do.
Also, it's hard to hit moving target that's not on the same plane
or elevation as you. Our company commander called in a couple
of gunships around 1420 hours. One of our friends was flying a
Shadow gunship, so he began hosing down enemy trails and
paths leading back into the jungle where no one could see them.
A few minutes later, we heard a huge explosion. Immediately I
knew he'd hit an ammo dump or a resupply point. I also realized
that they would stand and fight for that ground and their
remaining ammo and supplies. I was scared and I knew I was
scared, but it was an "all right" scared. I was on full alert. Every
nerve in my body was attentive: listening, watching, thinking,
searching for whatever might be happening. My eyesight was

acutely aware of the smallest movement and my heart slowed down, but it kept on beating hard in my chest.

That firefight began like so many others. We were constantly either stumbling onto them or they stumbled onto us. A couple of sniper rounds went off just ahead of our platoon. I had been told by our platoon leader to maneuver to the left and to come up online. As we started to flank to our left, sounds of the firefight began to get much louder. I had taken the point and we were moving very slowly, so everyone was on full alert. Our men were strung out in single file, so it had taken a few minutes to get everyone up and moving. We had not moved more than a few feet when a NVA soldier literally rose up out of the ground to my right, out from under a concealed spider hole. He had an RPG already up on his shoulder before I spotted him through the bush and tall grass. Less than 25 feet from me! I jumped away as he fired an RPG right at the spot where I had been standing, only moments before. It missed me by only a couple of feet, then went off as it struck tree a few feet to my right. It knocked some of our men down and a few were blown off their feet. My left leg felt like a pin cushion, with a burning sensation down both my legs. To this day I can remember looking down at my right leg. I was so pissed off! I was wearing brand new jungle fatigues, but now they were covered with blood and had holes in them! How did this happen? We didn't get new fatigues very often. I thought, "The nerve of these NVA and Viet Cong! They've ruined my brand new uniform!"

My left knee was hurting really bad. Blood was soaking my pants, running down both my legs. I shifted into reaction mode. In less than a minute, I'd slapped a compression bandage on my leg and tied a tourniquet tight to stop the blood flow. Now, I thought, we could move again. As we started to flank to the left,

WESTERN UNION TELEGRAM

158A EDT AUG 25 68 DEA309 PA402
P WA022 XV GOVT PDB WASHINGTON DC 24 1005P EDT
MR AND MRS HAROLD BOONE, DONT PHONE DONT DLR BTWN 10PM AND
6AM
    RTE 1 WILLIAMS IND
THE SECRETARY OF THE ARMY HAS ASKED ME TO INFORM YOU THAT YOUR
SON, SPECIALIST MICHAEL J. CONLEY, WAS SLIGHTLY WOUNDED IN
VIETNAM ON 21 AUGUST 1968 AS A RESULT OF HOSTILE ACTION, HE
RECEIVED METAL FRAGMENT WOUNDS TO THE LEFT THIGH AND LEFT KNEE.
HE WAS ON COMBAT OPERATION WHEN ENGAGED HOSTILE FORCE IN FIREFIGHT.

    HE IS HOSPITALIZED IN VIETNAM. ADDRESS MAIL TO HIM AT
THE HOSPITAL MAIL SECTION, APO SAN FRANCISCO 96381. SINCE HE
IS NOT REPEAT NOT SERIOUSLY WOUNDED NO FURTHER REPORTS WILL
BE FURNISHED
    KENNETH G WICKHAM MAJOR GENERAL USA C-3218 THE ADJUTANT GENERAL

AFTER 10 DAYS RETURN TO
THE WESTERN UNION TELEGRAPH CO.

20 N. MERIDIAN STREET
INDIANAPOLIS, IND. 46204

RR#1
WILLIAMS, IND

sounds of the firefight got much louder. I took the point and we began to flank as more RPG rounds came out of the jungle. I turned and yelled, "Get down!" We had been in the Ia Drang Valley for about two weeks on a company-size operation with approximately 100 men. Some of our men had gone on R&R; others were back in field hospitals or in various other locations. Immediately four men who'd been right behind me went down.

I fell down, too! A huge piece of shrapnel had just ripped through my left arm, while a larger piece hit my left leg just above the knee. I tried to crawl back toward my men as their automatic weapons opened up. I managed to crawl forward into a small depression that led me back toward other men who'd been knocked down. I knew we had been hit hard. Two of us were now dead. Others were wounded, much worse than me. The rest of our platoon came up on line and after a short firefight, the enemy broke it off and disappeared back where they came from, simply back into the jungle. I managed to pull myself up into a sitting position on the ground. Garry John Snyder came running up, screaming, "God! Sergeant, you're hit!" Blood poured into my pants. I turned to pull an ace bandage out of my rucksack. I saw our Company Commander heading straight for me and I just knew I was in big trouble with him. When he got abreast of me, he asked, "Sgt. Conley, was you the one who led this platoon to the left?"

I knew I should stand up to answer, but for the life of me I couldn't get my good leg under me. I just answered from where I sat. "Yes, Sir!"

He responded, "Outstanding initiative, young man! You did very well and it looks like you will get a few days off!"

As soon as he walked away, the field medic shot me full of morphine. As you can imagine, now I really began to feel good! I thought, "Wow! So 'my war' will be over for a few days. Whoopee!"

The medic managed to get a pressure bandage on my left thigh as I heard the choppers arrive. In just a few minutes we were flying far above those rice paddies. Heading for the hospital, I thought I heard horses galloping across those beautiful white clouds. On board were two other wounded men and the three dead, all of us from the first platoon. They flew me back to a firebase camp, then I was put onto another chopper and hauled back to Camp Eagle. I tried to tell them that I was not really hurt that bad. After a few days, I was up and out of my bed. The doctors fussed at me, but those cute little nurses were always smiling when they talked to any of us there. Yet, I knew things would not be the same when I returned back to the company. I'd been out of action for ten days. On the morning of my tenth day when I woke up, three new men had just been brought into my hospital room. They were from our company, A Company. I knew who they were, that they belonged to our unit, but I didn't know their names. I talked to each of them, then I made up my mind that it was time for me to go back to my unit. The guys back there needed me out there, not in here looking at and talking to pretty nurses.

I just walked out of that hospital, over to the helicopter pad and caught a flight back to our company, flying in with the supplies and mail going in. After I got back I found out that while I'd been gone, our numbers had continued to fall. Only seventeen remained of the original men in the company. The toll of continuing deaths resulted in me no longer wanting to make friends with any new men coming in as replacements.

After my return stateside, I was able to visit with Mother. She related to me what happened to her the night of her birthday, August 19th. She had gone to sleep and began to dream. She woke from a sound sleep, about 3:00 a.m., then reached over and woke up Harold, her new husband. She told him she had just had a dream in which I was wounded and she saw me being loaded onto a helicopter. They sat up the rest of the night because there was just no way was she going to be able to get back to sleep. Four days later, the Lawrence County Sheriff drove into their driveway at 2317 30th Street in Bedford, Indiana. He brought a telegram that said I had been wounded in Vietnam. After my mother died in August 2008, I was in her house looking through some of her things. I found an old shoe box where she'd saved every one of my C-ration box top postcards I'd written. I also found the telegram about me being wounded.

I sincerely believe Mother's dream came to her as I was wounded and then flown off to the hospital. My Aunt Alice told me that she also dreamed about me getting wounded in Vietnam. She watched while two angels stood beside me with blood running down my leg. She woke up, and was trusting the feeling she got that I was going to be fine, only needing a little help from those angels to get through the night. She never told me about any other dreams of me while I was in Vietnam, but I knew my Aunt Alice was a very religious woman with a strong belief in God and in the power of angels.

It has been many a year since my days in Vietnam, but I have never forgotten what it was like. I truly believe that once you have been in battle and hear the screams of your buddies and sounds of gunfire going off, you never forget any of it. Sounds of bullets hitting earth are much different than the sound of bullets hitting a human being. I have often wondered how it is that two men can be lying side by side and one is killed, yet the other doesn't even get a scratch.

In my dreams I still hear screams and sounds in the darkness, see flashes of light, think that artillery and mortar rounds are coming in. Our gunships, "Smokey" and "Puff, the Magic Dragon," fly in, lighting up the night sky with their cannons. I still see their red and green tracers as they sear the night sky.

Many nights I wake myself up, holding my breath so the enemy will not find me. I'm on alert; I try to not make any noise. I see parachute flares pop and mortar rounds give off light, as I watch the enemy creep through the tall elephant grass or over fallen jungle trees, through the undergrowth. I know I have to see them before they get us. It simply boils down to staying alive. Each one of us will instinctively kill to avoid being killed. They are trying to kill us and we are trying to kill them. Who gets to stay alive? I pray, "Oh, Lord! Protect us!"

Darkness approaches. I know we'll find dead men when the sun begins to shine through the jungle leaves, since daylight is when you get to see who still lives. Finally, I wake up. I realize, "That was my dream again, talking to me." I realize my night was all tangled up with screams and blurry vision.

Getting Ready for the A Shau: "PFC Dorsett Reporting, Sergeant!"

The 3rd Brigade of the 101st Airborne Division was on the move again by September 1968. We landed at a base camp called Camp Eagle, west of Hue City. Now I held the rank of Sergeant, and was the 1st Platoon Sgt. of our company. Our Company Commander was Cpt. William "Wild Bill" Burrier and our 1st Sergeant was Linn Sprinnoli. We had one platoon sergeant, an E-7 for Headquarters Platoon, one E-6 staff sergeant in the rear as a supply sergeant, and four E-5 buck sergeants. We, as buck sergeants, were the line company platoon sergeants in our company, the backbone of Alpha Company, experienced in battles and fire fights, as survivors from many months of fighting. Originally, 124 men and officers had flown out of Fort Campbell that cold December day in 1967. Now, only 22 of us were left. We were battled tested. We had cried, been wounded and watched as our buddies went to heaven. We knew we were not alone, that God had been with us every day, that His angels had protected us through long rainy nights. Our fears about dying had slowly faded away. We all thought that we were not alone because we knew those angels were with us. Also, as long as we could remember the faces and laughter of those who'd gone before us, they were still with us in our hearts. We knew we were the best of American's fighting men; we were proud to be paratroopers and Screaming Eagles.

A new concept was about to be tested: Airmobile to the Rescue. We would fly in on Huey helicopters, UH-1B's, and Chinooks, CH-24's. We called them our "stallions." We thought of ourselves as riding into battle, akin to the Crusaders. I certainly had no clue what lay ahead for us. On our first night in Camp

Eagle the 1st Sergeant came over, sat down and talked to all of the NCO's in our company. He said something big was coming down. He told us we had one day to "zero our new weapons" and get the right men in the right positions. We were going to fly into the A Shau Valley with "guns a'blazing!" in a couple of days.

My reaction was, "Wow!"

After the 1st Sergeant left, Sgt. Couch and I began to talk with Ellis and Sgt. Jimmy McGroarty. We talked for an hour about being understrength since leaving the Central Highlands, how long it took to train new men and get used to working with them. We didn't have time for that!

We were accustomed to going in by helicopters to "Hot LZ's." We knew we needed time to practice and show our men how to do what needed to be done. We felt that all the training and talking in the world was of no use if we didn't have time to train these new men right. We knew the A Shau, all the stories the Marines and the 1st Infantry Division already told about it. None of them were good.

Early on the morning of the 12th of September, I was told to go down to the helipad and pick up our new men coming in. Everyone was getting new men. I began to walk as I carried my ruck and my M-16. I'd gone about a half a mile when PFC Jerry Phillips of our company came by, driving a mule. He gave me a lift to the helicopter pad, over a mile from our tents and the outer perimeter.

Three CH-24's came in and sat down. Brand new men got off …. I saw new jungle fatigues, new faces. I thought, "They look so young." I had forgotten that I was only 19; I thought of myself now as a much-older soldier. A second load of men arrived. Each

Company Representative was called forward. I was the Sergeant for Alpha Company, standing beside a good friend from Charlie Company and another from Delta Company, when we began to hear names called out. I was standing with 20 new men behind me when I heard a name that sent a cold chill down my back. "Harry C. Dorsett," was yelled.

Someone nearby yelled, "Here!" I looked and watched as a young man with a very familiar face came walking up. He replied, "PFC Dorsett reporting, Sergeant!"

I simply reacted! I yelled, "Butch!" He was just practically my best friend from back home in Mitchell, Indiana. My short life flashed before my eyes: We had been friends my whole life and had been together until I left for the Army after my high school graduation. His Granny Carroll had taught me how to swim; I'd bought my first car from his father, Sonny. I thought I'd probably spent about half my childhood, my growing up years, over at Butch's house. We'd had sleepovers and attended school together and even played on the same basketball team together. I remembered when he and I had driven 100 miles down through Indiana to cross the Ohio River one night, just for the fun of it. All that seemed like an eternity ago. Now, he was right here, standing before me on the 12th day of September 1968, in Vietnam. Unbelievable! We hugged each other, right then and there. I spent about ten minutes talking with him. Then, I realized his sergeant had gotten all his men together and I had mine. We began to walk back to the company area. When we got back to camp and I had a few minutes, I sent a note to Butch's Granny, whom I thought of as my "Next-to-Best" Granny. I mailed it that day as we prepared to depart for the A Shau Valley.

September 12 1968

Dear Granny,

I received a card from someone (you) ...who has certainly brought smiles and laughter to me through the years. Now, Granny, you came through again. I opened my mail and I saw a small black Holy Bible. Yes, I knew I had a lot to thank God and the angels for, and I said a prayer and gave thanks to God. I said a prayer today that stretched across 12,000 miles to the heart of the people I love. Granny, thanks a lot for your card and the Bible. It has helped me this day in this foreign country in its torn-up land. Today, I also prayed for Butch, since he's now showed up here in our unit. He is and will always be one of my closest friends through the years, and I pray that he may face the many hazards of this coming year and overcome them as a man, and that he would be home soon.

Love,

Little Joe

Over the next three months I would stop by and talk to Butch every chance I got. I asked my friends from other companies to help him, to look after him if they could. We all tried to look after any of the new men, to train and teach them everything we knew. It was rough, looking into a new man's face and seeing that scared look, wondering whether he was going to be courageous. No one could tell until the lead started flying. To this day, I don't know how many times I saw Butch before I left, but I did check in on him whenever I could. Every time I saw him I told him, "Keep your fool head down! Don't take chances!"

In three days we would all fly into the A Shau Valley on a combat assault. All Hell was getting ready to break loose! But first, paint yourself this picture. Most of us were just American boys who only a year or two before had been playing some type of ball - basketball or football - all over America. Now that it was fall, in America autumn leaves of every hue fell all over yards, roads and farms. Many of us were simple country boys who'd loved a good game. In our branches of service we were trained in light infantry tactics. Some of us had even gone on to Jump School where we earned valuable wings, the Silver Wings of the 101st Airborne Division. We were the Screaming Eagles. We thought we were better than most anybody!

Now, 40 years later, I know we actually were good, but maybe not as good as we thought we were then. Many of us were bloodied in battles and fire fights. We were ambushed and run over by the enemy. We had forgotten what they told us long ago about that "enemy" before we got to Vietnam. This enemy certainly knew his way in and through the jungle and around his own backyard. We certainly found out that Charlie was good at what he did; in a jam, very good.

Finding any enemy in a three-canopy jungle was never easy. Sometimes, it was almost impossible. The enemy we were fighting was every bit a predator. It's very dangerous to look for a wounded tiger or a rattler in rocks who are in familiar territory and you are not. Our enemy knew where to hide. He also knew when we were going to be anywhere. Fixing on this enemy from any position was as difficult as finding a tiger or a rattler. Alpha Company, 2nd Battalion, 506th Infantry, 101st Airborne Division, along with Bravo Company, Charlie Company, two supporting companies of artillery and three companies of ARVN's (Army Republic of Vietnam) were all ordered into the same area. Our joint task was to assist the initiation of a "Search and Destroy Mission" which would utilize a series of company-sized helicopter assaults into the A Shau Valley, near the Laos border. Those of us in Alpha Company had already been sitting and waiting in the marshaling area alongside Bravo, Charlie, and Delta Companies for more than 40 hours as we listened to the company commander of each company. They used maps, photographs and terrain models to brief and re-brief us. Our preparations had been intense and meticulous. By now, we'd had so little sleep we were like the living dead. Our attack choppers and slicks, UH-1's, the Hueys, had been checked out, refueled and loaded once again. We had practiced various maneuvers five to six times: loading and sitting positions, unloading, then spreading out without running into another landing or a "stopped" Huey, practicing keeping our teams together.

We called the Huey's our "galloping' stallions" because they sounded like wild horses running across the sky. Each platoon had a sector and each squad had very specific assignments that had to be done exactly right. Everywhere I looked, no matter which direction, I saw new faces: brand new officer corps, from our company commander to new platoon leaders. It was obvious that most of these new men had never been on a combat assault; they certainly had never been shot at while flying into combat aboard a chopper. They actually were looking forward to their first invasion from the sky.

I saw some men sitting quietly, simply looking off in the distance; I knew these men had enough experience under their belts to know what lay ahead for us all. As for me, I was deeply concerned and apprehensive. I watched others check and recheck their weapons; watched their fingers move the selector switch from 'safe' to 'fire' and then to 'automatic.' I could not shake off the feeling that we were simply condemned men waiting to be dumped off into that valley. Although I had not fully recovered from my leg wound, I did feel like it was not severe enough to keep me from doing my job. As a platoon sergeant, I would not be running around like a private. I had been busy training these men over the past three weeks, explaining what they could expect to encounter.

The night before, I'd had a long talk with our new company commander. He asked me about my leg wound and how I felt. I told him I was "… almost 100 % … and more than ready to do my job." After a moment of silence, I added, in military language, "I am most anxious to return to action, to lead my men and my new platoon."

He looked at me hard, then finally said I could go. With a pause, he added, "Be careful!"

Although fears of death or capture were always with me in Vietnam, more than anything, thoughts of "failure to perform well" disturbed me more. I had almost convinced myself that I might not make it back home or return from this mission, but I did not want the "Old Man," our Company Commander, to know that. Within 24 hours I would, as our new soldiers would say later about that day, "heroically save the life of that new commander." My only request to him had been, "Sir, you can put us down in Saigon or Hue City or even Hell, but please, Sir, tell the aviation pilots and units, **please, put us down together, in one place**." I could not stress enough that we should not be separated from the platoon or from the rest of the company. I also prayed that morning, more than once, "Please, God, just keep us together."

Over the previous three to four days we'd been hearing rumors up and down the line that a large NVA unit was bivouacked in the western end of the valley. I looked at the map spread out in the Captain's Office, pointing to a small hill on the edge of the map. I said, "Sir, this is our destination." Within six months this hill would be known as "Hamburger Hill."

Puppy!

One memory that stands out was a new recruit with, of all things, a puppy! This recruit was a brand new private in our platoon and was just sitting on a rock, petting a small, skinny puppy. Who knows where he'd found her. I spoke to him, and he smiled as he responded, "This'll be my first helicopter ride."

I thought, "Oh, my God! Oh, my God!" Nevertheless, I replied calmly, "Have you never been on a helicopter?"

Cheerily, he answered, "Oh, yes, Sergeant! Three times yesterday, when we were practicing!"

I was overwhelmed. I didn't know how to respond, what to say to him. Instead, I just shifted the conversation to another topic. I thought, I'll just try to have a regular conversation with him. I asked, "Where'd you get that puppy?"

Still smiling, he said, "I found 'er. I gave 'er some C's. I'm gone keep 'er. She follows me ever whir." He thought of her as his pet now and she was certainly happy as a clam, sitting right there beside him.

Continuing the conversation, I asked, "What's her name?"

"Puppy."

Immediately I felt overwhelmed. I had to walk away from him. I could not remain there. I simply walked on, trying not to think about what I'd witnessed. Later, I'd realize I'd never even asked the kid his name. As we began to load the choppers, I saw that same private standing in line, waiting his turn to climb onto the choppers. Puppy was still with him, her head sticking out from the top of his rucksack. I only hoped that the dog would stay in the ruck until we hit the ground. The young man turned in my direction, saw me and yelled out, "We're finally going into action!"

He was all excited. I wanted to yell or scream, but I did neither. Three rows over, in Bravo Company, was a young man named Ted "Teddy Bear" Tilson who'd just made buck sergeant. He yelled out to me, "Hey, Machine Mike, see you on the other side!"

Over the next 30 plus years Teddy Bear and I would fight together in many other war zones. We would serve together as Ranger instructors at the Mountain Ranger Camp at Camp Frank D. Merrill; we would hike together along the Appalachian Trail, share a few cold beers and much of the rest of our lives together.

One day when I saw him at Camp Merrill, I called out, "Teddy Bear!"

He replied, "Machine Gun Mike!"

In conversation with my wife and me later, he told my wife, "He might be a funny kind of crazy, but he sure can run the Hell out of a machine gun!"

More on the A Shau

Teddy Bear would fly with us that day in 1968 into the A Shau Valley. We wished each other, "Safe trip!" We were both probably thinking the same thing. "How many more of these can we make and make it back, alive?"

The company briefing had not alleviated my concerns about this mission. The more I looked at the maps, the worse I felt. I was more than suspicious about the entire operation. Those in leadership kept talking about the advantages of a surprise attack, a quick lighting strike. They thought the enemy would not know where we were going to land or where our landing zones were going to be. Again, I looked at the company commander's map of the western end of the A Shau Valley. I was only a sergeant, an E-5, but I could only see three or four places large enough to land eight or nine helicopters at one time. We needed someplace larger than 200 meters in length for this operation. As I turned to walk away, I stuffed a brand new map into the outer pocket of my jungle fatigues. I knew I'd need it later; I was sure of that.

I talked to the company commander about my concerns and how nervous I was. One issue was how well communications would go when we hit the valley. I explained that the frequency we used always got jammed during battles. With only one frequency, and all four rifle platoons and their men using the same frequency, I just couldn't see that we'd be able to pull this one off... Too many people trying to talk on one frequency at the same time always caused a jam.

Another concern was our radios. PRC -25 radios seldom worked well in jungle terrain and could only transmit and receive at 4 - 5 kilometers. Someone, usually the battalion commander, was often overhead in a small plane and could transmit to a higher command. However, when four to six radios tried to transmit at once, no one could be heard. Additionally, the terrain where we were headed was problematic. The A Shau was down in a valley with hills and ridges all around, some of which were 300-400 feet higher than our landing zone. I took the commander over, opened up the map and showed him what I was talking about, explaining that the grid lines were very close together.

I got a chance to talk to our platoon leader and told him that our radios in all likelihood would not work at all in the early phases of this mission due to the fact that there was not a relay station on the ground close to the ridge line. Nor did I expect we'd be able to make contact with the forward air controller for at least a few hours. I had told the platoon leader that I had already told the "Old Man," our name for the company commander, the same thing. Then my mind told me, "Be quiet, quit worrying, and for God's sake, don't rock the boat!"

I kept trying to talk to myself, to convince myself that everything would be all right. Then I did something I only did once in Vietnam. Before we loaded the Huey's and started into the A Shau, I sat down and wrote a letter to Harold Boone, my new stepdad. I told him not to let Mother read that letter. I wrote that I was scared. Just before we headed out, I ran over, handed it to a company clerk, and turned to join my boys. The clerk yelled, "Don't worry. I'll mail it tomorrow, Sarge!" In 2012 I found that letter I'd mailed to Harold, tucked in with the C-ration postcards I sent Mother. It was so unlike any other letter or card I ever sent home. I never did lie to Mother, but sometimes I just didn't tell her the whole truth. "Mother, I hope you understand. I didn't want to worry you. I was truly scared and didn't want to go in that valley."

Now what to do? Something was really wrong here. I didn't think I was I just scared. After I went back to our platoon area, I quietly gave an order to my men. "Double up the ammo you usually carry: four hand grenades, instead of two. Plus, carry two more claymores mines per squad."

The night before we headed into the A Shau, we had a company meeting with 1st Sgt. Linn Sprinolli. There was very little time to strategize our plans. He wanted us to focus on how to get off the LZ (Landing Zone) fast. The platoon sergeant's job was to get our squad off the LZ and into the perimeter as fast as possible and in good order. Sprinolli began the briefing by writing the question "What would you do to grab the high ground?" on a large white sheet of paper.

One difficulty using helicopters to capture jungle high ground is that you generally have to land your troops in the valley. The enemy used mountain tops to dig in, putting in snares and setting traps with trip wires. Additionally, they would train their artillery on us as we attempted to come up the mountain. The enemy had learned how we operated and was able to predict where we'd be. As well, they knew those trails up the mountains like the backs of their hands. They used intelligence to their advantage to anticipate our arrivals and our strengths. They watched and learned our patterns of behavior, how we came in and how we attacked.

Our major difficulty, as infantry, was in trying to get up a mountain on foot. Anticipating our arrival, the enemy would have put in snares and set up traps with trip wires. They dug bunkers deep into the ground with tunnels running between them, set up with automatic weapons or RPG's. Just a few enemy troops dug in on a side of a mountain could inflict heavy casualties on a much larger number of men coming up the slopes. We talked about who would lead our teams and who was the best point man in the company. The squad in the lead was the best squad in the whole company. It was imperative that we find where "Charlie" was. Time was of the essence! We didn't have the luxury of time to practice; we were going in the next day. We talked about how to "prep" the LZ. The artillery would have to shift on time, with Huey's and gunships in the lead to take us in. Observation planes like the L-19's would spot the enemy and their movements and control the strafing and rockets. Artillery had the responsibility to get everyone into the right place at the right time.

Our first job would be to get as many men on the ground as quickly as possible. Then we had to move them away from the LZ because the door gunners would be throwing out lead from their M-60's as we scrambled out, onto the field of fire. This was going to be one hot LZ! My mantra was, "Get the strength out, get across the elephant grass, through the brush and into the edge of the jungle."

We looked for small trails, ravines or water streams that flowed into our LZ. We had learned that Charlie would use them to approach us while we were landing. As soon as we were on the ground, we should engage the VC and drive them out of the elephant grass, back into the jungle. We knew we had to push them back up on the mountain and away from where our brothers would be coming in behind us.

This time I knew Butch Dorsett, my best friend from Mitchell, was coming in with those troop carriers. Another company would be needed on the ground to help us do our job. I prayed, "God, help us! We've got to have room for the choppers to get in and the men to get out onto the LZ."

I knew that every helicopter shot down on the LZ would prevent another one from having enough room to land. Our company strength was just over 100. We would be out there by ourselves until the next lift could come in. I knew that after a certain number of choppers were shot down, the assault would be called off. I remember that I raised my hand and asked one question. "How long from when we land, before the next company comes in to reinforce us?"

The 1st Sergeant answered, "Maybe not fast enough."

After the briefing, we all walked out of the TOC (Tactical Operations Center.) A few more questions were asked and answered. I noticed a group of Special Forces troops, with their green berets and camouflage jungle hats. I thought, "Why are they here? Are they going in with us?"

I had never seen them working with our LRRP's or Recon Teams before. I asked our headquarters platoon sergeant, Sgt. Gaytan, why they were there. He responded, "Maybe they're heading out into the valley at last light and will be waiting on us to arrive after the sun comes up."

The 16th of September would be a day in which over 30 Bronze Stars, Purple Hearts and Air Medals would be handed out. We had clean clothes and new boots. We'd eaten two good meals in a row and now we were standing there listening as the UH-1 Hooey's warmed up. The stink of their fumes and the tension of anticipation hung in the air. Everyone was on alert, but we were ready to roll. Artillery was throwing shells into the valley as our Air Force raced overhead, making last minute strikes against enemy positions. We were more than ready. We had learned, "Remain calm, do your job and keep moving in front of the enemy. Lay down your own fire and get your men positioned in the right place."

Into The A Shau Valley
16TH -17TH of September 1968

The weather that morning was really nice. Everything went perfectly, just as we'd rehearsed it. No one stumbled; no one fell. No loose ammo fell out of our pockets. It was professional. As we walked up to the helicopters I heard strains of music weaving in and out, along with the noise of the chopper blades and their RPM's revving up. "Hey, Jude, take a sad song and make it be-eh-eh-ter!" was blaring out from the choppers' loud speakers. Only in Vietnam!

It was time for us to haul out of there. Each chopper was loaded up with six to eight men before two door gunners, along with the pilot and co-pilot, scrambled on board. Straps were handed to us by the door gunners which we pulled across our midsections; they were fastened it to the floor. The choppers roared and we rose up into the air. Like big birds, they picked up altitude and speed. Their engines screamed out, "Welcome to Air Mobile!" We were more than ready to attack the A Shau Valley. I thought, "Maybe everything's gonna to be all right."

As we took to the sky, I looked down in the valleys. I saw a light ground fog and a few clouds in the sky, but no rain in sight. I felt like we were in a picture, not "in" an actual event. Eventually, my mind drifted off, away from the sounds of the choppers, the Beatles singing. Thoughts of home drifted into my mind. I had been out on so many assaults, but this one felt different. Just before we landed on the LZ (landing zone), I looked over to my right and could see other helicopters in their big V formation. In the closest one to us, I spied that young man I'd spoken with earlier, the one who had "Puppy." She was still right there with him, her head sticking out of his rucksack. Her ears were flying in the breeze and she looked to be doing fine. My mind must have wandered again for a few minutes as the helicopter shifted around, preparing to take us in. I heard sounds in the distance. I shifted my line of vision out over to the left of the helicopter where artillery rounds were going off, where our Cobras were working over the jungle. Immediately, I shifted my attention to the job at hand. I realized we were going in! Rockets and artillery were changing and shifting over us to cover the side of the landing zone.

The first contact was made by Alpha Company, 2nd Battalion, 101st Airborne Division. We were leading the way! Men on board were silent; they broke out in nervous sweats. The smell of fear was pervasive. Everywhere. Choppers rose up and headed out over that beautiful, but deadly, country. After almost a year in country and so much blood, we believed we would find victory in this place. We would be calling the shots. We remembered, "Stay calm; do what is right. Don't get scared. Don't do anything dumb that gets your people killed."

Six helicopters came in and all of their troops jumped off, spreading out toward the jungle forest on the northwest side, just as we had discussed back at Camp Eagle. Our Huey's tried to hit as many LZ's as possible to throw off the enemy. I breathed a sigh of relief. The entire 1st Platoon and one squad of the 2nd Platoon had made it in! Artillery had prepped the LZ and three or four Cobras had come in with the choppers; they had unloaded all kinds of ammo, shot rockets past us into the surrounding area. All seemed very normal, but my gut told me otherwise. We knew from past experiences that the local VC and NVA would have observers watching us all along our flight pattern, on alert for our first wave. The next three choppers came swirling in, with dust flying as they neared the earth. Then I heard it! A rocket coming in over our heads! Terrified, I watched as it slammed into the side of a helicopter, not forty feet away. This enemy force was about platoon-size, maybe they were reinforced or up to company size! They came at us from the north, crossing a small stream. Our lead chopper was blown up as it tried to come in, exploding ten feet off the ground. As it turned out, this was the enemy's signal for them to attack.

All Hell broke loose in milliseconds! The angels of death were ready, for us and for them. The smell of fear was strong. We heard, "Two minutes to the LZ."

We could see smoke up ahead. We knew the first platoon had three squads of good men to lead this battle. We had told the new men what to expect, how fast things would change once we were on the ground. Every new man was assigned to an older experienced man. My squad leaders were reliable men: 1st

Squad - PFC Johnny Cox; 2nd Squad - PFC Donald Harris; 3rd Squad - PFC David Martinez. All had experience on hot LZ's. They'd learned quickly; the war had taken a hard turn since landing in the Central Highlands two months before. This fight would not be the same type of fight we'd had at Dak To, Pleiku, or Kontum. I knew my men would follow orders and could fight – really fight! They had proven it in the Tet Offensive more than five months ago. We had endured, having been overrun three times in the Hobo Woods and outnumbered in the Iron Triangle. We had learned our lessons the hard way. We knew we were combat soldiers, but we had never fought like we were going to have to fight here. Little did we know that we were walking straight into the Lion's Mouth here in the A Shau Valley. As we heard echoes of the artillery barrage and gunships ahead of us, we headed on in. Artillery shifted on the ground and elevated around the LZ. Smokey's laid down smoke screens and the Cobras opened up, sending rockets into the surrounding jungle.

The pitch of our motors changed as we abruptly turned down into the valley. Our door gunners opened up. I could see green tracers coming straight at us as we weaved our way into that valley. We were close enough to see the beautiful tall elephant grass, even ant hills sticking up out of the grass. I heard the engines whirl and scream as we slowed down, the automatic guns and the rounds going off. One chopper to our right and just a little ahead of us had landed; we were next.

Our chopper did not actually stop; it just hovered. We jumped more than five feet into elephant grass. We knew the enemy was near; their fire was pouring out at us. We began to automatically fire back. Another hot LZ! Men scrambled into formation, to push out. Now the enemy was pouring fire at us, but our troops on the ground responded with machine gun fire of their own. As the next lift landed right behind us, the NVA again opened up with RPG. One helicopter had released its men, then was hit in the tail and crashed. As the next one with the mortar platoon on board approached, their pilot and co-pilot observed the disaster on the ground, the LZ full of green tracers. They responded by pulling up and away.

I was facing north toward the mountains. I saw a rough line of NVA form a line as they broke out of the tree line, firing and running toward us. My first squad met them with rifle fire. Two of our M-60 machine guns hit them with a full load. As we crawled and pushed forward, we were hitting targets. That attack was stopped cold! Overhead, our second lift brought the rest of the company into the LZ and got out without more helicopters getting hit. They also brought in that mortar platoon which we now badly needed. Finally, our company was all on the ground.

Next would be Charlie Company, a very good company, with really good leaders. Within five minutes the NVA hit us again, this time with a much bigger unit. They came out of the same tree line, charging across the LZ, straight into our M-60's and those men who were already dug in. Again, the NVA were driven back. By now, I could see where bullets had cut down the elephant grass and hand grenades had blown out some wide patches of ground. NVA were lying in the open; very few appeared to be alive. However, this was no consolation to the men of the 2nd Platoon, since more than half of their men were either dead or wounded.

We were now smack dab in the middle of a very serious situation. I knew we could not take another charge. I called my radio man over, telling him to call up the chain of command; we needed artillery to be called in, to hit 50 meters into the wood line. Then, they should adjust their fire two times, for effect.

Two Cobras appeared out of nowhere. As soon as the artillery lifted, they shifted to the woods. These Cobras came in with "guns a'blazing!" They lit up the woods for a hundred meters. This in itself stopped the enemy from launching their third attack, as well as gave us time to cover and reinforce the 2nd Platoon. By this time I could hear our helicopters coming in from the east. I knew Charlie Company was there for us, but we had a clear LZ and the strength of the second company would get us off on the right foot. By early afternoon the rest of the battalion had made it. We started pushing out into the tree line.

Surprises, as a principal of war, are not reserved for a particular level of command. They can happen to someone in the lowest rank, as well as the highest. The 1st Platoon of Alpha Company had been the first to step off the side of those choppers that morning. I had a brand new 2nd lieutenant who had been in our company for about two weeks. He thought he knew everything. He had told me he was "in charge" and no buck sergeant was going to tell him how to run a platoon. We also had a new commander and I had attempted to talk with him regarding the map's gridlines and contour levels. I had tried to explain to him about why our radios often wouldn't work. He had also repeated to me, "I'm in-charge! And not about to listen to some Sargent!"

Our platoon had been the lead team. We'd begun our advance toward the jungle as the second lift came in. As soon as we heard the rocket, we jerked around and began to return fire, trying to maneuver into a flanking position. The 2nd Lieutenant gave us orders to move to the east, up close where we could assault them. As we tried to flank them, they kept up their fire power. Then, I heard the enemy's supporting fire open up, mortar rounds hitting the bottom of a base plate very near our front, their automatic weapons making strong growls as I watched green tracers cross the sky less than two feet above my head.

Within two minutes the second flight had been hit. The rest of the choppers unloaded their men and got off without being hit. Now, two platoons were on the ground and we had two officers with radios. Both officers were calling for air strikes and artillery to help us out. The enemy was soon hit with our artillery fire and by our air strike.

Immediately, the 2nd Platoon leader ordered his men to assault. Without hesitation men charged forward. Bomb explosions sent out echoes. Squads moved in with rapid, coordinated bounds, maintaining a heavy volume of fire for about 20 meters, until both their machine gunners went down. One gunner was hit; the other was stooped over to hang another 100-round belt on his machinegun because his assistant gunner was lying on the ground with mortal stomach wounds. About 40 meters away, the enemy rose up out of a small stream bed with their "guns a'blazing." They threw three to four chicom mines straight into the 2nd Platoon, screaming, shouting and charging forward at a dead run.

We had landed smack in the middle of two companies of an NVA regiment. For three days they had been waiting for us, using their time to dig in, prepare for the battle ahead, and pre-plot their rockets and mortars. As we landed their plan was to catch us in a vice. They maneuvered their artillery as we advanced, tried to get help in or evacuate out. As I watched, it was another one of those moments in Vietnam when you can see something happening, but just for few seconds, can't believe it's true. Your mind cannot process what's happening before your eyes.

Most of the 2nd Platoon were killed immediately. Lt. "Shit Head," the guy who "knew everything," had dropped his radio handset and was hiding behind a very large tree. I've always wanted to think that, at that moment, he was crying, since he had his head down. I really hoped he'd shit in his pants! He certainly didn't want to watch what was happening, much less lead anyone!

I knew we had to fight this one, here, right now, or we would all be dead in just a few minutes. I also knew we were surrounded. Running around was not going to do us any good. I crawled over and grabbed the radio handset and started talking on it. I don't really know who I called first, maybe it was the left leg artillery. I ordered them, "Drop HE (high explosives), close to our north side, then move across the streambed."

My plan was to adjust the blast, ten meters at a time. The radio operator back at Fire Base Camp sounded off to me from the other end, telling me he could not drop so dangerously close "without permission from above."

I could not believe what I was hearing! I would need an officer to place those orders! **In other words, the radioman was not going to send us any help without an officer of captain's rank or above to give them the OK.**

God, I was angry! Mad beyond words! I pressed the radio mike down for a couple of seconds and screamed, "That's the damn order you need or we'll all be dead here in five minutes!"

I also jumped frequency with the help of a radio operator who came to help me out. He called for the Bird Dog, to get help from above. The forward air controller took over from there. In just a minute or two, Snoopy came in a 'blazing! I got three men to throw trip flares as far out as they could, toward the enemy. I watched Snoopy cut a strip of green foliage, knocking down trees as big around as my waist, within 20 meters of our front lines and maybe 100-150 yards out, about the length of a football field. Meanwhile, I was running the steel curtain closer to us.

Now, we had the enemy on the defense, trying to outrun Snoopy's guns and our artillery. For three or four minutes we worked them over. Finally, three gunships came around our small landing zone, shooting rockets into trails that led back into the jungle. Within just a few minutes, we had control. I finally believed that we were going to live.

We had 60's and 82's, mortars known to us as "80 duce." They worked well in this type of situation. More helicopters returned, loaded with Headquarters Platoon and two sets of Mortar and Weapons Platoons. Within 20 minutes of them getting on the ground, the 60 mm. mortars were throwing their rounds on the remaining enemy as they tried to escape. Another load, and the rest of our company came in. Then, we were able to get some of the worst wounded out. We had survived another day, but dead and wounded men were scattered everywhere. The 2nd platoon was almost completely wiped out.

Right before dark I was sneaking around our outer perimeter, looking for claymore mines and booby traps. I was trying hard not to be seen or heard. Right before my eyes I saw that 2nd Lt. "Shit Head" and his radio man out just walking around on the outer perimeter, like they were on a football field. Obviously, they had no clue that any enemy might still be about. They walked toward two new troopers lying on the ground. The new troopers quickly jumped up, knowing they should stand and salute the lieutenant. To my horror, I heard machinegun fire from behind me. I watched green tracers slam into the lieutenant, the radioman, both of those troopers. They'd all been slaughtered! They were cut down, almost cut in half! Immediately, the four of them were dead. As if in a slow motion movie, I watched as six or seven more NVA soldiers ran out of the dark, headed straight towards our Headquarters, still on the attack, armed with AK-47's. Meanwhile, two more radiomen stood alongside the Company Commander, trying to rig up an antenna for the radio. I'm sure they didn't even see anything or hear the NVA coming.

This was beyond belief! I couldn't process what I was seeing unfold before my eyes. I had an M-16 rifle on me, but lying within two feet of me on the ground, I spotted an M-60 machine gun. I had been a machine gunner when I first came in country. Instantly, I grabbed it and began firing. I killed seven or eight men in less than three or four seconds before I quit shooting. Immediately it was so quiet you could have heard a pin drop. I couldn't believe what all I'd just been through. I knew that the 2nd Lieutenant and two of the dead men had been in the unit less than a week, but now they were lying there dead or dying.

One of those dying men was the new recruit I'd met earlier that day with Puppy. I knelt beside him. I tried to reassure him that he was going to be all right. I said, "We'll get you out on one of the first choppers coming in for wounded."

He pleaded with me, "Don't leave me, Sarge! Please, don't leave me alone!"

He didn't make it, but I was there with him when he whispered, for the last time, weakly and softly, "Please! Don't leave me, Sarge!"

By dark, the rest of our company and Bravo Company had set up a perimeter. As night fell on us, I knew I still had more than a month to go. It was going to be a very long hard mission ahead. In less than eight hours we had lost almost a whole platoon and two officers. Over the next three days we never lost another man. We spent days continuing to chase the enemy and finding trails they'd used. I found three booby traps, two snares and some punchi stakes in a bear trap.

This had been our 50th Air Assault Mission for Alpha Company and we would receive air assault medals for surviving this hot LZ. These days whenever I look at the names on the citations, I can't match many names with faces in my mind. But four days later, we were called on. "Move farther west, closer to the Laos border."

We were getting closer and closer to Hamburger Hill. On the 20th of September 1968 we took a four-company RIF (Recon in Force) right down the middle of the A Shau Valley, right along Highway #614, on what had been an enemy-built road originating across in Laos. Many called it the Yellow Brick Road, but to us, it was more like Hell's Highway. Men at headquarters, as well as Col. Bowers and the generals at MACV, thought we might make contact with the enemy along that road. After two weeks of RIF, all was quiet; nothing happened. The enemy simply moved out ahead of us. They left food, weapons, heavy equipment and their hooches. We found a hospital in a tunnel, still well-supplied with equipment. They even abandoned some seriously wounded men, certainly in no condition to fight us.

The contact with the enemy that they thought we would find really never took place. From some letters I sent home I had written that the 9th and 10th NVA Regiments were believed to be in that area. They just melted away, back across the border. We, as the 3rd Brigade, were able to locate a lot of equipment and all kinds of weapons, as well as food. However, very few of the enemy were ever caught. I really thought it strange that we found Soviet-built ground-to-air missiles, as well as some abandoned large artillery pieces. The enemy were building up for a real war, not just a little fight.

From that battle and forward, the realization of how many lives were wasted began to seriously affect me. Specifically, that kid with "Puppy," getting killed so quickly after getting to Vietnam …. My best friend, Butch Dorsett, would be KIA within a few weeks of my deployment back home. It seemed so senseless, leaving men behind to get killed when those of us who had learned so much were sent on home. New recruits coming in would have to learn those same lessons all over again at great personal expense. For those two men who died, as well as many, many others, I have written my book, Not Alone.

Three weeks later, we got finally returned to the rear base camp. Letters and post cards for troopers were there for those who were killed that day. One letter I assumed to be from "Puppy's" young man's family since it had his same last name on the return address. The company clerk and I pulled his stuff and a small Bible out of his rucksack and returned it to that address. I thought again about that young man, before our helicopter ride and about "Puppy." I never saw her again.

Once again, I stored more lessons in my brain. I didn't know it then, but later in life, I would become a Ranger instructor and even instruct men in a foreign nation. Opportunities would come for me to teach other men those lessons I'd learned in the A Shau Valley when I was 19 years old. Lesson # 1 was "Always be prepared! Be prepared to take control, to change what needs to be done as a situation unfolds before your very eyes, especially in a combat zone. Expect that the one that that is constant is change." Lesson # 2 was "Never allow your enemy to have the advantage of surprise, especially when fighting in the enemy's home environment."

Along the Laotian Border: October 1968

In little more than a month I expected I'd be headed home. I knew my birthday was coming up and my time was getting short. After returning to Camp Eagle for six days, they gave us our new briefing. We were heading out along the Laotian border. All of sudden, it hit me. Although my year "in country" was nearly done, I still had time to serve. It wasn't over yet. I'd been wounded, and I'd known fear, but now I felt different. It's strange when you have fought in major engagements and lived through them. I now realized that I was just plain scared. In the back of my mind was the question I was afraid to say out loud. "Would I really get back home alive, after all?"

I wrote Mother and Harold, telling them, "… things are tough here now," adding, "… since I got wounded, I pray all the time about making it home and walking those beautiful hills in southern Indiana once again." Although I was 12,000 miles from home, in my mind, I was back there in Indiana, with them. I hoped I would soon be able to return home, across the wide blue Pacific Ocean, by Christmas. All I wanted when I got home was to be able to buy a little place in southern Indiana, live in peace and quiet and raise a family there. In 2008 I found that letter in my mother's personal belongings, along with a small black and white photo of a hill in Laos. We had been told to take that hill "at all costs!"

No wonder I'd been so scared! I knew that the next day we would be going near Laos, on a Cobra assault with a lot of new men. So far, our days and nights had been awful. We constantly ran into snipers and ground troops who drew us into firefights, then they'd disappear.

On the evening of 9th of October we were in a small valley with a stream running through it. We had been on a RIF (Recon in Force) Mission, collecting intelligence. We'd seen a lot of signs of the enemy, but had not had much actual contact with them. Only two men had been wounded and sent to the rear. That afternoon, the supply helicopter flew in with fresh mail, more ammo, C-rations, as well as two new men. We had been down on the LZ. The company commander told me to take the two men with me and he would talk to them later. It was almost dark before we got back on the top of a small hill. Our Platoon Headquarters was a good way away from the rest of the company. We overlooked a small valley and trails. I told those two new men, "Sit down and stay right there, next to the radio man and the platoon medic," and "Go ahead and eat your rations."

Meanwhile, I walked out to our perimeter and began inspection. I made sure we had our claymore mines out and that they were well camouflaged. We had put out trip flares with hand grenades tied onto the trip wires. I found two dead spaces and made the men go back in, putting in more mines and trip wires, since there was only one approach to our hilltop, up a steep trail which ran straight up to the very top. A small ravine ran parallel with the ridge line. We were deep in rugged mountains, covered with jungle, just seven clicks from the Laotian border. We had found lots of signs and we knew the enemy was all over this area. The main questions I wanted answered were, "How many of them are out here? How close is their base camp and their supplies?

By the time I returned, it was getting dark. We held our platoon's central position. All of a sudden, the night's silence was shattered by machine gun fire! Mortar rounds hit the bottom of the base plate. Our platoon was caught completely by surprise! We were partially dug in with fighting positions and our machine gun fire was overlapped into the killing zones. I had almost reached the Platoon Headquarters where I'd left the two new men with our medic and radio man. I heard a mortar round coming in and I hit the ground. I was less than twenty steps from the radio as I heard the explosion. It lit up the night; shrapnel flew in every direction, waist high. All four of the men I'd left there were killed instantly. I took cover behind a tree, then yelled, "They are coming up the draws!"

It became one night of Hell, one of the darkest nights of my life. Already my medic and radio man were dead; two new men killed even before they had time to eat one meal in the field! The battle was on! We were more than 100 meters from the rest of the company. At least we had our squad radios and could talk to my higher command and to our mortar section within the company perimeter.

I thanked God that I knew exactly where my 1st Squad Leader's position was. And, I knew I was very close! I heard our M-60's barking back and the claymores going off. I began crawling to the 1st Squad. I could hear them fighting and shooting downhill. "Blaam! Blaam!" Our M-60's were shooting down our perimeter again, our weapons getting louder by the second. As I crawled into the squad sector, I grabbed the RTO and took his radio from him. I was trying to get an "order to fire" to our mortar team, but everyone else was screaming and talking on the radio. I yelled and screamed, "Get off the radio! Get off the radio!"

I contacted our 4.2 and ordered 80 mm mortars and rounds to be delivered as soon as possible. I heard the first round hit. Then, I yelled, "Drop 30 meters and fire again! Over!"

Another round went off on my right, but up on the side of the hill, near the trail. It was dangerously close to us, but at least it was on the correct side of the hill. I yelled and screamed in the radio, "Fire! Fire for effect!"

Over the next 20 minutes, I adjusted the fire up and down, then down to our right. The enemy was able to hit us three times that night. They did get close in, but parachute flares from our mortars and our M-60's moving constantly allowed us to keep them out of our platoon. All through the night claymore mines blew and trip wires went off. By 0300 when the final push came, they retreated.

I found out that the Mortar Platoon had some white phosphorus. I waited until I knew the enemy was 40 or 50 meters below us in a draw near the creek. I called for the mortar teams to drop five rounds of "Willy Pee" (white phosphorous) on them. I heard the rounds as they came in. The whole night sky lit up as those rounds went off! I knew the enemy was through with us and on the run.

Not long after, grey streaks began to light up the eastern sky and the night sounds went away. I realized it was my birthday, 20th October 1968, and I was still very much alive! For that I was immensely grateful! We had lived through the night. Although we had been hit hard in the early seconds of the battle, we held the hill. Only four men were wounded during the night. In less than one month I would be on my way home, and this platoon would have a new sergeant. All my men had been trained as well as I could do in such a short time.

In two days we were lifted up by helicopters and headed back to Camp Eagle. Over the next three weeks we pulled guard duty on the perimeter, worked with new men on movement and patrolling techniques, as well as helped them learn how to quickly react to near and far ambushes. I demonstrated how to roll with an M-60. I would give them the advice to take off the legs of their machine gun and use them for limiting stakes while doing their defensive positions in a patrol base. I explained how they could roll or shoot with the M-60 at ground level. I took men out on patrols close to base camp and demonstrated to them how to look for, see and find trip wires. I used a small flexible rice stem to show them how they could feel a trip wire. I tried hard to teach all of these new men what I had learned in one year. I did the best I could.

Orders: Head for Home!

Finally, the first week of November 1968 I got orders to head out. I looked up Butch's outfit to tell him goodbye. I would leave these Vietnamese battlefields to a whole new bunch of men and new NCO's, men who never in their wildest dreams would think that their year ahead might be worse that the year I had just put in. I left for Long Binh to process "out of country." By 30th November I was gone. It never occurred to me then that I might one day return to Vietnam, to many of these same men whom I was now leaving. For the time being, my year was over and I was glad to be heading home.

Butch's Platoon Sgt. told me he was doing very well and he would look after him. Butch and I had a good talk before I left, then I gave him a big hug. He told me when I got back to Mitchell to look up his first cousin, Donna Gerkin, because he knew she'd be glad to see me. I had known Donna since we both graduated from Mitchell High School in 1966, she as class valedictorian. I'd always thought she was very pretty and also, very smart. I told Butch I would follow up with her.

On the 25th of November 1968, we who were left, only eight from the original company, got orders that moved us to the 90th Replacement Battalion. We were flown in a small Caribou C-24 in three hops down country, finally arriving at Long Binh, not far from Division Headquarters at Bien Hoa. I could not believe how much things had changed there in just one year. When I'd first arrived in Vietnam, we had landed at the Bien Hoa Air Base, a sleepy little provincial seat. I had seen beautiful churches, stucco villas, and tree-lined streets left after the French were driven out. Peasants wore black pajamas and straw hats walked around, not visibly affected by the war raging around them. However, now the TET offensive had visibly changed this locale into a war zone. When we first pulled into base camp, I could almost taste the war in my mouth; I thought about how much the passage of one year had visibly changed everything. I could barely believe how huge the base was now, with lots of new buildings and for the better, passable roads. As soon as we arrived, we were driven 8 miles from Long Bien to Bien Hoa to get everything they'd kept for us when we first came in country and when we returned from R&R. We went to the building marked for "A Company," and located equipment in foot lockers or duffle bags. We realized that everything we'd left there had been opened up and rifled through; anything that appeared to be valuable had been stolen. We didn't think about filing a complaint; we just wanted to be gone from there.

As we looked at the check-in sheet listing our original company of 130 men, we realized we eight were the only survivors! We stood there and looked at each other. It hit all of us like a ton of bricks; many of our buddies from our company were gone forever; they had died here. Friends and families back in the states had sent sons, husbands and brothers off to war. It hit each of us like a ton of bricks: we eight were all that were left after one year. Out of us eight men, five had been in rear detachments.

We boarded a bus for Ton Son Nute Air Base, as the first leg of our homeward journey. Two days after arriving back where it had all begun for us, we were dressed in newly-issued, clean khakis and sporting clean haircuts with a maroon beret on top, but we were still wearing our old jungle boots. We heaved up our rucksacks as we quietly loaded onto the plane. The motors were already running; within just a few minutes, we were up off the ground. I sat next to a window and watched as we climbed higher and higher. The green that I knew was Vietnam fell away from view. I had made it. Tears of joy ran down my face.

Immediately, questions bombarded my mind. "Why had I made it? Why, God, I wasn't any better than anyone else, and maybe not as smart as some of those who had died in those jungles. Why me?"

I was happy to be leaving, but sad for my brothers in arms, those who remained, as well as those who had given their all. Those questions have remained with me the remainder of my life.

We stopped in Japan to refuel and were allowed to disembark from the plane into the airport. Our next refueling stop was the best of all: Alaska! The people of Alaska and their USO club had a very nice set up waiting for us there when we arrived. We could relax and enjoyed reading their "Welcome Home!" signs. All the people there were so nice to all of us. I felt like we were finally, once again, on American soil. We had made it! After we reloaded I was able to get some sleep. Next stop was California where we encountered the war protesters. People threw things at us, shouting, "Baby Killers!" as well as other nasty names.

I felt relieved when I finally boarded a plane bound for Louisville, Kentucky. Shortly before midnight I landed, still carrying my rucksack and a military duffel bag full of clothes. I hitched a ride to the Greyhound bus terminal, where I learned that my bus was not scheduled to go through my little town of Shoals, Indiana, until late the next day. I made the decision that I couldn't just sit around and wait for that but, so I paid for my bag to go as freight to Shoals. I had to be moving! I could see Interstate 65 just a few streets away; my thumb would get me home!

Within twenty minutes I had been picked up by a man driving a pickup truck. We crossed the Ohio River Bridge, then he dropped me off at the Salem Exit. Soon, I was picked up by a couple of young boys on their way into Salem. It had begun to snow. One of the boys asked me where I lived, where I was trying to go. I replied, "West of Mitchell, Indiana."

The boys talked quietly among themselves, then one of them asked me, "Do you have $5.00?"

I responded, "Yes, I believe I do."

They told me, "If you'll give us your $5.00, we'll take you on to Mitchell." That was certainly sweet music to my ears! I'd left the heat of Vietnam wearing short-sleeved khakis. Here it was wintry already. I was feeling more than a little chilly and my boots were wet. They drove on to Mitchell and dropped me off at right under our one stoplight in town, where the highway turned to go to Huron. I was almost home! I only had a little ways to go to get on to my hometown. I had almost made it. Within just three or four minutes a car passed by, then stopped and backed up. The driver rolled his window down and asked, "Are you Joe?"

He was Larry Tackett. A couple of years earlier I had worked for his father. Larry also had a brother who'd served in Vietnam. I climbed in Larry's car and he drove us to Huron. He took the left hand turn over King's Ridge, driving on to my mother's home on Ridge Road. Again, I sent thanks to my angels. I had made it home in less than three hours, safely hitchhiking 110 miles from the Louisville airport. I thanked Larry for the ride and stepped out. Old Rusty, Mother's big collie, began barking as he ran up to me. He almost knocked me down as he jumped up. I rubbed him behind the ears while I greeted him, then got him down as I headed toward the front door. The outside light came on. I heard Mother yell, "Harold, he's home! It's Joe! He's home!"

It had been a very long year. I stood there in the doorway as snow blew around my face and tears ran down my cheeks. Mother hugged me so tight as she said such beautiful words, "Come on in. You're home, now."

As soon as I got in the house, my stepfather Harold was right there beside me. He also gave me a bear hug. He held me a long time, then said a Thanksgiving prayer, thanking God for bringing me home.

I'd only been home two days when Butch Dorsett's family first received word that he was MIA, Missing in Action. To start with, I didn't want to believe he was missing. I thought, "Oh, maybe they just lost contact with his team or they got separated up in the mountains on a mission."

I wanted to believe that he and the team would be found. Two more days passed, then his parents received the notice every loved one dreads: PFC Harry C. Dorsett was KIA (Killed in Action.) He'd been lost in a big battle in the Thua Thien Province.

I could hardly believe it! Much later I found out that his platoon had been almost completely wiped out, ambushed in those rough and rugged mountains. I was overwhelmed. I cried out, "God, my very best friend from childhood, the buddy who I loved like a brother, is gone."

I felt such pain, such shock, such intense anger! My thoughts were that America was making so many mistakes! If we really wanted to win this war, we should just turn our Air Force and Navy pilots loose on the NVA, on all of North Vietnam. Instead, those of us with experience were ordered home. Such a waste of life! Why did the military take me and others who survived, with battle-earned experience, knowledge about ambushes and tactics, and just sent us all home. I thought, "By the time a new 2nd Lieutenant learns how to lead his men in a platoon, he's sent to a rear detachment job, getting him out of the field."

I felt such anger and frustration! All of us had just walked away when our time was done, leaving Butch and many others behind. Those of us who'd survived certainly didn't think we were heroes; we were just still alive. We'd just been told, "You've served your time, now it's time for you to go home!"

We were certainly glad to do so. I walked away and so did many other good men, wanting to be away from there, intuitively knowing things were going to be worse for those left behind because we took so much knowledge with us. We felt such ambivalence at leaving new men behind, without our experience to help them. I felt so frustrated, angry, and so, so sad. My best buddy, Butch Dorsett, was dead. I began to reflect on what came down to several more lessons that went into my Memory Bank and that I believed should have been taught to the men still there.

Lesson # 1 : We always had problems with firepower. It was my belief that the M-16 rifle killed more men in Vietnam than anything else. This rifle may have worked well back in the States, in a pristine environment, when tested in a "clean" foxhole, after having been shot just 30 rounds, when someone had just spent two hours cleaning it.

In Vietnam, we could depend on it to jam! Hell, it jammed all the time! Also, it would hang up on vines and in leaves as you climbed and moved around in the three-canopy undergrowth. We learned that it would only shoot a few rounds, then jam. Sometimes it might only fire one round, then jam. I cannot tell you how many times we found Americans lying around dead, still in a fighting position holding an almost fully-loaded M-16 in their hands. It was common to find two rounds still stuck in the chamber, side-by-side. Even in 2014, the M-16 still jams, wherever America has fighting men - in the sands of Iraq, in the Hindu Kush and mountains of Afghanistan.

I learned to love my M-60. I would rather fight with it than anything we had. Later, I taught men in all the ranks how to use the M-60: how to roll with it with their legs up under it, how you could still fire, even if you lost the trigger mechanism or the butt plate. I also worked with and trained with the M-14 rifle. It was important to teach students about cover fire, overlapping sectors of fire, how to find a secondary position if necessary to pull back, as a part of their fire plan.

Lesson # 2: Learn how to move on after firing on the enemy, before the enemy could zero in on you. Move on, to the other end of your log, your low place or to another tree. Don't just crawl up somewhere, shoot off 300-400 rounds of ammunition from one place and think you'll live there long! Many tasks needed to be taught about being out in the field: how to make fire charts, to cover those fire charts with claymore mines, how to cover trip wire with daisies chained with hand grenades, about "Willy Peter," our name for white phosphorous, for those dyed spaces on the range cards. Those troops needed to learn how to make changes "on the fly" when they found themselves in the heat of battle. When the core of Alpha Company left the field to go home, we knew we took valuable experiences with us.

Also, I don't think any of us were prepared for dealing with the enemy we would encounter. Our upper grade officers, military officers in general, always underestimated the NVA and portrayed them as weak, poorly organized and ineffective fighters. Out in the field we soon learned that our enemy was much better organized than anyone really wanted to admit. In my opinion, they were very savvy jungle fighters, using their territory to their advantage, digging into caves, utilizing tunnels between caves, etc. Additionally, since they were often on home territory, they had a big advantage over us. Furthermore, they gathered intelligence on us to prepare themselves, watching us, learning our patterns, and more often than not, simply waited on us to show up. They were very good at simply waiting on us to do our thing.

Lesson # 3: New men need good leadership and mentoring from those who have experience. As NCO's, it took us a year to learn from our mistakes. All the men of Company A left the field at the same time, leaving new men with some "Instant NCO" just sent in as a replacement. Few remained who could mentor incoming men. The two people in my company with the most experience, point man and compass man, finished their tours and returned home, only eight of an original company of 142 men and 8 officers who entered Vietnam in December 1967. It took me a long time to learn from my mistakes and from watching others also make mistakes.

To this day I think that is the motivation for me to become a Ranger Instructor and later on, an instructor at the Regional Training School. I made the conscious decision that for the rest of my military days I would teach and mentor young men, explaining things simply. Later, I helped train Republic of Georgia soldiers, the Iraqi Army and our reservists in the Georgia National Guard and Army Reserves. I always had a good feeling about training new men going into the field.

My attitude was "teach 'em tough." I gave them the straight facts about combat: War is not pretty, but if you understand what you may encounter, you can be safer. I also sent them in with a prayer.

Those cold December days in 1967 found me trying to get used to being home. I had to try to regain my emotional footing, as well as recover physically. Things began to happen very fast around me. I only weighed about 130 pounds and felt exhausted. Both of my shoulders and my back had callouses from where my rucksack had thickened the skin. I couldn't eat much food at a time; many foods were very hard on my stomach.

Butch's funeral was held shortly after we received his official death notice. Butch had asked me to look up his cousin, Donna Gerkin, which I did. She and I were both grieving over Butch's death, so we probably were not thinking very clearly. I had known her in high school; we both were single and began to date. She already had a young son. After a quick whirlwind romance, she agreed to marry me before I had to report back to Fort Bragg, North Carolina. To this day, I don't know why we married, except that I think we both felt vulnerable and wanted someone to belong to. Our families still remain friends, although I have always regretted that our marriage didn't work out.

We simply went our separate ways. Down deep, I have always felt guilty that I didn't try harder to make our marriage work. Our daughter, Carol Lynn Conley was born the 2nd of February 1970. As the years have passed, I have had the privilege to meet Carol, her husband and their child. It is my fervent prayer that she and her family have the best in life and all they seek.

Company B, 3rd Battalion, 11th Special Forces Group, Airborne Special Forces Tab

Way back when Paul Tolbert's body was brought home from Vietnam, when I'd still been in high school, I'd heard the Green Beret song on my car radio. "One hundred men will test today, but only three will win the Green Beret."

This song had inspired me as a young man looking for his way in life. I never met Barry Saddler, but his song set wheels in motion for me. Later, I would belong to Company B, 11th Special Forces Group. I have been asked more times than I can remember, "Which one was harder, Ranger School or the Special Forces Q Course?"

To this day I can tell you, "They are both very hard, more than demanding on your body and mind. God only knows, they are very intense, harder on any person, mentally and physically, than what anyone could ever expect to survive, much less survive."

Yet, I completed both courses in the same lifetime. The Special Forces course was first for me, so I chose to write about that one first. Why did we call it the Q course? Because of how many times our brains told us, "Quit!"

Those who aspire to the Special Forces refuse to take the easy way out. It's just not in our nature to do so. Special Forces training began in the piney woods of North Carolina, beyond Fort Bragg, in the swamps out beyond Pine Bluff. I was told, "This experience will forever change your mind about being a normal human being. This place will become like your second home."

181

Many books have been written about the Special Forces and their training. In no way could I tell about everything that happened there, but I will give you an idea of what it was like. We trained in the Uwarrah National Forest, in and around the communities of Troy and Star, North Carolina. We also flew down to the Ocala National Forest in Florida where we jumped into the forest in small units for about three weeks of training. Later, we would be sent to Patrick Air Force Base where we would assemble to go into Europe or to the European Command Center in Stuttgart, Germany.

My second wife and two sons were born near the Special Forces Training Site. For some, it would be where they would return after missions; for me, it became my second home. Friends are found there to this day. My oldest son, Robert Eugene Conley, lives with his family at Pine Bluff, near Pinehurst; my second son, Shannon Conley, lives close to Fort Bragg. I regularly return to Fort Bragg about once a year and try to make it to the Special Forces Museum in Fayetteville.

Special Forces trainees must spend many a cold night, damp night out in the swamps out behind Camp McCall, North Carolina. We learned about little places on the map, such as Troy, Biscoe, and the Uwarrah National Forest in the mountains. You learn to run patrols, set up ambushes and actions at the objective. Here is where you walk face to face with yourself. You find your strengths you never knew you had, get to know your weaknesses and find out how much you want to accomplish something.

Fort Bragg is between Aberdeen and Fayetteville, home to the Special Forces and to the Special Forces Operations Command. It is the home of the JFK Special Warfare Center and School, as well as the home of Iron Mike and the Green Beret. This is where men are selected to train to become a Special Forces Soldier. You might spend a lifetime roaming the world, but Fort Bragg is where it all begins. I sat there and wondered, "Is this how it begins or is this how we run away?"

In early spring 1977 I was released from the Mountain Ranger Camp and was sent back to Company B Rangers in Muncie, Indiana. I had decided to remain in Georgia and had enrolled in a Gainesville Junior College. While looking around for a home in the military, I found what I was searching for in Columbus, Georgia, with Company B, 11th Special Forces Group. I spent two years with them where we had a great time training. Many men were Vietnam veterans, so it was a great opportunity for me. I still attend all of our reunions; we always have a great time visiting with each other, telling stories about our youth and younger years.

I have often left a wife and children to go around the world, departing quietly for missions where I would be gone for weeks, even months, while those back home had no idea where I was or when I might return. I truly believe that being a Special Forces soldier or a Ranger is harder on wives and children than it ever is on the soldier. Only after I turned fifty, did the rigors of the action seem different from what I remembered: days seemed longer, nights feel colder, the ground seem harder, swamps were rougher on our bodies. I finally realized that it was beginning to take longer to recuperate between these missions. My body was trying to tell me that I was no longer the young buck I thought I was. My knees and shoulders ached after jumping into landing zones around the world. My body had really begun to age.

STABO RIGGING

I recall one of my last summers spent at Fort Bragg, North Carolina. I was assigned to Company H LRSU (Long Range Surveillance Unit.) This was a Georgia National Guard unit out of Newnan, Georgia. We went to Ft. Bragg in the summer 1998. It was hot, and I really mean hot. On several marches out to fields less than a mile away, men began to drop out. On a particular march over to Pope Air Force Base, three men fell out on the way. Those of us left had a quiet jump; d I landed with hardly a bump to my body. As I began to get up, I saw men lying all over the ground, like they had all the time in the world to get to the assembly area. I finally realized many of us were older and our bodies were telling us, "This is going to be a long, hot, summer camp!"

I wondered how many times had I jumped to this very same drop zone? How many times had I jumped and assembled in the same exact spot? I thought to myself, "When I was young and going through the Q course, it seemed more like fun, then!"

I have never forgotten my first night jump with our class. We jumped into the drop zone with a good wind at our face and slammed into the ground. The night was so dark I couldn't find any stars out. I was finally able to get my compass out and working, so I could head for the assembly area. We had a small creek to cross and water was running more than waist deep. We were being tested in a small group and it was our job to get into the assembly area quickly. I realized that my rucksack was bigger than me as I stepped into bone-chilling water, expecting it to be waist deep. What a surprise I got! I almost drowned, right there, sinking down, almost to my neck. The current was also much swifter than I had anticipated. My thoughts were, "This is not starting out so good." Finally, I made it into the assembly area. We'd begun with eight men, but only four arrived in time for us to move out, so we did what's called "Charlie Mike" meaning Continue the Mission.

Details have changed very little over the years of Special Forces Course School. It's still a contest of man against the mountain, against the weather, against the elements. It's also man against the temperature, whether cold or hot, against whatever the environment has to offer in the way of mosquitoes, gnats and flies that bite and leaches that suck. Somebody might twist a knee or sprain an ankle, but somehow we all kept going.

The basic structure of "tryouts for Special Forces" has remained constant over the years. It's a very rigorous course where you never get enough sleep and very little food. The first month feels like it lasts forever as a weeding-out time. Nevertheless, you make friends; you learn that it's not about you or your buddy; the two of you learn to work together to make it through. You learn how to work as a team in your platoon, how much each piece must fit together to work as a whole. My buddy was Capt. Sharber. My pet name for him was "Shrapnel."

Pervasive in the back of everyone's mind is the thought, "I can always quit." It was a known fact that of all who began the course, almost three-fourths of any group who started would not complete it. In our class of 126, only 18 students completed the course. At the midpoint of the Vietnam War there had been a big push to add more Special Forces men, but the turnout was very slow. A lot of the men in our class were already Vietnam veterans, so we knew what we were doing and what we'd be up against. Our course was hard and long. Eventually, the manpower and resources improved so that the number of men who graduated from each class began to increase. By the late 1960's the attrition rate dropped from 90% to 75%. These graduates were sent around the world.

Many of us returned to Vietnam to fight in the Central Highlands. Often we'd merge with the mountain people we affectionately called "the 'Yards." We lived with them and fought alongside them. Later, most of us would become part of 12-man teams sent into small patrol bases which overlooked valleys or were atop mountains. We ran patrols, often accompanied by as many as 100 men, some with young "Yard boys as young as thirteen. These base camps were strung out along the Cambodian and Laotian borders. At one time there were probably 250 base camps all over Vietnam. Those mountain "'Yards" became friends and family to us Special Forces troopers. They constantly and consistently proved themselves as very capable defenders of their homeland. One time I asked a 'Yards soldier to explain why he was fighting the North Vietnamese and the Viet Cong. His simple response was, "Because they are here. They came here to take from us: our land, our women and young men."

Some teams with 'Yards" were able to run covert missions across the border, attempting rescues of pilots and other militarily men who'd been shot down. These 'Yards proved themselves in every battle; we never questioned what they would do. Their loyalty was unquestionable and we knew they would fight alongside us to the very end. They showed us they were valiant fighters, more than capable of defending their homeland and native villages.

As the war dragged on, more and more North Vietnamese infiltrated into the south, traveling along the Ho Chi Minh trail. They would come down, overrun villages, force the native young men to fight, capture whenever they could the young women of the villages, to become slaves as the North Vietnamese came further south.

I had my own ideas about what I thought war was, but Special Forces School would teach me many more ways to deal with these warriors. As we moved north into North Carolina's high country, spending nights out in the cold, often with wet feet and wet bodies. We got blisters on our feet; sometimes, my boots and socks were so bloody that bloody water would get wrung out of our black wool socks. These mountains extracted their price out of us. Climbing up them, our thigh muscles would let us know they were being worked, but going back down, we'd have other difficulties. The fronts of our legs got super sore and we all experienced shin splints. This became a bone-chilling hurt that we felt clear through to the leg bones. In addition, we had to deal with intense mountain cold when we had to lie in wait to do a vehicle ambush. That cold would seep into our inner core; we'd get so cold, our teeth would spontaneously chatter. Another casualty of this was our jaws were constantly hurting from us trying to stop our teeth from chattering.

I was often selected as compass man since I demonstrated that I was good with a map and a compass. When I looked at a map, it was like "reading" to me. I knew I could get us anywhere on a map, so the men learned they could trust my map reading skills. I would work with the patrol leader; we'd make a terrain model and lay out a route to travel to our next objective. Then we'd have to "dig in." We dug everywhere we went and our instructors were always looking for an opportunity to teach us more. Yes, this training was hard, but living my life as a youngster had brought me to this very point in life. I was determined to become a Green Beret. There was never any question for me as to whether I'd make it.

Those six months after my first tour of Vietnam changed my life dramatically. My buddy Butch's death seriously affected me. Growing up, I'd spent almost as much time at his house as at any of my own relatives'. I felt like he was a brother. Many of our relatives had intermarried; my mother's brother Dago married June Dorsett. She died in childbirth, but I thought of her daughter, Georgia Ann, as a member of my family. Butch's death solidified my resolve to achieve further military training, spurring me on to become a Special Forces trooper, a Green Beret, a Ranger and even a Ranger Instructor. Over the next 35 years I would train and take many men to war. All of the lessons I learned in my first year in Vietnam were the basis for lessons I would teach soldiers over the next 40-plus years.

Many years later, I drove back home to attend the funeral of Butch's dad, Sonny. All the way there, I cried to myself, thinking about Butch and our childhood days, how we went sledding down big hills in the winter, how we'd make it around the sharp corner without a smashup. I thought about how both his mother and father came to watch us play basketball games at Huron High School. I did not know until I got to Sonny's funeral that he was a World War II veteran and he'd been awarded quite a number of Bronze Stars for his bravery. As I remembered

Butch, I think I felt some "survivor guilt", that I'd still been able to live my life in the Army. As soon as I arrived and saw Butch's mother, she reached out for my hand, held it for a moment, and then said, "I am glad you came home. It really means a lot to me, Joe." I finally felt a little relief come into my heart. I knew that I'd made lots of mistakes in my life and hadn't always done the right thing, but deep down, I loved Butch and his whole family with all my heart.

Michael J. Conley

Getting Ready to Take Hamburger Hill
5th - 9th of May 1969

Those six months after my return from Vietnam kept me on a fast track! I'd returned home from Vietnam in 1968 for Christmas, got married almost overnight to a hometown girl, then took her and her young son back with me to Fort Bragg, North Carolina, to get training with the Special Forces. Although she went back home to Mitchell, we created a daughter in our short time together. A month after her departure, I also left for Vietnam.

May 1st found me back in the 101st Airborne Division, 2nd Battalion, 506th Airborne, 101st Airborne Division. Four days later, May 5th, to celebrate my little brother Clifford's birthday, I finally got back up with my unit. Quickly, I began to hear about an upcoming invasion into the northern part of the A Shau Valley. They referred to this valley as "Apache Snow." This assault was to be another RIF (Reconnaissance in Force.) Previous assaults into the A Shau had been awful, but at least, those were over within just a few hours. Nothing I'd experienced so far would come close to the ten days we would spend battling our way up to the top of Dong Ap Bia Mountain.

The Montagnard tribe, the ones we called the 'Yards, lived nearby and referred to this mountain as the "Crouching Beast." This mountain stands alone, surrounded by jungle, rivers and streams. Trung Pham River borders the mountain on the north side, on Dong So Ridge. It is akin to the Tennessee Valley Divide that runs north out of Georgia, up through the Carolinas, and then further north into Virginia's Shenandoah River Valley. Along the south side of this mountain was the wild, raging Rao Lao River, similar to the Toccoa River in north Georgia. This was rough and rugged country, full of fast streams that ran far below steep cliffs. Its tributaries led off into the ridges, alongside many small paths that followed along the ridge lines.

We spent a lot of time fighting through that specific jungle. Vines and bamboo thickets covered whole sides of the mountain like triple-layers. I have included one of the maps that I carried as a platoon sergeant, to which I have often referred. Many times I would make notations on my maps regarding areas such as No Fire Zones, VC Palace or area of operation.

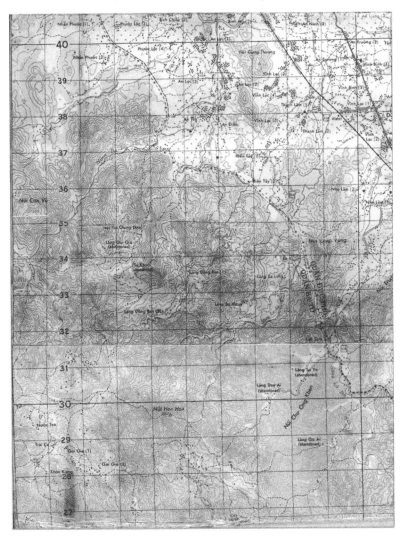

My memories of Vietnam are still vivid. I don't know why, to this day, my sleep is still invaded by those memories from Vietnam: faces, screams from the fighting, noises in the dark, whispers. All I know is I have never forgotten any of those dark days. Much of what we went through was affected by the timing of events, as well as weather events.

Shortly after we arrived in the valley, the rains began. Every day, each and every day, we lived through long, hard monsoon rains that lasted for hours. Additionally, we had to contend with fog. Every bit of that terrain was treacherous, but we kept on climbing. The enemy had had plenty of time to prepare for our arrival. Later, we would find underground trenches where they had built a bunker complex. They could resist anything we threw at them. We eventually discovered why. Just across the northern border were the VC supply lines with Soviet-made vehicles. Also, their captives or slaves were ready and waiting to resupply them every night. I always wondered why the U.S. didn't bomb the VC from the Laotian border or bring in other forces to prevent the VC from bringing in fresh troops and new equipment.

There were days when we hardly got off our hands and knees. Our life was one bit crawl, from one tree to the next, from a stump or root, to anyplace we could find, wherever we could reach out next, to whatever we could lay our hands on. We might only move 50-75 meters in one day, just crawling around. Nevertheless, we also had to constantly be on the lookout for booby traps and mines set along the mountain or in those steep ravines. The enemy knew quite well which routes we would have to use to get up to the top. I often look at some of those old maps that I carried in my ruck back then. In retrospect, I have spent hours looking at those maps, remembering our struggles, acknowledging our determination to see every mission through to the end. The more I look at the maps, the more I realize how intense our struggle was. Back then, I was a very young E-5 sergeant, determined to take care of the men assigned to my care and to do the job assigned to me.

Going up Hamburger Hill
8th - 24th of May 1969

In all my life I'd never seen a mountain like the one we were on now. We followed the trail, more like just a path, from the valley floor into the jungle. The jungle canopy was between 100-150 feet overhead. Only when there were gaps in the canopy could we actually glimpse some sunlight. That jungle was woven together like a basket; vines and bamboo were so thick that we couldn't push our way through it as we tried to climb. The temperature was super-hot, like maybe in the upper 90s or even 100, and not a breath of breeze could get through any of that bamboo interwoven with vines and briars. When people in America think of bamboo, they think about fishing poles, but the bamboo that grew in Vietnam and on this mountain was as thick as a small man's waist. Also, the stands themselves were thick, too thick to easily penetrate. We might try to push our way through or wedge open a spot between stalks of bamboo. Nevertheless, it took a concerted effort to be able to get through, push, wedge or chop through with a machete. That in itself was a job! Anyway we approached it, we had a really tough job.

When we went into a valley to run an LRRP mission, we would send out scouts, then backtrack to find if the NVA regiments had come in toward us. All the while, we kept finding lots of trails and roads coming from Laos. As we climbed the mountain along its ridgelines, we would often cut across gaps and low points in their roads. Whenever we were along the western end of the valley near nightfall, we'd watch as trucks drove through the middle of the A Shau Valley. We could hear convoys bringing in heavy equipment all through the night, down the valley on that same road. Yet, by dawn the next day, we would see nothing along that same road. We began to feel we were slowly being suffocated by that three-canopy jungle. I'd been sent back into Vietnam with the 101st Airborne Division. My assignment:

> Head toward the border;
> Cut off the enemy's supplies, trucks and men;
> Prevent the enemy from pouring into South Vietnam.

To this day, I still wonder why they sent in an infantry unit of 12 men to stop a convoy of over a hundred trucks and tanks pouring into Vietnam. Why did we not bomb them from the other side, from the Laotian or Cambodian border? Why did we say we tried to fight that war, but yet we stopped at a specific "line on the ground" because it was another country's property line? I am still asking these same questions today, as we fight in Iraq and other locations around the world.

This same mentality continues to eat us alive. We should have gone into Syria and taken out the headquarters units supplying equipment and the training units with professionals from Russia and China. In retrospect, it was hard for me to realize that when the Battle of Hamburger Hill began, there were people in the U.S. Army below the rank of major who actually did not know that the NVA were using Laos as a sanctuary to store food, clothing, ammo, and personnel. Only one mile across the border the Battle of Hamburger Hill would happen, but we could not even get one bomb across the border. The NVA continuously resupplied their men by crossing this border, waiting up in the draws and valleys that lead into other valleys, up a network of trails and paths leading to the very top of Hamburger Hill. Our government officials, as well as the NVA's top officials, simply kept sending more men into this meat grinder we veterans called

Hamburger Hill. Our top brass wanted to act like they didn't know what was going on out there. That was pure bullshit.

I worked long enough with the LRRP's to know they sent their intel to the higher, every day, then the higher sent this intel on to their higher every day. Nevertheless, congressmen and politicians chose to believe that the enemy we were fighting was little more than poor, uneducated, barefoot, hungry people trying to fight us with barely any weapons or ammo. The reality is that the NVA were well supplied by the Russians and the Chinese with trucks, tanks and more than enough ammo and weapons. They were well supplied, not only to carry on a war, but to win it.

On that first day back with the unit, I remember being told, "We'll go back into the valley on an assault into the western end of the A Shau valley." During the first briefing, we saw pictures of several landing zones. We were told how to use three different LZ's to get all our men in. I suddenly realized that although I had been gone more than six months, I had returned to a "continuation" of the last mission I thought I had finished, before I was sent home in 1968.

I think I should also tell you right here how this all came about. The people back in the rear, maybe some officers who had never even seen any LZ (Landing Zone), would decide where we were going to land. Next, another officer, maybe a major or higher, would take a ride out in a nice fat cat, a Huey, hovering about 3,000 feet above the LZ as he looked it over. But of course, he'd make sure the helicopter pilot wouldn't get him close enough to the ground to get shot at! He'd be so "committed" to this upcoming battle that he could say he went out there, but certainly he never goes close enough for any green tracers to "reach out and touch" him.

By this time, I certainly "know the drill." It's up to the blood and sweat of America's grunts to carry out what the highers have dictated, "… needs to happen." But never you mind, 'cause we knew we belonged to one of America's best units! We loaded up our rucks, carried extra ammo, shells and magazines. **Most importantly, we went into battle carrying water!**

Certainly by now, I did not think the U.S. Army was going to bring us water when a battle was going on! Newspaper people got flown in and out; wounded were actually picked up right in the middle of a firefight, but nobody thought to bring the troops on the ground, those in the fights, any water!

OK, I really do know the drill and the b.s going on here. My job is to keep as many men alive as possible; I've trained 'em to fight, now I have to keep 'em alive for the next however-many years. Again, I plan, trying to make sense of all this. As I brought squad leaders and team leaders together, I must have asked them a thousand questions. Then, my first afternoon back in Camp Eagle, we rehearsed how I wanted to do an airborne insertion, what needed to be done for an extraction, practicing different procedures during our movement phase. I questioned people about their duties and what they had been told to do, in case we encountered sniper fire, as well as what to do in case we were surprised by the enemy.

I advised them that I would do a final inspection before we flew out to the LZ. I would check their magazines, how many rounds they put into them and the condition of their weapons. I wanted them to actually show me what they carried in their rucksacks; I wanted to be sure they had what we were going to need for a battle. When I could, I talked to several different men, instructing them to carry a small "butt bag" where they could keep extra 40 mm rounds or hand grenades. In case someone had to send some more rounds out to men who needed them, then we'd have them. I explained that we would not have a five-gallon bucket out in the field to carry things in, so we needed to use what we actually had available. I instructed the squad leaders to set up inspections. They, in turn, planned and executed their plans with their fire teams. Now I believed I was actually teaching these men how things would work out in the field, in the heat of a battle, not how things were "supposed to work." I'd been told that the M-16's were working better with new ammunition for them, and the 30-round magazines now had stronger springs in the bottom. I must admit, right here, that I never actually saw those new 30-round magazines until I was on my way back to the states. (A soldier at a gate checkpoint had one.) Although I'd heard about them, we were never issued any of them.

I also advised our Company Commander that men in the unit had told me that only a few of our men had actually zeroed in their weapons. I returned to talk to the men, speaking to each one individually. This time around, I intended to do things differently. I wanted to get to know these men, to learn their names and learn things about them as individuals. No longer was I a rookie. I knew this time what we would probably encounter. I used a black marker to write out a time schedule on an old C-ration case. I explained that first, we'd get a warning order. I reassured them that I'd keep them abreast of each thing we would have to do for this mission. Over the past six months I'd been thinking about what I had been taught and more importantly, what I "had not been taught." What my men needed to learn was how to "NOT" make mistakes, because mistakes are what get you killed. I began to work out a detailed schedule to prepare for this assault. Each team leader was told exactly what weapons and equipment he should carry. I also began to talk with the assistant team leaders, explaining how I wanted them to use the maps at our disposal and to inspect each weapon.

Everyone was told that I expected them to "follow my orders," because one of my jobs was to keep them alive. The next day we had another air assault, then headed on up steep ridge lines closer to the top of the mountain. We were all drenched in sweat as we walked up a very narrow, twisted trail. I felt proud of my platoon, as they led the rest of Alpha Company, 2nd Battalion, 506th Airborne Division, 101st Airborne Division. We had been selected to lead the company because the "Old Man," our CO, Capt. Bill Womble, wanted us to be the point team and the first platoon in. All the men in the company liked this CO and thought he was a good field soldier. They affectionately called him "Wild Bill."

For all of the previous day we'd been on the move, searching the smaller hills. The battalion commander had sent two other companies off to the north, alongside a fast running stream which flowed down the mountain. Now, we were at the foot of that mountain, looking for the NVA. I had begun to think the enemy had just gone back across the border into Laos. I didn't think they were ready to fight us again, because I didn't think that they would fight unless they thought they could win and win big. I knew that things had changed a lot over the last year, after the TET offensive when we whipped the NVA. They had experienced setbacks in men and material. One question that still rattled around in my brain was, "Are they still not ready to fight yet?" By early afternoon we found more evidence of their freshly-dug bunkers and well-worn paths, but no sign of an actual enemy. Late in the afternoon we were ordered, "Turn and head north, further," deeper into that three-canopy jungle.

This environment began to look different to us. Brush, trees and jungle canopy dwarfed any smaller trees. It became really dark in there, everywhere you tried to look. Hardly a single ray of sunshine touched the jungle floor in there. The smell of death and rotting vegetation permeated the air. Soon, I felt my sixth sense kick in. I felt like we were being watched; I thought that our enemy was "out there" with their eyes on us as our leader moved forward. Although it would be completely dark in one hour, we were not moving very fast along this ridgeline. The path we were following led deeper into even thicker jungle. Shortly before night, the Old Man called in, telling us "to make a place." It was his way of telling us to get settled somewhere for the night. Although we were well into the jungle, the Old Man himself was just now coming into the jungle. It took almost an hour before we got to anyplace appropriate for us to settle ourselves. Since I was in the lead, we found a saddle between two hills to set up our NDP (Night Time Defensive) position, but it took the rest of our company quite a while to get in there with us.

Ever so slowly, the troops filed out onto the perimeter; each platoon had an assigned section of the ridgeline. The trail we'd been on went straight though the middle of our perimeter, from the six o'clock position to the twelve o'clock position. We were only about three-fourths of a mile from the Laos border, off to our west. I believed that the only way the enemy could hit us was to come up that ridge line or come down the hill along the same ridgeline we were now on. I pointed this out to the company commander and asked if we could put some teams out on both ends of our perimeters, for about 50 meters and use them as our LP (Listening Posts) throughout the night. He concurred, so I headed back down the trail with three of our platoon. It was really steep, so we were only able to cover about 50 meters. Finally, we located a small knoll that was not too steep. We felt that at least two men would be able to lie down here and rest, while one man could pull guard duty.

Almost before daybreak I got a radio call; the CO wanted us to go back up to the valley because they thought two other companies were going to use us as a blocking company. He then told me, "Be ready to take the 1st Platoon; head down in thirty minutes."

Right there I told him, in as few words as I could find, that the rest of the company "… would not be near ready to shove off in 30 minutes because they have to bring in their claymore mines and LP's," and, "most of the men have to eat some kind of C's before they'll be ready to go." I had known this CO for all of three weeks.

This time he fired off, "Don't be telling me what we ought to do!"

I replied, "Yes, Sir! We'll be on the move as soon as we can. I'll pick up my LP's as we move down the ridge."

Twenty-five minutes later we were on the ridge line. I knew we needed to go slowly, so the rest of the company and other platoons could catch up with us. I took the point man and we headed off together, listening, trying to be aware of our surroundings. Again, my sixth sense told me we were being watched and that the enemy knew exactly what we were doing. I thought out loud to my radio man, "This sure would be a good place for an ambush."

I wanted us spread out, with at least five meters between each man. I also wanted to be able to look up and down the side of the trail even though I knew it was very steep. My plan was, "Take it slow and easy." Twice I stopped the platoon, advancing forward alone, looking for our LP's who I knew had been left out there during the night. We had just spoken with them on the radio, only a few minutes ago. I'd told them, "Get ready for a link up; we're moving back down."

Expecting to run into some sniper fire, and more than likely, at least a squad of the enemy, I continued on, then stopping again, feeling sure I heard something up ahead. Then I thought, "That's just be our own LP (listening post.)" My training was telling me the enemy was near; the sounds from the jungle were also telling me the enemy was close to us. I looked down the trail ahead and saw a spider web just blowing in the morning breeze. My mind told me, "Stop! Something's going on here."

I knelt down to inspect the web. I could see that more than half of it had been torn through and dew drops were already sliding down the spokes of the web, then dripping off. I stood there and looked at that spider web for at least a minute. More of the web still hung from above, but finally, my brain processed the knowledge that whoever had walked under and through it was a whole lot shorter than anybody in my squad! My brain processed, "DANGER! Danger! Enemy near ... somebody through this, just seconds ago!"

The spider web had been hanging about 4 ½ feet above the trail. Somebody had passed through it as they went down this trail, some "bodies" a whole lot shorter than us! I realized whoever they were, were probably still really close by. I thought, "... they're just on down this very trail, towards the saddle where our guards are."

Time was of the essence! I had expected to find trail watchers or a sniper, but I sure as Hell didn't want to run headlong into a lead platoon of the NVA! I mentally shifted into Survival Mode. I slowly signaled a "Come Forward" motion with my left hand to my RTO (Radio Transmission Orderly) while scanning my eyes across the trail. I concentrated on what might unfold before me. Just as the RTO got over to me, I saw three NVA step out from the jungle. They were less than five meters from us! They were looking straight at us; I immediately reacted, shooting straight into them with my brand new M-16 rifle. Later on I'd realize that I'd never had time to zero it in.

Before we'd left camp I had taped three magazines together. Two were pointed away from me and the center one pointed towards me. When magazines are taped together, they kind of look like a big "Y" with twenty rounds in each mag. I'd learned I could fire all 60 rounds in less time than it takes to inhale twice. I hit that trigger and watched the bodies of the NVA fly backwards, morphed for all eternity into streams of humanity! Immediately, I switched to the other magazine, as I dropped down and rolled across the trail, away from my RTO. In less than a second, another five NVA appeared, firing small arms and a machine gun. On my second roll, I rose back up, blazing bullets once again sending more enemy on to eternity. This enemy had been surprised as we began moving down the trail. I think they intended to set up an ambush and wait for us, hoping to get our whole company inside their Kill Zone. After I shot that second bunch, I yelled back to my RTO, "Call in an air strike as soon as possible!" Meanwhile, I slammed in my third magazine. I just knew we were in for it now! I had no idea how many of them were out there, but I felt sure this would be a fight for our lives! I scrambled to my feet and ran back towards the RTO. I grabbed at him and we both ran for all "git out" towards the rest of the platoon. Hell broke loose on us all, not 50 meters from the company area.

Our 1st Platoon was all strung out. Many were just sitting with their backs turned toward the trail or propped up next to large trees. They looked like they were out for a picnic! The enemy hit on us from every conceivable direction. Many had scrambled on ahead, through the jungle, and had climbed overhead up into the trees. In less than five minutes at least a dozen of my men were dead and many more were wounded.

For nearly 20 minutes we had a major fight on our hands. I got men moving toward each other, so the platoon could move as a whole into a small saddle. The night before, two LP's had been in this same saddle, but now they were nowhere to be seen. With so many casualties, I knew we'd have to operate at less than half strength, so I had them form into three-man teams. We maneuvered ourselves around into a small circle less than 20 meters across, keeping our wounded in the middle with the RTO.

We knew the rest of our company was back up on the hill where they'd been engaged in battles all day long and doubted if they were in any better shape than us! The company did try to run a couple of RIF's down the mountain, to help us get out, but they weren't able to get close enough to even get to us. As an experienced soldier, I now knew that for all practical purposes, we were cut off from the rest of our company. They would not be able to get to us. I also knew they had been hit before they were even packed up or ready to start out from the NDP (Night Time Defensive Position,) so they were also in a really bad way. We all were in one big jam, to say the least! It was bad for any of us, any way you looked at it. Nevertheless, I have never been a quitter, and I was not about to start being one now. I made up my mind real quick, "We are going to fight right here, with what we have!"

I grabbed the radio and immediately called in air strikes. Then, I switched channels, and called for artillery back at Georgia, Blaze, Bradley, Currahee and Tiger. I also called the Eagles Nest, and asked who could actually call and talk to the Navy.

Over the next five minutes I had them fire, "Up and down, along both sides of the ridge," only 50-60 feet away. Those men from the Eagle's Nest saved our lives. I told them to drop plenty of HE (High Explosive.) We had so many chunks of hot shrapnel flying all around us that even my men were trying to dig in right there in that saddle.

We had five minutes to get ready for the fight of our lives! Where their base camp had been became a good spot for us. I do believe the enemy had 105's and a massive amount of other ammunition because, in over 22 hours of firing, they never left us alone. By now, I knew we were up against a very large force. For over an hour our company tried to get to us, but each time, they could only advance a few meters forward from their previous assault position before being driven back with automatic machine guns and small arms fire.

I got the CO, Lt. Col. Sharron of the 2nd Battalion, 506th, on the radio, advising him that I thought we could make it where we were, with the help of the artillery. I can remember thinking then how ironic it was that I could get higher up officers and the CO on the radio easier than I could contact my own company, less than 200 meters up that mountain. As dusk fell, I received a message from the higher, talking to me from a helicopter. He was part of the Hunter Killer Team. Two Cobras were hovering off to one side of our ridgeline. They had spotted more than a hundred NVA moving up the jungle trail headed straight toward us. "Bird Dog" talked to our higher and set things in motion, ordering those two Cobras off the mountain. They flew straight into our perimeter, with all their guns a'blazing. They raked that ridgeline back and forth! I'll never forget the sound of their mini-guns coming in off that mountainside. They stopped firing less than 20-30 meters from where we sat, dug in there on the saddle. That night, "Bird Dog" saved our very lives in more ways than one!

It was nearly dark when I spoke with Col. Sharron again. I asked him if I could speak to Col. Grange because he knew me. Then, I asked Col. Grange for permission to call in the FAC (Forward Air Controller.) Col. Grange asked me just one simple question, "Sergeant, can you do this?"

I told him, "Affirmative! I can do it right, Sir!"

Col. Grange gave me a verbal, "Then you do it, when you think you need it the most!"

I told the men what they could expect to happen within the next 10 to 12 minutes. Then I said, "Get in your bunkers and get ready!

The FAC came in, directly over our heads. When I could see his lights, I called out to him, "Whisper!"

I popped a trip flare so the FAC could pick up the light and smoke. We often would put a trip flare into our helmets and sometimes dig them into the ground because they would burn right through our steel pots. We used our helmets for a lot of things, but only in emergency would we ever put a trip flare into our helmet. The FAC called back, with a low, smooth voice, "I have your back. Hang on for a ride!"

Two of my men placed smoke grenades inside their helmets so the FAC could get a good sight on us. "Whisper" came roaring in, right out of the setting sun and right on target, right in the saddle between two large hilltops. "Whisper" had also called in two fighter bombers who struck less than half a football field away, with 150 pound bombs, cutting a very clean swathe through the jungle for us. Now we had a cleared field, up and down both sides of the ridge line.

We settled in for the night. Here is where experience from my first tour paid off. I told the men, "When it gets dark, do not fire your weapon. I explained that it would let the enemy know where we were. I instructed them to use their hand grenades to keep the enemy away from our perimeter. I also knew that the M-79 that fired a 40-mm HE and shotgun shell could mark where we were by shooting a small flare up through the trees when our parachute flares would not get through. I maneuvered myself around to all the men, whispering to each and every one. I wanted them to know I was there with them and we were going to fight this battle -+my way. I told every man, "Only fire your weapon to save your own life."

I gave them instructions about using their entrenching tools, as well as their Marine Corps K-bar, in case we had to do hand-to-hand combat. I told them to use anything that they could use to fight with, that wouldn't make a lot of noise. They listened and believed what I said; they were scared, but they trusted that I had enough experience and would get us all through this. I told every one of those boys that night, "… we will eat breakfast together in the morning."

I knew the enemy would come in to hit us, so I kept these men at the fire base camp. Before the last of our daylight disappeared, I'd crawled around and talked to each three-man group, passing out more ammo and hand grenades. I'd also given some grenades to the least-wounded men we had placed in the center. On the inside of our perimeter we placed five claymore mines. Two more faced back up the trail toward the company which was only one to two hundred meters away, straight back up the ridgeline. As an added precaution, our medics and some other men formed another secondary perimeter, inside the first one. If the outer perimeter fell or if any enemy got through, our men could crawl back to this secondary line. Everyone knew that tonight we faced the fight for our very lives!

Our second position was less than 20 steps across. We had dug bunkers for the more seriously wounded and covered them up. Our medic, the RTO and his assistant had gotten a whip antenna put up. Now, I believed we were in a good fighting position. The men had dug in where they could, then pulled trees and logs over on them. Everyone to a man had worked like beavers. We knew that when night came, we would be out there alone.

I could hear a little bit of noise around the perimeter. I moved about very quietly, just to reassure men in every position that it was imperative we maintain absolute quiet. I let them know that the smallest noise would lead the enemy straight to us. Again, I briefed each soldier, "Do not shoot your weapon unless it is absolutely a life or death choice. Instead, throw your hand grenades, and toss them in an arch so they (the enemy) won't know exactly where we are."

Night finally fell, and it fell fast. Anything we had been able to barely see totally disappeared from view. Soon we heard thunder up on the mountain. I knew we'd have a hard rain over the next couple of hours and thought, "... maybe that'll help us out." I also knew from having experience with being surrounded, that the enemy would sometimes exchange fire to find each other. That would certainly benefit us because it would tell us where they were. I also knew that our artillery and gunships would save us that night.

Of all things to happen at that moment, we got a call from our CO, Capt. "Wild Bill" Womble. (I think he might have been one of only three good company commanders I had in my life.) His RTO was asking if we were going to try to make it back up the hill to his unit. I remember thinking, "You are the same man who less than 24 hours ago told me to follow your orders because you knew what you were doing!" I thought to myself, "No, I am sitting right here, fixin' to fight a good fight." I respectfully responded, "No, Sir, we are here for the night. Since they (the enemy) are on higher ground, they would kill every one of us trying to get through the lines and back inside the perimeter."

Before midnight, a soldier shook my shoulder and whispered, "We can hear enemy coming down the other side of the hill toward our position."

Earlier that evening, I had shot off high explosives in that area, so now I ordered a fire mission. The first rounds came in from my right. A big blast and flash of light lit up the night. Next order, "Fire for Effect!"

They unloaded on the enemy, less than 50 meters from us. Shells were pounding on them, and blowing upward into the mountain, instead of over us. Five minutes passed, then our boys dropped three or four parachute flares. We could actually see the enemy crawling around out there, dragging bodies of their buddies back toward their top of the mountain. During the night the enemy probed us two more times, but just lightly, so we only used our hand grenades and our claymore mines to fight them. Daybreak finally dawned and the fog began to burn away. I told all my men we were going to blow the claymore mines behind us and head straight up the mountain for at least 50-60 meters, but our men up there would know it was us coming in. Our RTO called to the higher, and sent out a short message that told them, "We're coming home!"

Less than a minute later, our radio opened up. "Roger that! Come on home!"

I could hardly believe what my ears were hearing. No challenging passwords, no codes. The radio just opened right up. "Come on in, as fast as possible!"

We blew two claymores together to open up the jungle, then began to head out. Three men walked in front of our walking wounded; every remaining unhurt man helped another as we headed up that trail. The first 20 meters it was really wide open. No enemy shot at us as we entered the jungle. I knew we were very close to the perimeter. Ten meters later we were there! Our Company Commander was waiting for us, standing beside the trail. He was as happy to see us as we were to see him! Now, as I look back on this, I know it took us less than 15 minutes to get back to our company. It's almost unbelievable now to realize that not one soldier was shot at or killed along the way. We made it! Intact!

Two hours later, the big push came. The whole 3rd Brigade of the 187th Airborne, along with Alpha Company from the 2nd Battalion, 506th Infantry, headed back up Hamburger again. The fighting this time was brutal! It was intense and very loud; many good men died that day, but we would not be denied our due. After 16 days of fighting on our side of Hamburger Hill, American paratroopers began their final climb, up to the very top. We were not the first company, and we would not be the last, to make it to the top of Hamburger Hill, but we did make it to the top. There the fighting became very intense; some of the NVA had tied themselves up in the jungle trees so as to swoop down on us. Their snipers were hidden throughout the jungle canopy. Be that as it may, we still found the enemy wherever he was: down in their spider holes underground, up in the trees, out in the jungle.   Wherever we had to, we dropped white phosphorous on them.

Finally, around 1500 hours, everything around us became deadly quiet ... no moaning, no crying, no despair. I truly believed the angels had come to get many a soul. It was hard to believe it was over. We remained atop Hamburger three more days and two nights before receiving orders to march back to the valley. After more than two weeks of fighting for this specific hill, we simply walked off of it, and let the NVA and the jungle have it back. As a grunt, I felt really sad, as did most of the guys in my unit. As a company, we had gone on the defensive, holding onto that hill at all costs, guarding artillery and small base camps. Now, we were simply walking away.   It made many of us wonder, "What was all that sacrifice for? What about all those lost lives? Why? Why? Why?"

I must be honest with you, my fellow reader. Three days before we went back up Hamburger for that last time I wrote my mother and stepfather. I told them I was scared and I did not want to go. I had already been wounded once and was now back in country with a new company of men who were looking up to me to lead them up that hill. I wrote, "I'll do that the best I can."

I for sure didn't want to take a brand new platoon of men that we had not had time to train and who were still very new in country. I'd even told two other men I didn't want to attack that mountain. I thought we were crazy for even thinking of doing it, but I knew that if I did not lead these men up that mountain, then I would be relieved of my duties and another sergeant would be put in my place.   I was in a No-Win predicament.

In the 101st tradition, the word "retreat" is not known, especially in the line infantry or company. So I just made up my mind that, "By God, we will fight to the last man." I thought a lot about this after the battle. The only smart thing we did was sit there and watch them pound that hill with 1000 pound bombs.

Before I left Vietnam in late October 1969 I did know that the 101st had run a couple of more missions into the valley, but after all our efforts, we left that valley much the same way we found it. After the fall of the Special Forces Camp back in 1965, we gave the Viet Cong and the NVA control of the valley. That first time after Hamburger when I went home, we had not won the battle. After Hamburger this time, we went on to run more small ambushes. Never again was I involved in any other major battle in Vietnam.

Our next job was a RIF back at our fire base camp. By mid-October 1969 I was put on guard duty which meant I ran small nightly ambushes around Camp Eagle. One night I was called to the main orderly room where I was handed orders: "Return to the U.S."

I could hardly believe what I held in my hand. I would be going home, back to the good ol' U.S. of A. Soon I would fly south in a C-130 to Bien Hoa Air Base, and then on to Fort Bragg, North Carolina. The day I actually left I boarded a civilian aircraft in Bien Hoa, then flew on to Japan, then to Alaska. Our final stop was Pope Air Force Base in Fayetteville, North Carolina. I had served almost 18 months, but now it was over. I had received my first DD-214 on 20th November 1969. Over the years I would receive four more DD-214's and additional medals to pin on my chest. Although I was going home, I was not ready for civilian life. I know now that I was not ready to get out of the Army.

Indiana National Guard, Muncie, Indiana Co. D Rangers, Det. 1, 151st Airborne Infantry

The summer of 1972 I drove over to Camp Atterbury in Muncie, Indiana, for what I told myself was "just a visit." Yeah, right! I don't know who I thought I was kidding, least of all, myself. All of a sudden, I heard airplanes overhead. I looked up and watched as men parachuted from a small aircraft, then drifted towards the ground. Without missing a beat, I drove to their drop zone. Before I left Camp Atterbury that day, I had joined the 121st Infantry Battalion, Company D Rangers. This was and still is one the best things I ever did in my life! Then and there, my life was changed once again since the Indiana National Guard would be instrumental in getting me into Ranger School.

Later I would even become a Ranger Instructor at Camp Frank D. Merrill near Dahlonega, Georgia, the area made famous for gold mining in the late 1800's.

By October 1973 I received orders to report to Army Ranger School at Fort Benning, Georgia, for Winter Ranger Training. This was to prove to be one of the toughest things I would ever accomplish, but it certainly did provide the impetus to turn my life around. I needed to prove to myself, as well as others, that I could actually become someone worth knowing. Over the previous three years I had made many mistakes, hurting people I loved. I'd been married twice and had three children, but I'd really made a mess of my life. I wanted and needed to get back to what I knew I could do. After the second divorce I went back to live with my dad's youngest brother, my Uncle Pat Conley. To prepare for Ranger School, I began to train like I had never trained before. I got my mind right and my body in shape as I worked on my physical conditioning: running up and down hills, pushups and chin-ups on the old oak tree out front. I stopped drinking and smoking. Periodically, I'd have talks with my stepfather, letting him know how much it meant for me to be able to get back in the Army and become a Ranger. He told me he had known Rangers during World War II and knew they were the best fighting men he'd ever seen.

Late in October '73, shortly after my birthday, I found myself once again heading out to join up with the army. I hitched a ride over to Bedford to meet up with my stepfather. He was working for an outfit driving big semi's and had to do a run down to Bowling Green, Kentucky. He'd offered to let me ride along while he drove a load of limestone to a small college. We were both very quiet along the route, both lost in our own thoughts. When we were nearly to Bowling Green, he finally began to talk with me. I think he wanted to impart some fatherly advice. He started out with, "Joe, you've made some mistakes in your life, God knows you have, but this is your chance to do a good thing. Go on to Ranger School and be the best man in the class, and let the world know you are a good soldier." We traveled on a few more miles. Just before I got out, Harold added, "Go with God."

I was still a long way from Fort Benning, Georgia, but I was grateful for all the help he'd given, and especially for this blessing. To this day, I can't remember even traveling through the towns of Nashville or Chattanooga, Tennessee, but somehow I did. My next memory of this journey is in Georgia, in the town of Fort Benning, as I tried to get across post to a place they called Harmony Church. I found a piece of cardboard on the roadside and made a small sign on which I wrote "Harmony Church." I held it up for drivers to see, hoping I'd get a ride out there. Eventually, a soldier drove past, then pulled over to the side of the road. I had heard him slow down, so I turned and hurried over to catch this ride. The driver introduced himself as SFC (Sgt. First Class) Doug Perry; he was on his way to Ranger Camp also, since he was the Class Tactical NCO for the next Ranger class, my class. Although I was amazed at my good luck, in retrospect I was not surprised. Similar serendipitous events had happened many times in my life. As we drove along the way, he told me that he seldom stopped to pick anyone up. I think he was amazed that he had stopped for me, but I knew my angels were working, again on my behalf. Sgt. Perry told me that Capt. William H. Ohl would be our Class Tactical Officer, but students would learn to call him "Billy Hard Body." I would learn why as I got to know him and experienced Ranger Camp.

October 27, 1973, was the first day of one of the hardest things I ever completed. I was among 250 students who began their first day at Harmony Church at 0400 hours; we had to keep going until 2300 hours. We ran early and we ran long. We carried rucksacks loaded with more than forty pounds on 10 to 15-mile forced marches, running to the end of the line, then turned right around to do another. We'd leave Harmony Church in the dark and finish, still in the dark. Sometimes we'd actually leave on a forced march while it was still day light, but marches became our "every day, every hour" activity. All around us men dropped out and quit, deciding on their own that this was not for them. At the end of every day, fewer men were left to start the next day's march.

We each had been assigned a buddy; mine was Capt. Schreiber, but I called him "Shrapnel." We worked well together, helping each other in many ways, especially giving each other moral support. We trained with all kinds of weapons; I fired some I'd never seen before. The rifle range activities became very important since each of us had to qualify at sharpshooter level, or above. We had classes on finding buried bombs, then learned how to take them apart. We had to implement what we'd learned as we crawled through mine fields. We engaged in hand-to-hand combat and worked with the Marine Corps K-Bar, throwing these knives at targets at least 12-15 feet away. We worked on setting bobby traps and snares that would kill any man who encountered them. Each activities we did was graded. Early on, we began training on how to navigate by land. We were taught the Ranger doctrine: Train, move, fight; win as one team; never, ever, leave a comrade behind. Our days ran one into another; we seldom knew when a day ended or another began. We just knew to follow the drill, don't stop, don't give in, stay focused, stay with your buddy, keep the faith, and remember the Ranger doctrine: train, move fight, win. Never leave your buddy behind.

I trained like I'd never trained before. We left Harmony Church by the second week of November, headed for Camp Darby, named for a great commander in World War II. Here we learned about the obstacle course which we learned to affectionately call "the Darby Bitch." This obstacle course was designed by no man in his right mind! We had to walk across one end of a log to the other end and back again. Not to fret, these logs were positioned atop 40 foot poles, up above Mother Earth! We climbed up and down cargo nets, crawled through mud as explosions went off all around us and machine gun fire blasted only 12 inches above our heads. Our living conditions were out in the cold and in the mud. Men were constantly getting sick in this harsh environment. They got blisters all over, not just on their feet. Blisters so bad they couldn't stand up, much less move. Many just packed it in and quit.

On the other hand, I seemed to be doing very well. Actually, I felt like I was thriving! I was really enjoying myself out here doing all this stuff. For my first job as a patrol leader, I had to do a map recon, design a terrain model and take a 12-man team across a creek to the objective. The distance we had to accomplish was beyond anything I can remember, but it was my job to get us there. Every last one of us made it through the night with anyone quitting or getting lost. Consequently, I passed this first patrol and turned it over to my Ranger buddy, Shrapnel. Then, he did the "actions at the objective." Together, we got our team off to a very good start, passed both patrols, and made sure our men ate in a timely manner from with food or rations we picked up along the way.

We knew that rations were the lifeblood for our troops. If we couldn't find them hidden in the woods or were too late picking them up, then we wouldn't eat. Sometimes some teams didn't find their food and consequently, had to continue on without any rations. If a patrol leader was weak or his team got lost, then their timeline set everything else in motion for failure. I don't remember how many patrols Shrapnel and I made, but I do know I have never returned to Camp Darby. We left there on a very cold, rainy day, right before Christmas 1973. On our last morning there, we rose before dawn. We were given a warning order that, before we would eat again, we would march back to Fort Benning and Harmony Church. Shrapnel and I made it back with our troops by lunch! The number of men who had begun Ranger School was more than cut in half, and we were all in a mess, with bleeding feet, bruised knees and torn up bodies, but we'd finished. That was what mattered. We'd finished! Our next stop was Camp Merrill, Mountain Ranger Camp, in the beautiful north Georgia mountains near Dahlonega, Georgia.

Ranger School:
21st of October 1973 –
10th of March 1974

Late October saw us begin our tenure as Ranger students. The weather was nice and warm in the mornings, then cool in the evenings. We had to go on some early morning runs in brisk weather, but they weren't bad. We were all strong way back then. But eventually, all those long days and nights without sleep would take its toll on us. Class #4-74 had begun at Harmony Church in the pine tree forests of Fort Benning, Georgia. We were there three weeks, then we'd moved in the middle of the night to Camp William O. Darby about 14 miles out, but it might as well have been on another planet with very different terrain there. Now, we had moved on again, close to the Chattahoochee River with its billy bogs and wet clay forests. We were eaten alive by mosquitoes and pestered to death by pervasive gnats that got in our eyes and found any body crevice they could. They enjoyed us fat and sassy Ranger students! In the early days of December with wind at our backs, we slept as our trucks wound along those winding mountains roads into the Blue Ridge Mountains of Dahlonega, Georgia. We woke up after a six-hour drive to somebody yelling, "Get that truck unloaded! Get your stuff on your back or in your hand!"

Once again, we found ourselves at another Ranger Camp! Here, we were the 2nd Ranger Company in Dahlonega, Georgia. Less than 100 students remained from our initial class. Although it was only December, we were freezing to death in those mountains of North Georgia. We knew it would not be easy to pass whatever we encountered out here, but we each knew we would have to call on every bit of our endurance to find out if we had what it took to be a Ranger. That very first morning of Ranger School men began dropping out during runs or after the swimming test. We who had survived Harmony Church knew that even though other men had quit during our very first week of Ranger School, more would continue to leave quietly from here, too.

On our swimming test we had to swim 50 meters under water, dressed in full uniform and boots, while a 10-pound ruck and a rubber ducky were strapped to our backs. Every time any of us came up for air, he knew he'd better yell, "Rangers Lead the Way!"

Men had quit down at Camp Darby when they got inhumanely tired, tired of being eaten alive by those mosquitoes, being pestered to death by gnats. Our feet had stayed wet for days on end. Those gnats and fire ants just waited to ambush us as we moved through Palmetto brush; they'd be on us like a swarm of stinger bees. It was not unusual to be out on the firing ranges into the night if many men failed to hit enough targets. In a couple of instances men actually fell asleep on the rifle range if there was a lull in the action between targets or they might simply just drift off to sleep. We had buddy runs carrying a 40-pound rucksack and running ten miles on sore, blistered feet. We had blisters on the bottoms of our feet, on our heels and even on the backs of our feet. I had realized there, "No, this is not like any school in the military I've ever attended! This is Ranger School!"

The last night we were at Camp Merrill our Tactics Officer, Billy Ohl, and Tech Sergeant Doug Perry said it was the worst weather they had seen in those mountains in the 20 years they'd been running that camp. After surviving that night I thought, "Oh, yes, we will be allowed to wear our black and gold Ranger tab with white thread. We will forever be called Winter Rangers!"

But I have digressed. When we first arrived at Camp Merrill, our company was divided in half. One-half began patrolling beside the Ranger School, while the other half marched down to the mountaineering side of Ranger School. This lower area is beautiful, set down below black falls with repelling towers and sixty foot cliffs. During the CCC days in the 1930's rocks were blasted from these rock faces to build roads through these mountains. Here we learned mountaineering from some special Mountain Ranger Instructors who taught us knot tying, repelling and how to make two-man climbs from a lower mountaineering area. Most of the rocks there were constantly wet from water that continually oozed out from the mountain faces. Our ropes would freeze during that winter weather, but the other side of that weather was sure nice during the heat of summer. Many a good Ranger student failed to complete Ranger School simply because the physical training we had to endure was just too hard for his body or else the fear factor got to him. One thing we constantly worked on was the activity of two men carrying a wounded soldier on a litter down the side of the mountain.

Lower Mountaineering Area at Camp Frank D. Merrill

One particular time that I remember was just simply horrible. We had been there nearly three weeks and had been functioning on automatic, with little food or nourishment of any kind and few opportunities for any semblance of sleep. We had climbed Mount Yona, repelled down on frozen ropes, while clinging to the side of that frozen mountain. We felt like sheep out on a glacier. Finally, we had arrived to the point of being 12 kilometers out, for our last night on patrol for a vehicle ambush. All we had to do was complete this ambush and make it back to camp! Then, we'd move forward to our next phase, Camp Blanding in Pensacola, Florida.

This particular night was beyond horrible. A cloying dampness pervaded those mountains while the temperature continued dropping. Fog and clouds were so thick you could barely see your hand before your face. Now, we thought we are really going to freeze to death. We were lying out atop the frozen earth at our ambush site. We had been out there for over an hour, just waiting. I became aware of someone else out in that cold night air not far behind us. I felt sure it was a Ranger Instructor checking on us, to see how many of us were still awake.

The wind began blowing harder and I could actually hear it crying as it blew around Hawk Mountain. We had begun this journey by "humping it" in 20 degree weather from the FFU (Friendly Forward Unit) back at Camp Merrill. We had left before dark, continuing to walk for 36 hours. We'd crossed over the Tennessee Valley Divide, then pushed on down a side of Hawk Mountain near an old trout rearing station. We only stopped long enough to eat cold C's (C-rations.) We'd had to carry them inside whatever we were wearing so they wouldn't be frozen when we opened them up with our P-38's, our can openers. We were wearing either winter parkas or field jackets with poncho liners sewed inside. Fortunately, we kept our hands warm wearing wool gloves. By the time we were to prepare for this ambush we had been awake for nearly two days. Finally, we got to the side of the mountain where we were to wait to ambush a convoy. We'd been told they would come down this road before midnight. I prayed to my angels, "Please, make them hurry so we can get this over with, so I can get these men up and back on the move before they freeze to death."

Security teams had been placed out on each flank by at least 100 meters and around a curve on the road. Our linear ambush would be between two curves. We had teams in place, armed with M-60's, more than 500 rounds of ammunition, and in every belt, every tenth round was replaced by a tracer. The assistant gunners had already been busy, placing two claymore mines and four hand grenades primed with demolition cord and a blasting cap on each end; these were rigged to blow up simultaneously, and the claymores would overlap each other during the explosion. We'd also been busy laying booby traps on the other side of the road, placing trip wires to prevent the enemy from going back down the hill to escape. As well, everyone was supplied with hand grenades at the ready.

Our men were stretched out more than 100 meters alongside a well-worn gravel road in two-man teams and their weapons were concentrated on an area to provide overlapping fire once the ambush began. We were 32 strong, but we'd only had one day to practice and rehearse this ambush prior to crossing the FFU. This ambush was the highlight of the Mountain Ranger Camp training. We'd certainly had good instruction from some of the most experienced men in the world. Our Mountain Ranger Instructors made us students "do it right by the numbers" until we got whatever knowledge they were trying to impart, exactly right. Now it was time for us to prove that we Ranger Students could leave a designated place on a map, travel more than four miles across country, cross a 45 degree slope through mountains and the Tennessee Valley Divide, rappel down cliffs, traverse across streams of freezing water, crawl through mountain laurel thickets and rhododendron thickets. While on this patrol, we'd crossed two major roads, then slipped past the enemy's gates, pickets and patrols. We were now totally exhausted.

Our Ranger Instructor stopped us. I thought he was coming over to relieve me from my obligation as the point and compass man. I had led this team of Rangers to their objective site which now was only a few meters away. I felt such relief, thinking that I'd be able to go back to my assigned squad as just a member of the ambush. But the Instructor surprised me when he said, "You are now in charge of the ambush. You, Ranger Conley, are the new patrol leader."

I almost passed out, but I was too worn out to even react! My first thoughts were, "OK, let's get this ambush over with so we can get off this cold ass mountain and get back to Ranger Camp!" Thoughts of hot food and, hopefully, some rest, pushed me onward.

Our patrol had stopped the movement phase at what we called a "rallying point" or a rendezvous point. Now it was time for me to get to work as a leader and let my years of experience take over. Immediately I selected some of the best men as team leaders and began to give them very clear, concise instructions on how we were going to stay on the plan and the schedule, the same one we had rehearsed back at camp. I then led these leaders on a leader's recon of the objective, staying on the plan and the time line we had already established earlier. As a team we'd already discussed this specifics of this site; exactly how we could use the mountain behind us and the road ahead of us for an ambush site. First, I took the all the team leaders and two security men down the mountain until we found the gravel road. As I stood there looking at the road and where we were, I realized we had come out within 20 meters of where we had made plans on the map; I knew what the grid coordinates were that we had planned on when we'd been back at Camp Merrill.

I took the left security team or LP (listening post) off to the left about 100 meters; I showed them exactly where I wanted security to put their explosives and their trip wires next to the road. Meanwhile the Ranger Instructor was listening to me, watching what I did and grading me, but I forgot all about him. I was too busy to think that this was another grade for Ranger School. My instincts took over and I operated on automatic. I explained to the security team leader that, according to the operations order they had given us, the convoy should first appear on our right. Security would seal off the KZ (Kill Zone) with claymores and hand grenades, ensuring that no vehicle could get escape. Secondly, they were to set up an M-60 to stop anyone from coming into the KZ to rescue those in our trap. It was my intention that no one would escape the ambush, from the KZ nor would a rescue team enter.

Then I went back to my platoon and got the right security team leader; he and I walked over to his site, just around the curve. We traversed up and down the ambush site, discussing where they should put claymore mines, fragmentation grenades and a couple of smoke grenades. We also discussed how to use the lower side of the road, by booby trapping the two small ravines and a smaller, shallow ravine which led out of the KZ. I told him to put two trip flares alongside the road there, so anyone attempting to escape would trip them and we could see any escapees. I took time to explain to him how the enemy would try to escape: by going down the hill, then using those ravines or small ditches to crawl away from the light and shooting. I also walked the KZ with the ambush commander instructing him to put at least 22 men on the ground with weapons and machine guns. Finally, I directed each team to use their own particular KZ; they could expect to have cover fire and overlapping fire for at least 25-30 seconds.

Then we leaders all walked together, about 40 meters back up the side of the mountain, to find the rest of our patrol. As we pulled out, two men remained behind armed with a radio and with their eyes on the objective. We entered the patrol base and found men cleaning machine guns and rifles; some had been industriously organizing all the rucksacks into lines and had also put a special colored Kim Light on each squad's rucks. (They used a Cyalume safety light which utilizes three different colors; in this way, each squad's men could find their own rucks in total darkness without having to use their flashlights.) All was well, here. In just a few minutes, while the team leaders talked to their teams, I told the Ranger Instructor we were about ready to proceed with the ambush. He then took me aside and talked to me very quietly in the darkness. He advised me: another cold front with more snow was coming, in according to his last situation report from higher. He said, "Before the night is over, we may be in for a very rough time."

I went back to the patrol and talked to them, again, this time whispering. I wanted to encourage them, but also to advise them as to the gravity of the situation. "Men," I said, "we must do it right the first time tonight because we not want to go through this again." It was common knowledge in the Ranger Department that if any of us students failed the first time he tried to accomplish something, the Ranger Instructors could and probably would make you go back up the mountain, put in another patrol leader and we'd be made to do something all over again. I spoke a little louder as I told the patrol "Let's go do it right, the first time, men!"

Then I led the Ranger students down the mountain and into the ambush site. It was just getting dark, a time known to us as "BENT" (beginning evening nautical twilight.) Our left and the right security teams broke off from the rest of the patrol and assumed to their chosen positions. Then I also picked out two sites where snipers could see the road. Using their starlight scopes, they could not only watch the ambush site and give the rest of us instruction and advice, they could also fire into the KZ if we needed their assistance. Our security teams did radio checks as soon as they got into position. I went up and down the line of men, looking and watching as night began to fall, making sure the men were using their limiting stakes for sightings into this KZ. I also dispensed "words of encouragement" to each man as he lay on the cold wet ground, telling them "…remain quiet," but admonished them to "… please, stay awake. Don't go to sleep, no matter what!"

Everything was ready, so I sent the report to higher that we were in our assigned positions and in "Waiting Mode." By now, it was very dark; I could hear the wind in the distance howling like an angry beast as it screamed, coming around the side of Hawk Mountain.

We were all set and into position by 2100 hrs. We had 30 minutes until the set time for the ambush. I prayed aloud, "God, please let this convoy come on time!"

I knew we were in for a very long night where we would have to, quite simply, endure all that lay ahead. Over the next 30 minutes, the wind began to die down some, but clouds were descending closer and closer to the ground, increasing the fog.

Only periodically did the moon appear to any of us through that cloud cover; in the gap only a few, weak moonbeams actually penetrated through to the earth. Soon, fog enclosed our whole area and cold began to permeate our surroundings. Our small platoon was stretched out more than 200 meters and our security teams were another 100 meters beyond the end of our kill zone. I knew these men were beyond cold, with wet extremities that were freezing: feet in cold, wet boots and hands in cold, wet mittens. Equally as damaging, I knew they were very hungry, almost starved.

Ranger students were always hungry because we burned up more calories each day than we were able to put back into our bodies. We ingested about 1500 calories daily, but burned up two to three times that many on a daily basis. We'd figured out a way to keep C-rations instantly available, using the warm-jacket method. While out on maneuvers or traveling along a trail over the mountain, we'd place a can of C-rations inside our field jackets or parkas and keep it there for three or four hours. Then, whenever we had a break or changed position or leaders, we'd have a chance to grab a bite of something warmer than frozen!. We also used this same technique to keep our canteens from freezing, so we could sip a bit of water. Bitter cold water is much better than frozen water, every time.

I've often wondered if the Ranger Instructor called his higher, calling in the trucks and convoys so we could get that job on the road, get the ambush done and off that mountain! It seemed like a long wait, but in about 20 minutes, I began to hear what I thought was the sounds of trucks coming through. Even though that wind was howling like mad, I still thought I could hear trucks. Maybe I was really feeling the vibrations of their motors in that cold mountain air. Finally, I decided, "It's on! They're coming around the mountain, they're through Cooper's Gap.

Now, they're on the other side of Sassafras Mountain."

Our security team sent the code word to our radio operator that the convoy was within earshot. Within two to three minutes word came over the radio, "They're in sight!"

We saw lights penetrating through the fog. I could see headlights off in the distance as they rounded curves farther back on the mountain. I knew they'd have more vehicles behind their lead vehicle. My Rangers lay in silence, with fingers on triggers. I knew men with M-60s were ready to get rid of as much ammo as possible. We certainly did not want to carry any back up the mountain after this ambush. A call sign came from the right security guard. Three broken squelches were heard over the radio, then passed on to me, followed by the message, "… four large trucks and two smaller trucks just passed right security."

I knew that spacing between the point truck and the last truck was little more than 100 meters. I told both team leaders and the ambush leader, "Hold your fire until my signal. I'll blow up the claymore mine to initiate the ambush." I wanted as many vehicles as possible into our KZ zone.

I looked into the fog and mist and waited to see lights of that first vehicle. They would be coming off of a curve just as they came into my line of sight, out of the fog and mist. I watched as each vehicle passed me, then saw brake lights come on as they slowed down for the next curve on my left.

I was waiting for the left security team to radio their code words, "Heat! Heat! Heat!" which was our alert that all their vehicles were now in our KZ. As soon as I heard those code words, I squeezed the clacker in my hand. That claymore mine exploded. "Ba-la-a-am!" Noise and bright light ripped across the side of the road and into the mountainside. The rest of our platoon cut loose with everything that we had rehearsed. Over the next 30 seconds, all Hell broke loose out there! Then I shot a red pin flare into the air. As quickly as it had started, it was now over with. The entire area became eerily quiet. My team leaders yelled, "Search teams, do your work!"

Two teams of men moved out into the KZ as a large parachute flare went off overhead. Each team moved down onto the road, with machine guns facing out. They began to back up toward the rest of our platoon. Quickly the search team radioed back out, "Kilo Zulu Charlie!" meaning Kill Zone Clear.

We knew it was time to get out of there. In turn, I radioed my message, "Zero 36 Charlie!" through the RTO to the higher.

Now, teams of four to six men headed toward the rallying point. First, all team members and weapons were accounted for, then squads checked in with each other. They spread whatever ammunition they had left among themselves, so everyone had a basic load for any fighting which might now ensue. I was so glad it was over with, more than ready to hand over this leadership role to another Ranger. It was still dark as I felt a strong hand touch one shoulder. I recognized the voice of SFC Doug Perry. I asked myself, "What is he doing here?"

I had not seen him out on our KZ or during our ambush. He spoke very gently, but firmly to me. "Now, Sgt. Conley, get 'em home before they all freeze to death out here on this mountain!"

Much later on, after I became a Ranger instructor myself, I came to realize that Perry had ridden in with the vehicles that we were waiting to ambush. Later, he waited with the Medevac vehicles at the gap where we crossed, in case we needed help getting anyone one back into camp.

We made formation to begin our journey back to civilization. Not one person quit or shirked his duty. We headed out due north, out of the rally point, with our faces straight into wind and snow falling harder by the minute. No one could see more than five feet ahead. We were 32 Ranger students strong, with one Ranger Instructor. Each person followed the man ahead of him.

I was carrying a Silva compass I'd acquired during my first days of Ranger School. I'd stuck a piece of luminous tape on it, so whenever I opened it up, it glowed. As we moved along the mountain, the arrow bounced around seeking north. Each man struggled onward, slipping on the icy paths and falling. I tripped many times as more snow fell and ice began forming along our paths. We also had to climb over fallen trees and limbs. The temperature continued to drop as the hours passed.

Three hours after leaving the ambush site we finally got to the gap. Here the wind was blowing at 40 miles an hour and snow began sticking to our faces. My thoughts turned to those men of the 101st Airborne Division during World War II who were surrounded at Bastogne during winter. I wondered what it had been like for them. My mind traveled even farther back, to Gen. George Washington and his men at Valley Forge during those dark winter days during the American Revolution. I wondered if I was dreaming, but I never quit moving forward; neither did any of my men. Everyone stayed two steps behind the one in front; if a man fell down, the comrade behind him would help him get back up. We were going home! We were not making any attempts at stealth. We were not thinking about an enemy hearing us coming through. Nothing would stop us from getting to our destination! Between the men loudly encouraging each other and the wind howling around us, it truly did sound like a freight train coming straight at us in that area known as High Tower Gap.

The weather was screaming inhumane sounds in our ears. Like an angry beast, it screamed all around each of us, while the brutal weather assaulted our faces and eyes. When our eyes watered, the water froze as soon as it oozed out of our eyes; our breath froze as soon as it departed our noses and mouths, onto the scarves we'd pulled up for protection. Nevertheless, we kept moving forward. We walked slowly, crawling and clawing at the side of that mountain to get through the pass. As each one crossed that Tennessee Valley Divide's gravel road, I again spoke words of encouragement. I was standing on the side of the road in the gap. Gently, I said to each one as he passed me by, "I know you can make it back! We are going to make it together. Keep going! Don't think about anything else, just get home!" Although I thought about saying, "Don't quit," somehow, I just couldn't get those words out of my mouth. I just could not say, "Don't quit."

Less than 100 meters beyond the gap, two trucks and two ambulances with medics and hot coffee were waiting for us, but not one student quit or asked for comfort. What was left of Class 4-74 were not quitters. We had become Rangers! At any place in our future, we might fall down, we might get knocked down, but never would we ever think of ourselves as quitters. I can be honest with you, dear reader. I brought those men home through the most direct and shortest route I could find! I figured that no one would be out to ambush us while we tried to get back inside the FFU. No one in his right mind would be out there in that blizzard!

Five hours later, as we neared the FFU near the headwaters of the Etowah River, SFC Perry again materialized out from the snow and the wind. He reached across and found my almost frozen hand, grabbed it and shook it. Then, he said some wonderful words, "Great job, Sgt. Conley! Now, we can go eat some hot blueberry pancakes and have a hot cup of coffee!"

I had promised my men that we'd live to share breakfast, and it was within our grasp! We still had over 400 meters to hump through, but it was all downhill, through the middle of Mosby Army Airfield. Nothing, but nothing, would stop us now! I don't remember eating those blueberry pancakes nor even drinking a cup of coffee, but I do remember going to sleep in a little hooch with heat. I had a long dream and a good sleep. I certainly needed to sleep for a very long time.

Christmas Leave, 1974

The nightmare was finally over. After twenty days at Camp Merrill, we departed for Fort Benning, headed back to Harmony Church where we'd first begun Ranger School. We didn't know that within 24 hours we would be released for a 10-day Christmas leave. Shortly after our arrival at Fort Benning, we were told, "Fall in." We came on in and ate a meal. Capt. Billy Ohl told us we had a leave that would begin at 0800 hours.

I was surprised at this, but I did know that each of us certainly was in serious need of a break. Few of us could barely walk; all had serious mobility issues with our feet, from frostbite and blisters, twisted knees and ankles. Any way you looked at us, we had problems walking. Finally, I realized they were giving us a reprieve before sending us on to Camp Rudder for the Florida phase of Ranger School.

The following morning I took a taxi to the Greyhound Bus Station in Columbus, Georgia, where I purchased a ticket home to Bedford, Indiana. I had already called ahead and talked with Harold, my stepfather. I told him I was headed for home that day on a 10-day leave. As soon as I got on that bus, I went straight to sleep. I slept straight through for the next six hours, even through a stopover in Atlanta. Finally, when we stopped in Nashville, Tennessee, I got off to get something to eat. I continued on that same bus to Louisville, Kentucky, then transferred onto another bus. Finally, after 14 hours of traveling, I arrived in Bedford, Indiana. Harold was waiting at the bus station to take me on home.

Mother and Harold had bought another home down near the town of Huron, on the Old Brantsville Road, near where Joe Tolbert lives today. I rode alongside Harold, as he talked with me. Finally he said, "You look like you've lost near 20 pounds!"

I laughed at this remark because I knew I'd lost **more** than 30 pounds in less than 70 days in Ranger School. But I knew it was well worth all that effort. My first night home I slept at Mother and Harold's house. During the night it snowed a bit. The next morning, after a good night's sleep and breakfast, I decided I'd drive down to Huron to visit some friends I hadn't seen in quite a while. School was already out for Christmas vacation. Word had gotten out that I would be back home, so a lot of people came by to visit. On one of those cold mornings, one of my best friends, Allen Wade, came over. He and I had become very close three years after I returned home from Vietnam. Together we'd drunk beer and smoked some weed, but never anything really bad. This time around, Allen and I went out for a drive around Huron, then, as it began snowing harder, we decided to drive on over so I could visit his folks. He told me, "They'll be real glad to see you."

We drove almost a mile past Huron to where he lived. I'd spent one night at my mother's house, but I was really restless. I wanted to get out of that house and go somewhere else, so I was more than agreeable to go with Allen to see his folks. As we drove, the scenery began to look like a winter wonderland, like a Christmas card. By now the snow was coming down pretty hard and had begun to blanket tree limbs, evergreen trees and twigs alongside the road. The scene before us looked like a screen on a Walt Disney movie.

We got to the Wade house where Allen's parents Jody and Norma Jean lived with their other children, Teresa and Rita. Since all the kids were out of school on Christmas break, there was a holiday spirit in the household. I had known Jody because he worked with my stepfather Harold at the gypsum mines near Shoals. As soon as I walked into the Wade house, I immediately felt surrounded by the warmth and love of this family. I felt so comfortable there, among friends. We all talked about where I'd been, and I told them about Ranger School. After a while, Jody asked me if I'd like to stay for dinner and the night, even though he was about to leave to go to work in the mines. He said the weather was getting worse, and thought that soon the back country roads would be impassable. His wife, Norma Jean, chimed in, adding, "I've already fixed a big meal for the family. You can just stay 'n' eat with us 'n' spend the night here."

I thought, "How nice is this? I have been home less than 24 hours. Already, somebody has asked me to spend the night and is going to feed me home-cooked meals!"

I did believe God's will was working there that day, providing me with what I craved, a homelike environment. Norma Jean probably thought I looked like a lost puppy or a starved young man. I remember that during dinner I kept apologizing to her, explaining that I couldn't eat a whole lot at one time because my stomach was not used to a big meal. Nevertheless, I sure did give it a good try! Although many years have now passed since that winter of 1973, I have never forgotten Jody Wade's nice family. They treated me like I was a one of their own family. In our neck of the woods, people treated each other with kindness and compassion.

Not only did I spend that night, I remained there five nights! And, I loved every minute of it! Allen and I went squirrel hunting up on the ridgeline, where I used to run cross country while in high school. He, his sister and I all played in the snow, enjoying snowball fights. Allen and I got in the car and drove around a little, getting as far over as Mitchell, but mostly, we just stayed pretty close in, passing the time together. One night, before I left to return to Fort Benning, I asked Allen what we wanted to do with his life. He told me he wanted to be like me! To be an Airborne Ranger! I could hardly believe what I was hearing. Allen told me he'd grown to love me like the brother he'd never had. I had not ever told him this, but for a long time, whenever I saw Allen, I thought about my little brother Clifford. I suppose right then, we'd both been on the same wave length for a long time.

The days and nights passed by fast. Soon my body regained the weight I'd lost, especially with Norma Jean's good cooking! After we'd eaten a couple of meals, she took her guitar down from where it hung and began to play, first some country music, then some church songs. Then the days and nights really began to fly by. I was gaining weight and strength, and finally began to believe my prayers would be answered. I felt in my soul that someday, I would graduate from Ranger School.

I even wondered if I might ever be able to become a Ranger School Instructor. I wanted to dream about a future. I knew I needed to now return to the military and find a home there, to heal my body and soul. I knew I'd come home from Vietnam after that second tour with a really, messed-up mind. I had become a journeyman electrical lineman, but I did not like that job. I had made good money, but I had not been happy. All I had wanted in this world was to have a second chance. Back then I thought, "Just, please God, let me get back to the military!"

The last day before I left for Fort Benning, GA, it had been snowing a little. The roads seemed better than they'd been. I wanted to drive over the Williams Bridge and on to Port Williams Church where little brother Clifford was buried. I asked Allen to ride with me over there, but he had a date with some girl up in Mitchell. His sister Rita said, "Joe, I'll ride with you over there."

When we got to the church, I went into the cemetery and talked with Clifford. This was not the first time, nor would it be the last time, I'd talk with Clifford like this. I'd talked to him all the other times when I'd come home from the military. I just remember that while I sat in the church yard, it began to snow again. That evening I told my little brother, "All I want to be is an Army Ranger Instructor. Maybe one day, I'll be good enough to get full time duty as my job."

Little did I know then that it would be more than 30 years before I'd again see any of those family members again. In the summer of 2005 I drove up to Indiana to visit my mother. While talking with some friends, I found out that Jody Wade's wife Norma Jean had passed away and he'd eventually remarried. Their son Allen never did join the Army, so he didn't get to become a Ranger. I found out where Jody and his second wife had moved and drove over to visit them.

Jody and I went for a drive back to Huron, past his old home place and on over to Port Williams Church. He and I had a long talk, again standing in the graveyard where Norma Jean and my brother, Clifford are now both buried. We stood there a long time and never said a word. Finally, he explained that although he really missed his wife, after a while, he felt like he had to go on with living. I told him I totally agreed with his choice to remarry. I added that after Vietnam I felt numb from all the pain I'd seen, the killing and death I'd witnessed, and the frustration I felt over Butch Dorsett's death. I told him that now I had a good wife and I hoped this time I had somebody who would love me for who I am. I said I was proud I had gone to college, became a school teacher and had been a coach for basketball and football. Now, I was finally able to enjoy a peaceful and quiet life after all those years I'd spent in wars. Jody and I spent four to five hours together. He asked me to drive him down to some of the places where he'd fished and hunted when he was a young man living below Shoals, and we both remarked about how fast our lives had gone by. I told him I had some regrets about how my life had gone, but living my life as a soldier was not one of them. Before I left Jody at his home that day, I met his wife and remarked, "Please take good care of my ol' buddy, Jody." Right her, right now, I want to say to you Jody Wade and all your family, I thank you for what all of you did to help me go down the road of life. I hope God is as good to you as He's been to me.

Jody and Norma Jean Wade with their grandchildren, 1992

Finishing up Ranger School: Camp Rudder 1974

I arrived back at Fort Benning, Georgia, on the 3rd of January. The following morning my Ranger class flew out of Fort Benning on a cold windy day to go jump into the swamps of northwestern Florida, known as the East Bay Swamps, near Pensacola, near Elgin Air Force Base. The Florida Phase of Ranger School would last 18 days. I now know if I'd not had that Christmas break and the opportunity to heal my body, I could never have passed this phase of the course. Never again in my life would I feel so cold. The temperature in the air was above freezing, but the water temperature was 40 degrees or below! Our feet got so blistered that the skin pulled away every time we changed our socks. We went through worse conditions than anything I'd ever experienced in Vietnam.

Finally, I began to see a payoff from Mountain Ranger Camp. The actions at the objectives were not so far away, sometimes within 3,000 meters for one night's travel. Our job was to "get it done and be well hidden" before daylight found us. Only 50 students remained from the original 250 who'd started, with only two platoons left to stumble on. Before we left Harmony Church, Capt. Ohl and SFC Doug Perry called us all together in a classroom. Things had gotten pretty bad for us as a class and we had lost many classmates. Nevertheless, they inspired us, telling us, "You're the best! You have to stay together and help each other make it."

By now, each of us certainly knew our strengths and our weaknesses, as well as those of each of us. Now came that part of our training when we had to really develop teamwork by picking each one up emotionally and helping carry each other along to the end of this training. We talked to each other constantly. Even if someone begged to be allowed to quit, said they couldn't take another step, we tried every way we could find to rally each other. We felt we were all brothers.

We developed survival skills by learning to trust one another. We knew we had to find the objective in the swamp, such as a small house or a bridge crossing. We had to practice "how to do it." We'd come in close, then stop. Next, we'd lead a leader's recon to within 100 meters and put "eyes on the objective." Next, we'd make any necessary last minute changes from the original operations order. We'd come back in, then two teams would attack and seal off the objective with artillery. We'd gather information, reorganize the teams, back up, split up and head for our rendezvous 600-800 meters away. Again we'd split up, this time into three or four smaller groups, rendezvous again at a pre-arranged spot such as a trail junction, so an enemy couldn't track all of us at one time. Before we'd rest, a team would backtrack and do a "dog leg" over our own back trail, then lie in wait to see if the enemy were tracking us. As I've said before these were all graded activities.

If a team was carrying wounded or dead, it took longer to cover 300-400 meters. It was also harder to be quiet. Our Ranger Instructors would designate two or three men as "wounded," so we'd have to do first aid on them, then maneuver around while carrying them. Even these actions were graded.

Tying knots and crossing streams became a huge part of our lives. Whenever we came to a stream in the swamp, we'd have to stop the entire patrol. We'd do a leader's recon to locate the banks of the stream. Then, we'd rig up our rope and select one man as the "Far Side Life Guard." It was his job to swim across the current carrying one end of a 120 foot rope and get to the other side. Once he got up the opposite bank, he'd have to find a good "anchor point" or a very strong tree on which to tie his end of the rope. He had to be sure that his end of the rope was secure, far enough away from the edge of the stream and not at risk of giving way. He'd signal us by pulling three times on the rope; our job was to "take up the slack." We'd use our pulley system to tighten the ropes on our end, then prepare to cross the stream. Each man would hold onto the rope with one hand, while holding his rucksack with the other. Using the pulley system, we'd cinch each man across the stream. When the last man came over, he'd bring the end of the rope with him, then we'd pull tight, so the knot of the other end let the rope pass through. Finally, we'd retrieve our rope, roll it up and continue on our way. During some patrols we might cross a stream two or three times in one night. It was important that we kept our ropes from getting tangled up.

Of course, in the midst of all this, no one is getting much sleep. Sometimes, men would fall asleep and not realize the rest of the patrol had moved forward. Maybe someone just simply fell down and drifted off to sleep. A thousand other things might go awry. Our patrol might get broken apart, so we'd have to stop and send two rangers back to find whoever was "lost." Any actions regarding reclaiming a trooper was risky because everything had to be done as quietly as possible. We had to use the utmost stealth; we couldn't call out to find someone or to find out what had happened. If any yelling or hollering took place, it was referred to as a "Ranger screw-up." Additionally, we had problems with our radios. We'd experienced terrible reception while in the mountains; here we were again, with radios not working.

Finally, after being out in those swamps for 82 days, we came upon a small airfield on Eglin Air Force Base. Trucks were waiting for us there. Those of us who remained from Ranger Class 4-74 were driven back to Camp Rudder. We had made it! I was graded and ranked in the class, then we all voted on who would win various awards. The following day was our graduation, the 24th January 1974. Forty-two of us graduated. I was selected as recipient of the Merrill's Marauders Award. My fellow classmates and our Ranger instructors had trusted me "to do the job and do it right," as I led students off that mountain range during a driving blizzard of snow, ice pellets and high wind. I was chosen by fellow rangers as a leader, and a great compass man. This award meant so much to me!

"Rangers Lead the Way!" became our Motto.

RANGER CREED

Recognizing that I have volunteered as a Ranger, fully knowing the hazards of my chosen profession, I will always endeavor to uphold the prestige, honor and high "Espirit de Corps" of the Rangers.

Acknowledging the fact that a Ranger is a more elite soldier who arrives at the cutting edge of battle by land, sea, or air, I accept the fact that as a Ranger, my country expects me to move further, faster, and fight harder than any other soldier.

Never shall I fail my comrades. I will always keep myself mentally alert, physically strong and morally straight and I will shoulder more than my share of the task whatever it may be. One hundred percent and then some.

Gallantly will I show the world that I am a specially selected and well trained soldier. My courtesy to superior officers, neatness of dress and care of equipment shall set the example for others to follow.

Energetically will I meet the enemies of my country. I shall defeat them on the field of battle for I am better trained and will fight with all my might. Surrender is not a Ranger word. I will never leave a fallen comrade to fall into the hands of the enemy and under no circumstances will I ever embarrass my country.

Readily will I display the intestinal fortitude required to fight on to the Ranger objective and complete the mission, though I be the lone survivor.

RANGERS LEAD THE WAY!

Less than a year later I would be back at Camp Merrill as a Mountain Ranger Instructor, leading other young men, future Special Forces and Special Ops team leaders, through their tasks toward graduation from one of the most toughest courses I ever completed, that of the military's "Ranger School." From there I headed back home, assigned to Company D, Ranger Detachment, 151st Airborne Infantry. I was stationed out of Muncie, Indiana.

Company D, Ranger Detachment, 151st Airborne Infantry
Muncie, Indiana

Mountain Ranger Camp Frank D. Merrill

I became a Staff Sargent (SSG E-6) and for the summer camps I taught classes to many an Indiana National Guardsman as to what and how the rangers had taught us. One of the men promoted with me after Ranger School was Jerry W. Ryan; during summer camp at Camp Atterbury he was my second in command. Together we taught over 600 men how to rappel out of helicopters, how to do fast roping along with our stabo rigs. We went out patrolling, crossed streams and survived hostile environments. Sergeant Ryan and I made four parachute jumps, but we had too much air assault to keep track of that summer.

I worked that summer at Camp Atterbury, Indiana, and on long weekends I would return to Bedford to stay with my Uncle Pat Conley. He was my father's youngest brother and the only living child out of four. He needed me as much as I needed him. He was quite elderly by then and needed someone around to help him out, fix a meal once in a while, and just be nearby on a regular basis. He became the father I never had and I loved him with all my heart. I knew I needed to be around him and wanted to learn as much as I could about the Conley family tree. He had five daughters who are Connie Beasley Crosby, Hallie Conley Coulter, Hattie Conley Armstrong, Peggy Conley Ritchison, and Patsy Conley Sons. His wife, Grace, had passed away so he was basically alone. His girls treated me like the brother they never had, and for that, I will always be grateful. As for me, they became the sisters that I never had and I always felt very close to all of them. I had always wanted a sister; now I had a whole handful of them! I had gotten divorced again, so I stayed with Uncle Pat over the course of the summer, until I left for Mountain Ranger Camp. Over the years, whenever I have returned to Indiana, I've often stayed at Connie's house. To this day, I feel very close to these cousins and they have always treated me as one of the family.

As summer turned into fall, I was notified by the Indiana National Guard and the United States Army Ranger School that I had been accepted as a Mountain Ranger Instructor. I was to report to Fort Benning, Georgia, by the end of January 1975. Just nearly a year before, on the 24th of January 1974 I had graduated from Ranger School and won the Merrill's Marauders Award. Now, I was going back to Ranger School to train students and help start the special operations teams that would later become known as America's "best fighting men."

I needed to get away from Bedford, back to doing a job that I truly loved. On that last morning there, I told Uncle Pat, "Good bye," gave him a big hug and headed for Fort Leonard Wood, Missouri. From there I would journey on to Fort Benning, Georgia. I stopped to say goodbye to my favorite cousin Connie Beasley and to tell her I was on my way. I had a very good 1974 Grand Torino Ford and was looking forward to a new chapter in my life. Connie and I said our goodbyes and I thanked her for a wonderful Christmas; I told her I would miss the family and her father. She hugged me in return, told me to be careful and to let her know where I could be contacted. I promised to write as soon as I was settled.

As I headed west to Fort Leonard Wood, I thought about Uncle Pat. I was only able to see him twice over the next year; he passed away on the 10th of June 1976. I really truly loved that old man and thank God for all those long talks we had together, for what he did for me, what he told me about our family, how they had been raised in a rough and tumble world out in Oklahoma. His youngest daughter Connie has kept up with our lineage and in this way, I've found out a lot of things about my family tree. Connie also stepped up to the plate while I was gone by going to see my mother, took her out to eat, and in Mother's last days, visited and talked with her in the nursing home. At this point of the book I want to thank the Conley girls for making me feel like their brother and for all the help they have given to me through the years, along with letters to they sent me while I was away on deployment overseas. Peggy's son Tim taught me how to knap an arrowhead and spear points. He was very good at making them. Whenever I needed a helping hand, Peggy's boys were always there to help me.

Our local newspaper, The Indianapolis Times, wrote about me rejoining the military. Here is an excerpt from their article which appeared in July 1974.

SSG Conley joined the 3658th Maintenance Company of the Indiana National Guard at Bedford, IN, then joined Company D Rangers At Muncie. He went to Ranger School at Fort Benning, GA, and received The Merrill's Marauder's award there. Last summer SSG E-6 Conley Taught survival and escape to guardsmen at Camp Atterbury, IN. After survival instruction, SSG Conley sent the guardsmen out into the field to find their afternoon meal. They came back with wild berries, fruit and greens, even pine needles for tea, as Conley had taught them. But none of them brought back meat. SSG Conley would usually bring a live chicken or two to demonstrate how to kill and eat wild game for survival. He would break the bird's neck, then bite off the head and drink the fresh blood, because "...the blood of wild game is the most nourishing part of the animal for survival," according to Conley. Conley would then demonstrate how to clean the chicken by skinning it and how to cook it in the field in less than ten minutes.

Asked how the men reacted to his chicken demonstration. Conley said "Some of the guys threw up." Conley said it is easy to show what you can find in the wild in the field, but in a real survival situation, "you must have the will to survive. If you have that will to survive you may do many things you never thought possible, even drink the blood of a chicken." When he finishes teaching summer camp to the Indiana National Guard, he will be heading off to Fort Benning, GA, to teach Ranger students at Camp Frank D. Merrill near Dahlonega, GA.

Late in January, 1975, I drove out of Lawrence County, Indiana, and headed west. I had never been to Fort Leonard Wood so I obtained a good road map to guide me. The roads were dry and it was a clear, but cold, winter day. I felt this drive would afford me time to do a lot of thinking. Somewhere along the way, I began to talk with God and asked him to be with me in this new phase of my life. As I crossed into Missouri, almost immediately, a unique feeling overtook me. Out of the blue it occurred to me! God was with me, right now! I had asked him for a second chance and it was being delivered to me! I had been married two times and now I was divorced for the second time. I felt like my children were lost to me. Although I had worked at being an electrical lineman, my heart had not been in it either. I had wanted to go back to the military. Here, on this trip to Fort Leonard Wood, I was getting that second chance.

Over the past three years I had made a lot of mistakes, doing many things that a young man should not do. Friends, neighbors and relatives who loved me a lot had all tried to help me lead a better life when I was there. As I've looked back and remembered how badly I behaved, I now realized I was really confused and had no sense of direction. I had dated some very nice young women, but I had no feelings for any of them. In my heart I felt cold and lacked any semblance of initiative. I turned to "childish things" and reckless behaviors. I smoked a lot of pot and even took to raising a couple of small bushes of the stuff in my yard. Eventually the police found them, and luckily for me, there were no lasting consequences or legal complications. I'll always believe it was because I was back home, where I'd grown up, and local law enforcement cut me a break because I was a returned Vietnam vet. Many times I'd work all day, then go to a bar in the evening to hang out and drink until I got drunk or forced me to leave so they could lock the doors. Somehow or other, I'd always make it back to my Uncle Pat's house for what was left of the night. There was no happiness in my life; I was totally miserable. I sure was not happy with the way my life had ended up.

Finally, I believe, my angels began to penetrate into my funk. My thinking began to change. I realized, "It's time to put these childish things (behaviors) away and do things differently. I need to become a better man. I can, with God's help." I'd begun driving over to the graveyard where my brother Clifford was buried, just to talk to him and pray to God. Eventually, I told my relatives that I was going to try to again get back into the military, if they'd let me in. I was making strides in changing my ways and believed I could do a good job there. I believe God and my angels blessed me with another chance to change my life.

I continued to drive, to reflect on the changes that had taken place in my life. Eventually, I arrived at Fort Leonard Wood where I remained for two days. Then came the orders I'd been longing to receive: Report to the Ranger Department, Fort

Benning, Georgia. The next morning I headed for Georgia, reflecting on my new opportunity. My drive was uneventful and I reported in on the 30th day of January, 1975. After one night at Fort Benning, I received the next morning another set of orders: Report to the 2nd Ranger Company, TSB (Training School Brigade), Camp Frank D. Merrill, Dahlonega, Georgia. Telephone number, orderly room included. This was definitive confirmation that I was now a freshly-minted Ranger!

In less than a week Ranger students reported in for the Mountain Phase of Ranger School. We had so many students in this class that they were broken into two phases: one class was assigned to Patrolling Phase, the other to Mountain Phase. In this way, all of these students would be working at the same time. I was assigned to teach the Mountaineering Phase. My job was to teach rock climbing, survival tactics and mountaineering procedures. My fellow Rangers praised me for my ability to read a topographical map well. Students and I were constantly out on patrols on Mount Yona. I instructed these men on how to lead two-man climbs, as well as execute night rapells with a "wounded" man tied to a stretcher.

I found out I enjoyed teaching; in fact, I loved every minute of those days and nights. The weeks sped by and before I realized it, spring was showing herself on those mountain bushes. Our classes continued to grow so substantially that we were having to work fifteen hours each day. It was imperative that these students master these skills to complete the Mountain Phase. I came to realize that working in those mountains and teaching was what I was born to do! It was the most fun I had had in my whole life. In March of 1975 Army reporters sent my hometown newspaper the following report:

Vietnam Vet Teaches Mountaineering

SSG Conley went back on active duty in January at Camp Frank D. Merrill located in the Smokey and Blue Ridge mountains near Dahlonega, Georgia. There Conley is teaching mountaineering. He has already taught two classes of 42 men. He teaches mountain climbing, repelling, fast roping, aerial rescue with hoist and airborne operations, the jump master's duties, along with rescue techniques. Repelling is the method to come down a sheer cliff or mountain by lowering yourself backside first, down a rope. Another rappelling method is the one in which you come down with your face and head first. At the start of the mountaineering class, SSG Conley and another Ranger Instructor staged a fight on top of the mountain. The other instructor ordered Conley, "Get off!"

Conley came running down the mountain while firing his M-60, running all the way to the bottom of a 60-foot cliff. "It looks very difficult and frightening to the Ranger students," Conley said. He added, "If they see it done the hard way, then it it's not so hard for them when they have to try it the easy way."

Mountain Ranger Camp Frank D. Merrill   Patrolling Committee June 1976

Front Row Kneeling: front to back and left to right MSG Don Stafford, Capt. (Wild) Bill Walsh, Cpt. Maynard,

SFC Doug Perry, SSG Steve Crawford, Capt Mike Flack, SFC Moose Monroe, SSG, Richard Dudley,

SSG Mike Conley, SSG Barlowe, SSG Schultz, MSG Mike Smith, SSG Lonnie Miller, SSG Nelson, SSG Bill Miller, SSG Udo Taring, SFC Cheshire, SFC Stanley Fox , SFC Gibson, SFC Chuck Thomas, SSG Hughes

As the Ranger assigned to the Mountaineering Phase, I worked in the lower mountain area, at Black Falls. Eventually, we moved over near the small town of Cleveland onto Yona Mountain for more advanced training. We Ranger instructors would pick our Ranger students up at Mosby Army Airfield, then march them or run them from Ranger Camp along the road, past Mt. Zion Church. This was quite a way to start the day as we encountered adventures along these mountain roads which were often covered with snow or ice. We'd run over the mountain, finally coming out not far from the community of Suches. I loved this part of our journey since I thought we were in the most beautiful part of the Tennessee Valley Divide.

During the Patrolling Phase of Ranger School I noticed many beautiful flowers such as the Indian Slipper,(Pink Lady Slipper) a member of the orchid family. Sometimes we would come across a snowy orchid growing near wet-weather springs. This orchid is also referred to as "showy" orchid because of its definitive markings. Meanwhile I was developing a real interest in botany, so much so that I purchased a plant identification book so I could learn even more about different kinds of flowers and trees that grew along the Blue Ridge Mountains. Years later, while attending

North Georgia College, I enrolled in a botany class where I was required to turn in a flower collection. But I have digressed from my duties as a Ranger instructor.

Many of our patrols entailed me getting an afternoon off to pack my rucksack and eat a meal. Then I had to report to the TOC (Technical Operations Center) where I'd meet up with either a captain or master sergeant. That officer would hand me Mission Order with a list of my trainees. Then I would go to a small roofed shelter where they were sitting, waiting to be picked up for their next assignment. I began calling out names, then assigned the positions of patrol leader and assistant patrol leader. I gave them the mission statement and warning order.

My job was to grade each student over the next two days as they attempted to complete their tasks. I assessed their behavior, how much anyone complied or complained. Did each one follow orders; was he a team player? A compass man would be selected from the patrol; then he would select someone to assist him in building a terrain model with anything resources at hand.

Almost all these students carried a small bag of toy soldiers to use for model layouts. They had colored the helmets with black for Rangers and red for the enemy. The terrain model should show the route to their objective and farther out, where they would stop for a debriefing. These jobs could eat away many hours of a day; every person who would be going out on patrol had a job to do. When it was approaching time to actually go out, around midnight or shortly before the mission was assigned, they would do their final rehearsal for Actions at the Objective. It was always a sight to see those Rangers, with faces painted black, green and tan, moving quietly along in good patrol order headed for the FFU (Friendly Forward Unit) wire for "passage of the lines."

It was my job to grade each student on everything. There were rehearsals and inspections all along the way. Each instructor taught as the students progressed through the procedures. It took lots of talking to students, through each and every phase. They each knew they could ask for help, but they also knew that it was their primary job to "mostly" run the show.

I would sit down with the patrol leader to discuss what things we might want to know when we passed "over the lines" into enemy territory. I had my own way of getting this information over to the students and patrol leaders. I wanted them to realize they needed to know lots of things. They had to know how to ask their questions, as well as what questions specifically to ask. They had to realize: the enemy is out there waiting for us. Some questions to be asked of those on the wire were "Have any other patrols been out on their wire passage in the last few hours? Has there been any noises out there? Who is guarding the wire; how long have they been there? Will they be relieved by another unit any time soon? Did those on the wire know if there's been any contact with anyone or gunshots since they had been on the wire? Can they send out a quick reaction team for us? Can they help carry out our wounded men in case we got hit?"

We also had maps, but we also wanted to know if there were any places that might have a footbridges or crossing points that those troops on the wire would know about. I was always very careful to ask the students to find out if the FFU (Friendly Forward Unit) had any targets already zeroed in. That would be insurance for us if we got hit because they could they call in artillery or mortars for us as cover for us to get back inside the wire.

In most military operations Murphy's Law takes over, long before any shot is ever fired. Things may begin to go wrong during the planning phase. Confusion, sometimes even total chaos, totally takes over and should be expected. Errors begin to compound themselves, even before you have an opportunity to meet the enemy. Events, such as unexpected weather, bad maps which do not match the terrain, all impact a mission with unforeseen results which no one could have predicted. Sometimes a vital piece of equipment, such as extra batteries for the radios or an antenna, are not available or were lost. Perhaps correct information maybe is missing, resulting in a break in communications.

The issue of "time" played a huge role at Ranger School because students were always under a time limit in which to do anything. Compound time limits with compromised physical abilities of these students who were closer to exhaustion, more likely than not. It was hard for them to do things right the first time through; more times than not, they had to do it everything all over again. Remember the old adage: Practice makes perfect. Many times, when they were so very near the objective, after making a long, hard and exhaustive climb toward the objective, yet they'd completely gone around it. The objective might be only a few meters away or down in a small ditch where someone couldn't see. These errors might be the reason why a battle is won or lost. Weather also changes very fast in mountainous terrain, requiring last minute changes to be made.

Any host of unexpected and unremitting problems make up the fractional aspects of war. My job was to illustrate these stresses and difficulties through my own experiences and relate them to the students so they would have a better understanding of how to deal with them whenever they occurred. After looking over the objective, last minute changes must be made during the leader's recon and during final planning. They must be sent down to the each one to ensure that everyone knew exactly what was going on, who was doing what, and what specifically each "part" was.

One such example is dealing with wounded troops. It's very hard to train students who have never had to deal with wounded. When you have men who cannot walk, the others have to be aware of what all must be dealt with to get your patrol back across friendly lines. Other considerations would be "Can we get smoke or white phosphorus, gunships or Hueys to extract our wounded" from the route we'd be following. Someone might break a leg, get snake bit, suffer serious wounds from falls or become very ill with all sorts of ailments. As well, I also began to learn from the older Rangers, specifically from people such as SFC Doug Perry who knew where all the landing sites and evacuation points were so that a helicopter could get to us in a hurry. SFC Doug Perry knew more about these mountains and the terrain in here than any other person I ever met at Mountain Ranger Camp.

When crossing the FFU, we stepped off into another world. When we were on the line, we'd ask, always, always check about the passwords. Make sure the password we'd been given matched what they'd been given. Passwords can be changed after you leave one unit if another unit comes in to take their place. A new password may have been brought in. In addition, there were "challenge words" which can be changed at throughout the day: at noon, at midnight or at other times during a day.

Our job as Ranger instructors was to ensure that the students understood that once we were beyond the lines, we would be in enemy territory. One thing that sticks out in my mind to this day that I was learned in the Ranger School was to appreciate exactly why a certain action took place. I learned to see a situation through my own eyes and to comprehend what influenced that action; how to make a decisions quickly and stick to it, yet know when and why to adjust it. Later in life, when I became a high school basketball coach, I used my decision-making techniques learned in Ranger School. If my game plan was not working in the first half of a basketball game, I was smart enough to shift gears and make adjustments that would help our team win a game. So, too, with a battle or war. Someone can make plans, but you must be able to change that direction in an instant on the battle field, to carry the day.

Another aspect we taught was how they should space themselves out. During the daylight, they should be ten meters apart as a general rule in mountainous terrain. If enemy were thought to be close by or we were in enemy territory, we kept what was called "Ranger file," with six men in a V-shape, then a space and other six men, and so forth. If we came under fire, we could maneuver against the enemy, using this two-team technique. Each Ranger student carried about 60 pounds in their rucksacks, consisting of their own ammo, food and water. At that time we were eating C-rations, although later in my tour we would get

LRRP rations which consisted of dehydrated food that we'd add water to, let them sit for 20-30 minutes, then eat.

Mountainous terrain is tough; climbing mountains in any kind of weather – heat of summer; snow and ice of winter. As well, the weather could change very quickly. We could depart from Ranger camp on what I thought was a beautiful day; one hour later, it might be pouring rain. The students never got enough to eat since they spent so much energy doing all we required of them; they were always more than very tired from lack of enough quality sleep, let alone enough sleep time. Usually after an action at the objective or a raid we could let them sleep two or three hours, but security had to always be maintained which meant that someone had to forego their share of extra sleep time. If we began to witness a lot of things going awry, an instructor might ask the ranger leader what he thought about this situation or if he might want to change his mind about something they were trying to accomplish, such as a specific route they were trying to use. All in all, it always came down to what decision the patrol leader chose to make. We instructors would grade them or encourage them. We instructors would never tell the students how to do their jobs, although we each tried very hard to help them, often finding ways to get them extra food. Sometimes we might show them things they could forage from the woods at specific times of the year. I tried to take a lot of time to teach my students things that I had learned, teaching them to utilize their environment – the woods, creeks and streams, to supplement what was in their rucks. My upbringing in rural Indiana, hunting for wild mushrooms with my uncles and Grandpa Byrd, and in general, living off the land had taught me how to survive in any environment where I might find myself.

The patrol leader was graded on how well he answered questions that the Unit Sargent would ask him or how well the whole patrol performed during a certain section of the day. The men running the friendly forward unit would always have a multitude of questions to be answered: How many men were going out? What types of weapons did we have? Had we made any contact with the artillery? Did we have an overlay they could see? They would also show us theirs, in case we needed to see it. Sometimes it would take us an hour to get through the lines on the route that had been planned for the team. Shortly after getting into enemy territory we might come to a halt, lie or crouch down on the ground, then settle in for a while to let the night sounds or the terrain settle down around us. These students were learning that stealth is a Ranger's greatest alley. At that time I might put another Ranger student in charge of the Movement Phase. Performing filtration or exfiltration, being close to the front lines, is a very dangerous position to be in and is one of those times that everything must work right or a whole team can get wiped out or captured.

We crossed the Etowah River so many times in my two years at Ranger Camp that I knew where to direct students to cross so that no one would get completely wet. This was especially important during winter months. We would head north, sometimes cross the ridgelines that head toward Conner Mountain, then get on a ridgeline heading northeast, go down through a saddle and back up along a trail heading almost due north until we could get to the top of Sassafras Mountain. From there we'd cross the Appalachian Trail, well-marked with white rectangular signs on the sides of trees. Many students found this amazing, as most of them had only heard of the trail; only a few had ever been on any part of it. The Appalachian Trail was marked on every map we carried; students would then make a map recon to be sure which draw they should use to get down to a small gravel road known as the TVD (Tennessee Valley Road) where we would do a leader's recon if an early morning ambush was planned. After walking for four hours in below freezing temperatures, we'd leave a few Rangers behind as the rest of us went down to look at a road to find a good place for an ambush. It took a lot of teaching for the students to understand what had to be done. Eventually, we'd work it out together; sometimes, it took a few hints from me or another instructor as to why one place might be a better place than another. Then, shortly before daylight, maybe in the early morning twilight known as "the beginning of nautical twilight" we would move men into place for an ambush. We'd set a security team off to both sides of the road, sometimes 100 meters alongside the same road we were on. Then, it was sit and wait and listen for the trucks or motor vehicles (of the enemy) to come along the road. Sometimes, if we hadn't thought the students did it very well, we'd make them do it over and over, again and again, until they finally got it right. We were trying to teach them what they'd need to do to pull off a successful ambush, save their own hide and hopefully, that of many others under their command.

Thirty years later I would find myself in Iraq running a MITT team. One of the things we were all scared off were IED's, what would happen immediately after one would go off and how to react to these situations. I had been teaching students how to deal with similar situations back in '75 and '76 at the Mountain Ranger Camp.

We instructors often sat around talking to students and with other Ranger instructors about how to do these activities right and how to make them more effective. One things I really hated to do was to force students into the KZ (Kill Zone) or ambush site to search for any enemy lying about on the ground. I was never comfortable with that part of it. Instead, I would show them how to do a doubletrap or create secondary explosions, follow the first explosions and set off by hand. We would set off one explosion in the road, disable a truck or jeep and lay there, not firing a rifle or making any noise. After a few minutes another jeep or truck would appear; they would look and listen before going into the kill zone. If their buddies were begging for help, those onlookers would eventually make their way out into the KZ to start helping get their comrades out. We stressed with our students, "No! Wait! Stay quiet! Wait until as many people as possible are out into that KZ before you set off more explosions on both sides of the zone. Have them crisscross each other, to maximize their effectiveness."

If we were using the claymore mine or call in the artillery on them and adjust fire using white phosphorus or fragmentation shells know as HE (high explosion) and then slip away very quietly without ever firing one round. Often when I had enough Ranger Students and an assistant Ranger Instructor I would leave them behind while we would all gather at the rendezvous site and make sure we were not being followed after we left the kill zone. Another thing we begin to teach each of the classes coming through was about a hide site. A whole patrol might travel for three or four hours after hitting an objective or an ambush and then go into their hide site. This was a place where we would get very close together and get quiet and take care of wounded men or to recheck our ammunition and resupplied would often get delivered to us in these place. We could stop and change socks and redistribute the ammo to every one having a basic load. We had a lot to do like taking care of medical problems like blisters or yellow jackets stings. There was always the threat of a snake bite at the ranger camp in the summer time as they were the Mountain Rattle snake in these areas known as the Timber Rattler. These snakes were a very long and dark rattle snake that did not like ranger students walking close to them. At night during movement phase if we heard a rattle snake buzzing we would turn right or left and leave him a big space without us being in their way. There was so much to teach and these were the best years of my life at the mountain ranger camp. I learned more in those two years as a soldier than I learned or built onto over the next twenty five years. We also tried dog legs and checking back on our own back trial as we traveled through the mountains. If we had a chance in enemy territory we would bobby trap or put up frag grenade's or trip flares on our back trail. If the enemy got after us and tried tracking us and if we were carrying wounded men things would definitely get hairy. We would drop off a couple of Ranger students with a claymore mine and let them set it hooked up to a trip wire or leave them with the clacker to ambush the enemy or trackers on our trail. My suggestions if asked by the ranger student was to hit and slip away without any one ever shooting at us or given up your stealth by using exploding bombs or artillery after using an IED. **Never ever shoot until it is the very last resort one has**. Once you shoot at them they will know where you are. Never ever shoot unless it is the last thing you can do to cover a patrol on the run.

Jeffersonville and the Steam Boat Days

During the summer of 1976 I was selected to go on training trips with the Ranger Department. One of the most fun times I ever had away from the military was our team was selected to go to Jeffersonville, Indiana to the steam boat festival in the fall of 1976. The Golden Knights were there and they were skydiving into the Ohio River and we with our U-B 3 life rafts with Johnson motors on the back of them would fly up the river and pick them up and sling them in to the back of the boats. ON THE MOVE SOMETIMES AT 22 MPH.

We also did repelling off from a bridge that crossed the Ohio River and it must have been at least one hundred feet out of the water and we would race to the water and sometimes we would do a free fall as the Austrian repel would admit us to do and then about twenty feet out of the water we would put the brakes on and land in the Ohio river. It was summer time and the water felt so good and cool.

We all had a great time.

I will never forget what a weekend we had and what a wonderful time on this trip. Years later as a Ranger Instructors I look back and think of those good times and some of those great times and recently we all met at the Mountain Ranger Camp and they did a commeration to the Ranger Instructors of the early and mid-1960's and there were my friends and buddies that I had taught Ranger school with in a picture hanging there in the old snap link. One of my closest friends and a buddy who fought in the Vietnam War was there by the name of Ted Tilson (Teddy Bear) We went on to three other cities and did more demonstrations and even faked a couple of fire fights for the children and young people but it was all in fun and we enjoyed that part of our training. It was early fall by the time we all got back to Camp Frank D. Merrill and I did not know it at this time but my time at the mountain Ranger Camp was almost over.

I would stay at the mountain ranger camp for two years and in January 1977 there was a big cut back in the army.

A new president had been elected and he was cutting back on the military. Jimmy Carter from Georgia was elected president and he said the nation needed healing so they set down a RIF (Reduction in Force). We were not the World War two veterans'. The nation had welcomed them back with open arms and a noble light. Unfortunately this favorable depiction did not span to other conflicts. Veterans of the Korean War are all but forgotten and invisible and the military tried very hard to get rid of as many of the Vietnam veterans as possible especially combat soldiers. My own personal feeling is that the Vietnam veterans on the other hand, receive potentially the most lasting and negative portrayals of all the soldiers and wars. Now I was going to the Company B, 3rd Battalion of the 11th Special Forces Group and go back on reserve status. I would go to college and get a degree as a school teacher and try to take all the things I had been taught in the military back out into the world to be a good man. To do good deeds and help people where ever I could. I wanted to help heal that nation and the same time I thought I was going to reevaluate my purpose in life. I was now ready to settle down get married and have a family. I wanted to get an education and be a good citizen. I was more than ready to reclaim my role in society.

I got out of the regular army on Jan. 30, 1977 and over the next four years I went full time and even took extra classes so I could graduate as soon as possible.

My college years went by very quickly. I think that I made more mistakes on test and worked and extra forty hours a week to get by but somehow I managed to get an Associate degree in Biology. I had been on the student government at Gainesville Junior College and ran on the college track team there. At North Georgia College I joined the ROTC and took military classes and worked a lot with the undergraduate students and became the commander in the Order of Colombo. Mostly I had turned to books and I loved learning.

I was thirty plus when I graduated from North Georgia College. Three weeks before graduation I found out that I could not become an officer in the regular army because of my age. I was now too old! That was a low blow to my psyche.

Within a few days, however, I was called into the Commander's Office to talk with Col. Ben Purcell from Claxton, Georgia. I knew him as a veteran of Vietnam, and admired him. He had been shot down and captured, kept as a prisoner of war for more than four years. We had a long talk that day.

Col. Purcell told me, "It's time to get on with your life... You brought a lot of good things to North Georgia Collage; the underclassmen look up to you."

He asked me what I wanted to do with my life. I sat there for a minute and thought about it and told him I wanted to be a school teacher and a basketball coach. I was very disappointed about not getting my commissioned as a second lieutenant. I had thought I would get a commissioned and I would go back in the regular army as an officer. I had that in my head the last two years that I attended North Georgia College. I had dreamed about it and what it would be like to go back on active duty. Now that was gone. I had my goals and I know I had made a lot of mistakes in my life but I was willing to keep trying and I also felt like I was making a lot of progress in development of my mind and maturity .

Four days after leaving Col Ben Purcell office I had a phone call from Cherokee County Georgia asking me to come down for a teaching interview with Mike Johnson the School superintendent and a Mr. Tony Ingle head boys' basketball coach and a Dr. Casey the school principal. I was actually going to graduate from college and get a school teaching job and become freshman basketball coach in Cherokee County Georgia. Welcome to a brand new world. The truth was I had never been a basketball coach before and all of this was going to be new to me.

Company B, 3rd Battalion, 11th Special Forces Group

B Company, 3d Battalion,
11th Special Forces Group (Airborne)
Association

I was going to college at Gainesville Junior College and I needed a unit to fit into. I looked around and heard about a unit down in Columbus, Georgia. I drove down there and sat down and talked to one of their recruiters. He was very glad to meet me and took me in to a office and introduced me to a Captain Hal Williams. Now this is a very big man and his arms were the size of small limb on a tree. We talked a few minutes and I found out he lived in Dahlonega, Georgia and he was in charge of a team of Green Berets. I joined this very elite group of men and have been associated with them through the years.

Now as fall arrives my wife and I start making plans to go to our reunion in late August or early September. I have belonged to this group for many years and we have a great time together. One of the Last units I belonged to in the Army Reserves was at Fort Gillem. Georgia and my Sargent Major was a Green Beret and we had served in this unit many years before and he ask me if I would like to come to a reunion and I was so glad to find men and share our experiences with. Oh, by the way some of these men are kinds looking old but I am still one of the youngest of this group. There is a General McCollum and his wife and when we all get together it is a wonderful time. We have had reunions down in Columbus, Georgia and over in Savanna, Georgia and last year we went down to Jekyll, Island where we all enjoyed our time and commandership together.

Last evening I was talking to Fast Fred one of my friends I served with in Company B and he was laughing and talking about the time we all went to Cleveland, Georgia and about us working on the side of Yona mountain and then he started telling me about me leaving the unit and going out into the country side and coming back with some live chickens and a box's full of very large trout. I thought I need to tell this as part of the book. I do not know how much of it is true but they (as the boys I worked with) tell me that I did come back after dark in a snow storm I and brought back at least a half dozen chickens alive and a full box of fresh trout and it was snowing at he the tent of a GP Medium we had a fire going there and we set there and laughed and cooked chicken and roasted trout over a spit fire until at least after midnight. I came back up the mountain and the wind was howling and everyone was glad when I returned and it was the best night we ever had. (I do not know as it has been a many of year but Fast Fred swears to me on the phone that I did it.)

I was able to get orders from Company D. Rangers out of Muncie. Indiana and they sent me to Company B, 3rd Battalion, 11th Special Forces Group in Columbus, Georgia in late February 1977, I went to drills and we were able to parachute and planned on going down to Florida for the summer camp. We flew down on C-130's and parachuted into the Ocala National forest not far from Ocala, Florida. We spent the next 14 days in the swamps and the horse ranches along the St. Mary's river. One of the teams were caught trying to get on land and the photo ops and newspaper asked them many a questions and one of the men who would later become a great friend of mine is Fast Fred Updike told them it was all a game and he had no commit. They all got their pictures on the front page of the newspaper without telling anyone why they were there.

Over the next three weeks we ran all over the Ocala National Forest. We even visited the Silver Springs and saw monkeys in the trees. We were being chased by the Battalion from the 82nd Airborne Division from Fort Bragg, North Carolina. We would be hidden deep in the jungle and here they come over in C-130's and then we would have our men out on the edge of the great orange plantations and they would call us and tell us where they were jumping. An hour or two later they would tell us where there men were putting their parachutes and in which directions they would be heading. As team leader with only 12 men and a good map and compass we could easily out distance a large company in the jungle and we would set up ambushes. Large companies would use trails and at least large beaten paths that maybe the tractors would sue going back and forth to the orange groves. We would cut across their path and then when they would stop for a rest we would move around them and actually put four man teams into three different directions and we would set up our ambush sites with fake hand grenades and dummy clay more mines with artillery simulators going but we would never shoot at the other side everything would be electrically controlled and we would never ever go into a kill zone. Later in Iraq I wanted to be turned loose to use our method of fighting on the enemy but by then we were a much better loving society and we would not be allowed to booby trap or sneak around a do really bad things to the enemy. We would never fire our own weapons only us electricity and blasting cap to make it look like we were near. They were supposed to catch us but we played games with their minds.

Of all the great times I had in company B came to play in my mind later in my life when I was sent to the republic of Georgia and I was in charge no not really in charge more liked I helped over 3,000 Georgian Army men get ready for a show down with the Russians up in North Ossetia. I went back to my youth and remembered how we had played real games and I did truly believe that with a combination of Long Range Recon and penetration into the enemy strong hole on the right terrain and in the right place we could actually stop a large army with only about 3,000 men I felt later in my life we could actually inflict a lot of damage on a very large force like the Russians tried to bring against the Republic of Georgia. This story is in a later chapter.

I love company B, 11th Special Forces Group and I still have many friends who always meet and have a get together every Augusta or September and we set around a laugh about all of those parachutes and helicopter rides we did as young men. We often tell stories and every one laughs about freezing to death or falling through a small creek in the middle of winter. We even went back up to Mount Yona, where I had worked as a Ranger Instructor and we spent a whole weekend up there doing two man part climbs and also doing night repels and the water was freezing and the ice cycles were hanging all over the place and we had a blast later in the night when we build a small fire and cooked five chickens and a half dozen very large trout that had found its way into our small ice boxes we took along. What a feast it was and before morning the snow came down so soft and pretty that by daylight there was a least two or three inches of snow on the mountain. That would be my last drill and also the last time I ever worked on Yona Mountain. We all had a great time and we will always know in our own hearts some of us really did enjoy or days in a uniform.

I stayed in this unit for the next ten months and then in December, 1977 I got out of the reserves and out of the Army. I would not do anything but go to college and get my degree and later I got a job working at Amicicola Falls State Park with Henry Johnson as a park Ranger. I would spend the next five years out of service only I belonged to the Ready Reserves and I did not have to go to summer camps.

United States Marines Corp (Reserve) 1984-1987

I had been teaching school for two years and had been coaching and things in my life were going pretty good. After my first year as a school teacher in Cherokee, County I had started to date Dolores Little and over the next two years we had found our love and our place in life was to be together. I heard about a Marine Corp Reserve unit that was out of Dobbins Air Reserve Base in Marietta, Georgia. It was only about 20 miles away. I had driven to Dobbins Air Reserve Base and they told me how to find the Marine Corp recruiter on the other side of the base. I drove around to the Navy side and found a very old building and inside I met SSgt John DeGarris and E-7 Gunny Williamson. I set down and talked to both of these men for maybe an half hour and they told me I could return to the military as a Marine. I would return as Sgt E-5 in a Stinger unit. I would be assigned to a FAD (Forward Area Air Defense) unit. I would also learn how to fire the Stinger and we would go to other Marine Corps bases to learn how to fire and how to use them. This all sounded real exacting to me and I had missed being out of the military so I thought it was the right thing to

do. We would have drills once a month and sometimes muta 6 we would go in early on a Friday evening and pack our sea bags and be ready to leave early the next morning in the Marine Corps meant leaving at 03:30 am and travel to faraway places but be ready for some real training. Dobbins which was near our home and we could also know that I would be gone for two to three weeks each summer with the unit. I joined up that day and one month before Dee and I were married I had also joined the 4th Marine Division. I was not expecting to go on summer camp and told them I was getting married but would have a short honey moon in the Bahamas. Less than one week after returning from our honey moon the Marine Corps said and called me and told me the orders had coming down we were on our way to Germany for training near Hohenfels, Germany. My first month of marriage was a one week honey moon and three weeks of Marine Corp training. OK It sounds funny but I loved that summer. I had walked into an office and with my discharge papers and asked them if I could join up in the Marine Corp Yes, I was able to Join the Marine Corp and I loved all the great training and the exacting places I was able to go with them.. Where I underwent desert training with them. I enjoyed the Marines and learned a lot about them and their ways. I only served three years and in that time we went over to Cherry Point, down to Camp Lajune, North Carolina and over to Hohenfels, Germany one summer for camp. The next summer we went out to the Mojave Desert. I loved the desert and the training was great. I lost almost fourteen pounds and I learned about desert survival.

My last summer 1988 we were sent to train in Alaska. We went to work with the Alaskan National Guard. We ended up in a fort south and east of Fairbanks, Alaska. The name of the fort was Fort Wainwrights and it was a very small place but the whole time I was there the salmon was running up this creek behind our barracks and the small creek was a milky color because of the glacier melt stream but the salmon would never stop coming up that stream. On our way to Alaska we went up the inner passage and we saw glaciers and even went by bus passed the highest mountain in North America. Mount McKinley. I enjoyed the Marines and learned an awful lot about their heritage but I had a wife now. I wanted to spend some time with my wife and coaching was taking all the free time I had so I took a break after the Marine Corp. One of the last things we did together was go to a Marine Corp birthday party over in Rome, Georgia. Little did I know thirty years later I would take a hero of mine by the name of W.A. Presley to a Marine alumni meeting and there I would meet some of the men he had been with when they attacked and walked upon the shore of Iwo Jima. I was also introduced to the Code talkers and had a wonderful time talking and listening to their stories of World War II.

Summer school and summer coaching basketball teams was getting in my way. I decided to get out of the Corp but had a great time and a couple of very nice letters from my commander was sent home with me. I would spend the next five years out of the reserves or any regular army. I became a school teacher and a basketball coach. These seem now like my busy years. We bought a home in Dallas, Georgia. Dolores and I were getting along great and we started snow skiing in and around the great state of Colorado in the winter times and we had some great years. Our life and our love grew stronger and we went places in the summer time and even joined a time share place and we both enjoyed us going out of the country.

Company H LRSU
Georgia National Guard, 1997-1999

One morning I was returning from Albany, Georgia where I was teaching and coaching as the Defensive line coach on a football team and was also the junior varsity basketball coach and the assistant on the varsity team. I first heard helicopters over my car and then soon I spotted these helicopters going over my head and going in the same direction as I was traveling. I almost knew they were going to jump out of this UH-1E just ahead of me. I actually saw six helicopters flying in formation I even saw the door open and the jumpmaster stood in the door way and I watched as the sky begin to fill with parachutes.

My life had changed again. I had missed being in the army. I missed the excitement of the jumps but most of all I missed the comradeship of the men I used to work with. I drove up to the drop zone and introduced myself to their company commander.

I told him I was very interested in joining a new unit. He told me to bring in my DD-214 and he would find a slot for me. One month later I was assigned to the Company H LRSU in Newnan Ga. I turned out to be a good unit.

Over the next three years I would go overseas for summer camps. I also went to the Republic of Georgia, to Stuttgart, Germany, and inside of Bosnia Herzegovina. I made one trip to Fort Bragg, North Carolina and saw my children. It was also the last company I would ever jump with. After all those years I had a total of 286 jumps. I will never know how many jump master duties I had.

In late fall after returning from a four jump summer camp while I was running down in a garbage dump and near Newnan, Georgia I dropped to the ground with a torn left Anterior Cruciate Ligament (ACL) tear. I would never jump again. One of the most common knee injuries to paratroopers and football players.

I would spend my last summer camp at Fort Bragg, North Carolina. How strange it was to go there as my ex-wife's parents, Jesse and Maude Nelson, lived there and so did my two sons, Robbie and Shannon. This was the only time I remember both of my sons coming out to St. Marie Eglise to watch me jump. Afterwards, we all went out to eat together.

Left to Right Shannon Conley, his half-sister, SSG Conley, Robert E. Conley Summer Camp 1999

RTI Macon, Georgia
1/122 Infantry 1998-2002

One of the best jobs I had in the Georgia National Guard was being sent to a school in Macon, Georgia. I was there to be schooled trained of being in the infantry. Yes, it might sound funny but I was never attended a course of being in the United States Army as an infantryman. I had been schooled trained as a wheel and track vehicle mechanic so once I was in the National Guard they decided I needed to go to Infantry School at Fort Stewart, Georgia.

While attending this course I met a lot of my old time friends and they would laugh and cut up about me being a student in an infantry school. One of my long times friends was a Staff Sergeant Hawk and a Staff Sergeant Lopez who had been with me in company H LRSU back in Newnan, Georgia. By the second week of a four week course they had pulled me out of the student's class and had me to become a platoon leader on the field managers. I would act like I was a patrol leader and would show and talk to the men in our class. They finally became aware of what was really going on and all the students loved to stay in the field with me. We ran patrols, actions at objective and set up clover leave recon missions. We had day light and night time missions using some of Americans new toys that made being in the infantry a lot more fun. Our radios that we had used in the Vietnam War were much out dated and we were able to use and new radios that was almost unbelievable and they could keep track of us back in the operations TOC (Tactical Operations Center) as we moved.

Another thing at RTI we were taught how to use the BFV (Bradley Fighting Vehicle) as a support to the infantry units moving on the ground would have up armored Humvees and scouts that moved and then behind them were the mechanized units and then on the next level was the 108th Armor units and we learned how to use all of these units as support for our Infantry units while going to school. Things at Fort Swampy was lot different than anything I ever saw in Vietnam and twenty years- thirty years had passed since then.

Yes, I could read a map with the best of them. I could out run most of them and when it came down to sitting up an ambush or actions at the objective I was a good leader but people like SSG Hawk, and SSG Lopez, SSG Palmer and SSG Keith Hunter were much advanced to me in the way things were done in the new modern army. In my peace time military theses few men would become some of my best friends anywhere. We would almost all of fight in Iraq and some of us would even go into Afghanistan. I would go back to Company H, LRSU and in two months I received order to report to Macon, Georgia as an Instructor. I was given a promotion back to Staff Sergeant E-6 which I had lost many years before.

SSG Michael Conley, SFC Steve Hawk at RTI in Fort Stewart, Ga. Jan. 2000

This being sent to Macon was a big blessing in disguise. I was still teaching school and coaching basketball but he National Guard was good money in the summer months while we went to summer camps and it also let me take all kinds of courses on line to help with my military education. The first tings that happened after I received a job there in the National Guard was I was able to go over to the Bibb County School department and they found me a job teaching at an Alternative School under a Dr. Swint as my department head.

I would spend two years teaching there at the Bibb County Alternative School and we had a great science department. My students were able to have a greenhouse. I would teach Botany, Chemistry, and Physics. I also taught Biology where we had a greenhouse and we did all kinds of stuff in our school yards as planting flowers and roses and small flowering bushes. My chemistry classes had a chance to make divinity candy, homemade ice cream and all kinds of candy for different occasions. I also went to Mercer University for three semesters and was able to complete my specialty degree in education. That way I was able to male more money as a school teacher. My second year at the school I was voted as the teacher of the year from the other teachers and everyone loved what our students had done to improve the school grounds and also helped some of the inner city students to get jobs at Lowes and Home Depot working in the outdoor grading section. I really did enjoying my teaching there and loved working with some very intellectual teachers that cared a lot for the students and we helped a lot of them get back on track.

I took teachers and the students on road trips or field trips to Atlanta, Georgia where we would spend the day at Zoo Atlanta and also we went to visit the historical museum where a lot was taught about the history of Atlanta and the battle of Atlanta during the civil war. I was able to take some students down to Callaway Gardens down near LaGrange, Georgia and we visited the Hills and Dales there to walk around the gardens and through their green houses. I spent two years teaching in Bibb County and I was close to my National Guard Unit and also to the school where I was teaching.

By the year 1997 my wife Dolores and I had purchased some land in Cherokee County near where her mother and father lived. We cleared the ground and built a horse barn and built a road into the place we were going to build our home. In the summer of 1999 we had hired a home builder to start to work on our new home. By the late fall he had the house completed and we were able to sell our home in Dallas, Georgian and move to Cherokee County so we could be close to her parents and also closer to her job. Our property bordered on her parent's property.

I could already tell that Dee's father was beginning to be sick and not doing well. I just could not put that together. I was able to get a job at Brandon Hall School in Fulton, County near Dunwoody, Georgia as a science teacher and head basketball coach. A friend of mine here at Chattahoochee called it "a very well to do school" This was a completely a different kind of school. It was a very private school. The upper crust or the society were sending their children to this school to get a real education. Some of their parents had attended and graduated from Georgia techs and the Duke University here in the south. Spouses had their spouses that worked at the CDC (Center for Disease Control). I do know they had a very good athletic department but they had never won a state championship in anything.

I was not the best teacher at Brandon Hall School but I did work very hard to become a better teacher and my field of work improved a lot while teaching there. I was hired as the assistant Varsity Boys Head Basketball coach my first year and the following year while I was there and they hired me to be the head basketball coach we had a record of 54 wins and 4 loses. My first year as a head coach the Brandon Hall panthers won 25 games and lost 4. We lost in the state semifinals to the Furtah Falcons by 3 points. In my second year as head coach we had a goal to become the state champions from the very first practice on. We had only lost two of our seniors and we were going to be good. I knew that we were going to be very good. I had a great feeling. They loved to run drills and all the men worked hard to becoming better athletes. They really reminded me of my first coaching job ever as the freshmen coach at Cherokee County. Those boys had heart too.

My Mother and Aunt Alice summer of 98, petting the horses (Precious, Shadow, Champ. Lady and Cody) at Dees mom and Dad.

As the year and basketball season was under way we had made it to the Christmas tournament with a 9 wins and 0 losses. We met the Furtah Falcons in a Christmas and we able to beat them in an overtime game on their home court. The next time we met them was on our home court and we beat them again by 5 points. It was a real game but I knew we would play them again on their court near Woodstock, Georgia. Sometimes it is harder to win on a good team's court then on your own home court. By the end of February our team was at 21 wins and 0 losses.

We would meet them for the last regular season game of the year. What at night that was on their gym. They led the whole game until less than 20 seconds on the clock as we took a one point lead. Our center had completed a wheel move and made his basket and was fouled by their pivot. Then after they had called time out he stepped to the line and made his free throw although he was not a good free throw shooter. This was our only lead of the night. They brought the ball down the court and in the last three seconds a strong forward moved into the lane and tried to make a big layup. He was not fouled and he did miss the game winning shot. We had finished the regular season 22 wins and 0 losses.

Our walk through the state playoff was like watching Hoosiers. A very good long time ago basketball story about a small school in Southern Indiana that made it to the state finals. We made it to the last game only by winning two overtime games. I almost knew all along we would meet Coach Friez (freeze) and the Furtah Falcons. They had been the years state champions and they were a really a good team and they were coached by one of the better coach's in our state. We would meet again on their floor.

I do not have my play book at this time but I do know that at half time they had a double digit lead on us .I knew my boys and our team could play better but mostly we had as yet not gotten into a fast paced game or the full court defense and denied the ball to their guards. Slowly over the third period we begin to eat away at the lead and with only one minute left in the third quarter my guards had penetrated their defense and drew two fast fouls on their center. This is a game changer. We finished the third quarter still seven points down but we were on the right side of the foul calls. Now we could start shooting free throws and everyone knows a well-coached Indiana team or coach can do a good job hitting our free throws.

The fourth quarter began with the falcons making a three point basket. From that point on we hit their team with a full court press and the 1-3-1 half court trap and the game begin to change. We made some quick baskets and then the momentum came to our bench. I set two of the starters down and two sophomores who were both very good outside shooters went in.

The falcons were trying to cover up the inside game and they were also protecting their center from fouling. With a turn over and a layup we had cut it down to five. With four minutes to go. Then for one minute we lost our sight and our way. They were back up by seven points at three minutes to go. After I called time out I set the two young men down and told the team" this is our game". "We have to take it because they are not going to give it to us".

It all came down to their last three minutes. My team had fresher legs and we also had experienced four overtime's games through the season. We had something in basketball that is not taught. We had confidence we were going to win. The last three minute I let them play. We went through four different defensive moves. I let the captain of the team make that decisions but I gave them hints along the way with hand and arm signals. We picked them up at full court. Then we did another half-court trap and scored off from that with a layup. The team went into the 2-1-2 full court trap and we caught a long pass down court without them getting a shot. With less than 20 seconds to go. We had the ball and down by two. Our final shot was where our center who had the ball and tried another layup but he was fouled by their pivot. That fouled their big man out of the game and our center stepped to the line and hit both free throws to put us into another overtime game. I felt good. Knowing we had not lost one overtime game the whole year, and their big man and best player was now fouled out of the game.

The next five minutes was a game for the ages. The Brandon Hall panthers team did everything right. We took a nine point lead and they scored the last two points of the game because we refused to foul them. We had outscored them in a nine to two run as we won by 7 points. **We had finished the season with a 28-0 record. Not one loss. The perfect season without a loss.** I would never coach another Brandon Hall game because as summer came on I went to Fort Stewart, Georgia to train the Georgia National Guard and while training soldiers to set up an ambush a trip flare in my right hand went off. That was all my own fault for really not paying close attention to what I was doing. I was to suffer second and third degree burns over my hand and wrist. This is the worst pain I ever felt in my life.

I was put onto a six months LOD (line of duty) and that took me off the teaching and coaching at Brandon Hall. Little did I know it would be another seven years and many miles of travel before I would ever step back onto the basketball court or a classroom? I would finish up my six months at an Armory in Canton, Georgia serving with the 108th Armor, and A Company 1/121st Mechanized Infantry in Winder, Georgia. With the help of Captain of Lipper and Lt. Col Rick Barr I was selected to go to the republic of Georgia as the senior operations NCO in early months the following year 2004. I would be gone almost all of the next five years.

Going to the Republic of Georgia in 2004, Bringing Spotty Home

In the late winter of 2003 while serving as a Platoon Sargent with company A 1st Brigade of the 151st Mechanized Infantry in Lawrenceville, Georgia I was called into Captains Michael Lipper's office. I had been put on LOD (Line of Duty) medical leave after summer camp. I had suffered second and third degrees burns on my left hand while doing a demonstration during our annual summer camp down at Fort Stewart. A trip flare had gone off in my hand and I had suffered one of the worst pains I had ever had in my whole life. For six months I went back and forth to Fort Gordon, Georgia to the burn unit and as they worked on my hand I had been assigned to a unit here in Canton Georgia with the 108th Armor Battalion Company B but in January I had been sent back to my own unit in Lawrenceville, Georgia as a platoon sergeant of a company full of Bradley Fighting Vehicles and I loved my platoon Sargent jobs and had been working part time for the state of Georgia National Guard.

I reported into Captains Michael Lipper office on a Monday morning in late January and he handed me a Message from the Global Distribution.

"LTC Rick Barr, our Bilateral Affairs Officer in the Republic of Georgia, has succeeded in gaining approval for a Georgia Army National Guard NCO in the pay grade of E7 or E8 to assist him as the Operations NCO in Tbilisi Republic of Georgia. This is a six month TDY assignment with tour dates of 24 April-19th of October 2004". It also had a phone number to SMS Bradford at the Dobbins Air Force Base less than twenty miles from my home.

There were rumors at that time about us (the Georgia National Guard) going to Iraq and also going out to Fort Irwin, California next summer for rotations to see if we could get ready and pass inspection on going to Iraq. So I had been with Alpha Company first foot of the 48th Inf. Brigade working on giving extra classes and working on the arms and qualification ranges in our company. I had been taken off the medical list in early January and was looking forward to going back to work as a school teacher at Brandon Hall School. The year before our basketball team I had I was coaching the varsity team had been the state champions. We had gone 29 wins and 0 loses and had a very good team coming back. That year they had to start the season without me and had put another coach into my position as varsity coach. I was thinking and hoping that by the fall of 2004 I could go back to my school teaching and coaching job. This was not to be. I would never go back to Brandon Hall where I had coached for two years as a varsity head coach and had a record leaving there of winning 51 out of 55 games and my last year as a varsity coach was an undefeated season. I reported into Captain Michael Lipper back at Company A 121st Infantry Battalion. He was my company commander and a very close friend. He asks me if I would be interested in going back to the Republic Of Georgia. When I was in Company H LRSU in Newnan, Georgia we had gone over there for three weeks and trained their men in surveillance techniques. We had been over there together once before to help the Georgians build an army and help this small republic gets it feet on the ground. At the time we were there I was serving in a Long Range Surveillance Company down in Newnan Georgia. Its name was called Company H LRSU of the Georgia National Guard.

There was an opening with the Ministry of Defense and there was also a friend of ours from the North Georgia College days who was over there and his name was Lieutenant Colonel Rick Barr. I put in the paper work and within one month I was selected to go to the Republic of Georgia. I lift our home on the 24th of April, 2004 and arrived in Stuttgart, Germany on the 25th of April. I stayed in Stuttgart for two days under the European Command and attended a Team Meeting on orientation to the Republic of Georgia. I departed there and headed for Tbilisi, Republic of Georgia on the 28th of April. 2004.

My arrival in Tbilisi, Georgia is nothing like I really expected. I was taken immediately to the American Embassy and a guard from the U.S. Marine Corp met me there.

He handed me a Check-in List. For the next six hours he never left my side. I met the American Ambassador and also the Deputy Chief of Missions. I was given a briefing on Georgia's current political and economic situation and the effects of the daily life in Georgia. I spent one hour in a security briefing with RSO. (Regional Security Officer) I received my Embassy I. D. and went over Emergency Action Plans. I met and was introduced to my Interpreter (Patta) and I was also introduced to the Post Language Programs (Eka) and one of the last things they did was sent me into an office to receive information regarding procedures for sending and receiving telegrams and incoming mail and phone calls. Security was at the highest level everywhere I went in the American Embassy compound. I was then taken outside to a motor pool and my Marine Body Guard took me to meet LTC Rick Barr over at the Metechi Annex. After climbing eight flights of stairs I arrived and reported in to Lieutenant Colonel Rick Barr.

In Honor of all Newcomer.

The Ambassador of the United States of America
and
Mrs. Richard Monroe Miles
request the pleasure of your company
at a buffet dinner
on Wednesday, August fourth,
at six-thirty o'clock

Casual
R.S.V.P.
98 99 67, ext. 4101

3rd Delisi Side Street
House No. 3

1st SGT Michael Conley

JCTP

CHECK-IN LIST
U.S. EMBASSY, TBILISI, GEORGIA

Name: _Michael Conley_   Arrival Date: _April 14th, 2004_

Agency: _____   Sponsor: _____

Welcome to Tbilisi! Please meet personally with each person/office on this list and have him/her initial this sheet after your briefing.

Executive Section (Second floor; top of Chancery grand staircase)
___ Arrange for call on the Ambassador and/or Deputy Chief of Mission within one workday of your arrival at post.

Amb.'s/DCM Secretary

Political Economic Section (Second Floor, top of Chancery grand staircase)
___ Briefing on Georgia's current political and economic situation and the effects on daily life.

Pol/Econ Chief

CLO Office (First Floor, Chancery)
___ Meet with CLO-discuss resources (household help, dependent employment, schools, outside activities).

Community Liaison Officer

Systems Office (First Floor, Chancery)
✓ Request log on for computer access.

E. Chvika
Systems Assistant

Regional Security Officer (Ground floor, Chancery)
✓ Meet with RSO for security briefing.
✓ Receive Embassy I.D.
___ Read Sections of Emergency Action Plan pertinent to your office and family safety.

Regional Security Officer

CONS Office (Ground floor, Chancery)
___ Meet with CON Officer for briefing on consular portion of the duty officer's responsibilities and on post visa referral program.
___ Receive information on Post Language Programs.

CONS Officer

Tbilisi Employee Association (Ground floor, Chancery)
___ Meet with Manager (membership, deposit, and fees)

TEA Manager

Information Programs Center (CAC Tower, Chancery)
___ Contact the office to receive information regarding procedures for sending and receiving telegrams.
___ Pick-up radio and charger from telephone technician. _Maggy Reddx IPC at 4/22_
___ Visit mail room, receive explanation of pouch and mail procedures and guidelines
___ Contact telephone operations to ensure that you are added to the telephone list.
___ Request log-on for classified system.

Information Programs Officer

HR Section: (Eighth Floor, Metechi Annex)
___ Arrange for TM Eight-Arrival Cable.
___ Arrange for FSC/P13 - leave accounting form for American personnel.
___ Complete SF-1190 - foreign allowance grant for post differential, Post allowance & SND.
___ Complete Emergency Locator Card and return to the personnel office (one copy will be forwarded to the Foreign Service Lounge and one copy will be retained in your Personnel file at Post)
___ Copy of the Passport required.
___ New TSP address sent to Charleston

HR Assistant

There were a lot of things that went on over there but the thing that made me the happiest happened one morning going to the American Embassy on a cool July morning. There on the side of the rode was a medium size dog that had been run over by a car or small truck. Now in America that might not seem like a big deal but over there they weren't many cars and a lot less dogs. Matter of fact seeing any dogs in Republic of Georgia was like seeing a Black Bear in the North Georgia Mountains. They were not many dogs. Only a very wealthy society can have dogs because if there is little food around they will be few dogs around. The Republic of Georgia was a very poor country and not many dogs. As we drove by I saw two little small patches of white and they were lying still but then I thought I saw one of the small bundles of white move. We backed up and I got out of the car and there next to its mother were two dead puppies and a real thin skinny puppy and she was covered with fleas and she was alive. "Oh no I said to Patta my driver and interrupter" what am I going to do with this puppy"? I really already knew what I was going to do. I gave her a name and put spotty into a small rucksack with her head hanging out and took her into the American embassy with me.

While I was there I ask people at the embassy if they had any flea shampoo or something to kills fleas. No not one bottle of anything. I ask the American ambassador if he could get some sent in from Germany on the next plane. He said he would check on it. I left there thinking sure he will. I had never in my farthest mind believed an American Ambassador would do that for me. I thought I'll never hear anything about some flea shampoo. That night after midnight the phone rang in my room and I answered it. I had a call from a Lance Corporal United States Marine Corps from the American Embassy and he said there was a package for me to pick up at the front gate. I drove over there at 1:00 PM in the morning and brought the shampoo home. They had flown three bottles of Flea Shampoo from Stuttgart Germany to Tbilisi, Georgia. I had this little dog that was starving to death and eat up with at least a thousand fleas and I put her into the bath tub and washed her for at least twenty to thirty minutes. They were dead fleas everywhere.

I gave her three baths that night and each time I dried her off and combed her skinny little boney body until she would go to sleep on my lap and then I would give her another bath. Finally before daylight she went to sleep in the same rucksack I had carried her home in. OH no Raymond ha ha made another mistake. My wife calls me Raymond from the TV series of Everybody Loves Raymond. The rucksack had at least one hundred fleas in it and she got another round of fleas on her. But not to worry she would soon become my best friend in Georgia and she went with me everywhere except out on missions or away from the capital. Later I had a chance to phone my wife Dolores and I told her I had a new friend and she had big brown eyes and she was sleeping in my bed with me. Every day after I would get home from the Metchi Annex I would take Spotty for long walks and we would find a small twig or a stick and she would play with it and even drag it for a ways as we walked in the quiet neighborhood that we lived in. I could walk to the LTC Barr's house in five minutes and he would laugh and he soon got to calling her my guard dog. Yes, he was sure I was crazy. Spotty was my closest friend and we did so many thing together and went on long walks and watched the river run past under the bridge not far from where we lived. Three months later the problem came on how to get spotty home. I asked everyone I knew there if they would take her and no one would take her. I offered Patta and Maumka $200 to take care of her. They were good friends but both of them turned me down. This is a very poor country and leaving her behind was a death warrant. What else could I do? Well I thought about taking her home. How much trouble would that be? I found out it would be both a lot of trouble and cost a lot of money.

Spotty had to have a passport and they had put a chip under her skin. I had to go back to the American Embassy and get permission to bring her home. She was quarantined for 40 days and given many shots to bring her home. I had a very special lady (my language teacher) working at the embassy that was able to fine me a used dog carrier and on the last morning in Georgia I walked out onto the rain coming down and we walked out onto the run way with a dog in a small dog carrying case and paid for her a trip to America. On the way home she had a passport specially made for her and they put a chip into her neck and she road on the plane and we stopped at four different airports on the way home.

I always got to see her and pet her and take her for a short walk when we stopped. While on board from Paris France on a Delta aircraft to Atlanta Georgia a flight stewardess came by and gave me a small short note that said "Spotty is doing well and enjoying her flight" I thought at the time how nice this lady was and how good it was going to be to get her home where she would be free and could run and live out in the country of Cherokee County in the foothills of the North Georgia Mountains. Spotty and I finally made it to Atlanta Georgia it had been three different airplanes and a twelve thousand mile trip from Tbilisi, Georgia to Atlanta, Georgian but we were home. My wife was there to meet me and we had to go to three different places and get my luggage and then to pick up spotty. It was so good to come home and my wife gave me a big hug and said "I can't believe you would bring a dog home from over there" Honey I am a Ranger and we don't leave our friends behind. I told her. We drove about sixty miles north of Atlanta and arrived here on the farm.

This is a beautiful small farm. There are about five acres and a small lake near our house here with a creek running down the property and a barn up on the hill. There are trees and woods to play in and fields to run through and places where she could roll and play. She found squirrels and ground hogs to chase and often went walking with me and followed the horses when I went riding. This would be spots home for the next eight years. She has been a good dog and loves the life in America. When my father in Law (Bill little) went to a nursing home and my Mother in Law Marie Little was left all alone. Spotty on her own stated staying over there and keeping her company and being a guard dog for my mother in law. Marie was so good to Spotty. Never did a dog get any better treatment then spotty did while she lived there. The truth is at my Mother in Laws house everything gets fed. The birds, the stray cats and even a Possum and a raccoon come up on her porch at night and eats. Spotty was happy and a very well-adjusted Russian mutt. She grew up to be a beautiful dog and a great pet. The birds and the squirrels would take her food and she would not even bark at them and she was just a good loving dog. Everyone that met her always said spotty was a good dog.

Spotty's Passport and a Picture. She also had a chip in her neck

This is mount Kazbaucki very near the Russian border

During her last two years she got so she would wave at me when I came up the drive way. She would lift her left front paw and put it up to shake hands and it always looked like she was waving. In the summer of 2012 a very bad year here for mosquitoes. It was a very hot here and the mosquito's population just exploded. Spotty came down with heart worms and became very sick. I had given her medications ever month. I have been taking her to see a Veterinarian not far from here but she has been getting very weak even though I put her through the treatment I don't know if she is going to make it.

I will miss my little dog from the Republic of Georgia but I know in my heart we had some great times and she was as loyal a dog as any man could ever have. She will be buried here on the farm not far from our horse Cody who passed away late in the fall last year. My life and road is getting shorter but my friends and horses will always have a special spot in my heart. It will be so sad but good memories when we have to put her down. Good by spotty. I loved you girl. Tomorrow I will take her to the vet and I know it will be like burying one of my buddies from the war days.

I did take her to the vet and she told me she had Addison's disease and we put her on medicines to help her out. My wife Dolores has been very upset with me for spending money on her. The heart treatment took a lot out of her but she has slowly gotten some better and got so she could run and play again. My mother in law Marie went to a hospital for a knee operation and was gone for almost four weeks and spotty never once in four weeks did she ever come over to our home. She was always there at my Mother in Laws when I went to feed the horse named lady and most of the time she would be sitting by the American Flag. She would wave at me as I came up the drive way. She was feeling so much better I begin to think she was going to make it. On Thanksgiving Day 22 November 2012 she was running and jumping around and acted like s are going to make it girl' and I sat beside of her and petted her for a long time. She laid her head in my lap and set beside of me and then she got up and went over to Marie and laid her head on Maries lap for a few minutes as I was getting ready to leave. The following day I saw her and spotty did not act sick and was running around. The last time I saw Spotty she was sitting on the porch watching me leave and go down the drive way. The next morning 24th of Nov. 2012 my wife called me and told me to go back to her mother's house I had been on the way to Antioch he felt so good. I told her spotty 'maybe you are going to make it girl' and I sat beside of her and petted her for a long time. She laid her head in my lap and set beside of me and then she got up and went over to Marie and laid her head on Maries lap for a few minutes as I was getting ready to leave. The following day I saw her and spotty did not act sick and was running around. The last time I saw Spotty she was sitting on the porch watching me leave and go down the drive way. The next morning 24th of Nov. 2012 my

302

wife called me and told me to go back to her mother's house I had been on the way to Antioch Church for men's breakfast so I turned around. Spotty had spent the night indoors at my mother in laws place and momma said there was something wrong with spotty. I said a prayer to God on my way back and told God I loved Spotty but I did not want the little dog to suffer. If it was time to go please Lord Take her but don't let her suffer. She was dead when I got there and she had been sleeping in the kitchen and I found her lying there. I spoke her name and then touched her. She was cold and stiff and I knew when I touched her I had lost another one of my friends and a good buddy. I was sad so very sad but I talked to the Lord while I was digging a grave and I thanked him for little spotty dog and for all the great moments we had had together. I know it doesn't sound right but I thanked him for taking her so she did not really suffer that I know off very much. She had been a very good and a loyal dog. I am so glad even though I could not save all the little children while I worked in Georgia I do believe saving spotty was a very good thing. I buried spotty down on the farm where Cody our black horse had been buried. No one came to help me or say anything kind over her as I laid her in her grave. We had come to America alone just me and her and she past with momma being the only one close. I know one should not feel toward an animal like you do toward human beings but I will miss my spotty dog and I know in my heart she was loyal and a happy dog. She gave us her all and she loved me and momma. We sure did do a lot together Spotty. Thank you for the journey. You were a good dog. My wife was going through some paper work yesterday and we found spot's pass port with her picture. She traveled far from where she was born. I loved you Spotty. Thank you for the journey. You were a good dog.

SFC Michael J. Conley NCOIC at the American Embassy at the time of the death of Ronald Reagan. meet and greeted many who came to pay their last respects to a great Man.

I had been serving and working in the Republic of Georgia for five months when things really begin to go wrong. I was working in the Ministry of Defense and working with the Republic of Georgians Army. I was working under a great and very brilliant man by the name of Lieutenant Colonel Rick Barr and the call came down something big was coming down the pike. Over the next week of August 17, 2004 the world would be aware of the trouble a little country can have with its being neighbor the Russian empire better known as the Soviet Union. I have radio messages and newspaper clippings and things I wrote my wife from Aug the `6th through August the 27th and the kind of work we were doing over there has been copied from newspaper clippings and off the computer taken at that time.

Hello from over here near the village named Erdivi, South Ossetia
Death Toll Rises as Clashes Continue
Taken from a Newspaper clippings: Tbilisi Republic of Georgia
Overnight clashes between Georgian troops and South Ossetian militias, which   also include mercenaries from Russia's North Caucasus republics, have already resulted in six Georgia soldiers' deaths despite a ceasefire agreement signed by both sides on August 13 2004. Georgians officials say dozens were killed from the South Ossetian side however Tskhinvali denies these reports.   The Georgian village of Erdivi has become a major target for South Ossetian militias recently.

8/17/2004 10:51 Eastern Standard Time   E-mail to my wife while serving in the Republic of Georgia.

Can't say send me back; get me the hell out of here. I don't know when I will be back. LTC Nick Janjuvia a friend from Ranger school days and a Georgian is coming up tomorrow with three American Soldiers. General So So is the most incompetent man I have ever met. Please Dolores tell me the things I said about Captain Michael Lipper was not true. I am so sorry I ever said what I said This General So So is a third grader compared to Captain Lipper and I so wished he was here with me now with SSG Blow and our three squad leaders I had back there in Company A first foot. Captain Lipper and I with our company could hold them off for days with our Bradley's and our units. He is really a very good company commander. Things are worse here and it will not be long until dark and night sits in. I have had two or may three hours of sleep in two days. Teams are coming in tomorrow and Captain Phillips from the air force and he is in charge of the helicopters back in Tbilisi and he has moved them up close to Gori. I am taking only Paata and one officer and going higher into the mountains terrain and gets a good look at the river crossing tonight. When I get back I will have three commanders and will be reviewing troops and giving them a warning order to their commanders, this is the third night and it is very dangerous situation. We either find a way to stop them here or all will be lost.

Two days later
8/19/2004 24:52 am Eastern Standard Time
To my wife: Dee: Please understand: I am OK but have been pushed very hard. I love you and have been without computer for two days. I have just talked to three gentlemen in civilian clothes and they brought me some small items and some much need materials from the American embassy. I also have the maps that I have needed for three days. We are now working with the 11th Mountain Brigade and staff at this minute. We are deeper into the mountains north of Gori and I have found the

place to make our stand. I am north of Gori about one hand space near Rocki Pass and south of Java by 14 KM near Tskhinvali. This is where we are and tomorrow morning with the help of our American helicopters we will make a stand. This is where we are and we are not going to back up any farther. We must make our stand here because once the Russians gets their tanks onto the open planes and past Gori we could never stop them with what we have to fight with. I also know today is my Mother's birthday and tomorrow is your Mother's birthday. I cannot call or send anything. I am so sorry. I am a soldier and will do well. You said in your last e-mail you took my e-mails to church and let them read them and had a prayer for me. Dolores oh I love you so much but God is with me it's the men. This is the men I have been training and I know their families. They are like my men back at Alpha Company. These are my boys. I don't want to waste it in this pass. Last night we lost seventeen men killed and more than forty wounded. It's not what the paper said but I know how many men got killed. I know them and I know their faces but that is not what the paper reported in Tbilisi. I may not call or be able to text you for a couple of days.

Two Pictures of me and two Helicopter pilots in Georgia Tbilisi Republic of Georgia Thursday, Aug 19th, 2004 Newspaper from Tbilisi

The fighting was described by officials Thursday as some of the most fiercely fought in recent days. They said the Georgian forces had captured a very strategic area and held it at bay against the Russian forces and mercenaries. The Georgian forces and one commander from the ministry of defense said "They were ready now to hand over the control of these heights that there force had just won near the Rocki Pass and the South Ossetia River. The Georgian president Saakashville said in a televised address to his nation that the Russians tanks and armor units were withdrawing and heading back north through the valley shortly after noon today. This has drawn fierce criticism from Moscow as they said it was and escalation in force bringing helicopters into the picture. As the president spoke the Russian news agencies reported that heavy fighting still continues for the control of the strategic high ground near the pass and that the peacekeepers were on their way into the area to get pictures of the Russian tanks in the valley.

8/20/2004 Written to my Wife. I found this on my computer after I got home.

Dee: It is now 09:45 and we have handed over the concept sheets and Battle plans to a Major from a forward Army Officer Troop command. It's now in his hands and we are pulling our soldiers over to a small village now three kilometers from here next to a small river for washing and getting drinking water. I need some shade and some rest. We thank the Russians have moved north more than 60 km in the last twelve hours and the danger is past for now. We will still be under pack and weapons at the ready but there has been a cease fire and I was not there but LTC Barr said maybe things will calm down now. I have asked these soldiers to do and done all a body can ask of these young men since last Monday morning once we started to head north. I as a soldier could not ask neither nor expect any more than these solder's and these brave young men and soldier's then they have given. I don't know why. I don't know how good, but I do know that when there're country ask them to step forward they were there and some I believe in the end some 18 men gave their all and scores of men have been wounded. I don't know when I will be back in Tbilisi. I am only asking for prayers now that maybe we can have a peaceful and a quiet weekend. Pray for a quiet weekend. This is a chance for Peace at Last in this area for a while. Soon in just two more months I will be coming home to you. To love. To peace. To come home to the quiet in the beautiful hills of Cherokee County. My fighting days are nearly over and I thank God it's time to quit all this fighting it is hard on a man's nerves. I will be seeing Spotty in two or three days and maybe we can get a walk down along the river. Another battle is over. Love Michael

I stayed in the Republic of Georgia and ended up going over to the Black sea and seeing and staying at Batumi on the shores of a beautiful sea. We stayed there for three days and four nights and picked up a convoy and with the help of their military and our trucks we were able to move a lot of equipment over two hundred miles. We moved everything back to Tbilisi and to the military post not far from the capital. I saw where the oil pipe line was being put in and where it would empty into the tankers coming into the port there close to the Turkey border and then headed back for Tbilisi. I begin to thank things were getting quieter and we could get back to working with the little villages and getting a water well dug and water to a small village before I had to leave. It was already changing weather there and winter comes in hard and quick over there. The American Salvation Army and the American Red Cross I saw over there did so much good in helping these so poor people and our Doctors and medical teams came over there and helped these poor Georgians get medicines and medical attention. While I was there I also saw churches being opened for the first time in three hundred years and people were going to church and helping each other. In reality I loved Georgia and the summer I spent there will always be in my heart and mind as one of the best times in my life while we were trying to help this small country stand up for peace and love of their own people. I can hope in some small way I helped a nation and a people who appreciated every little thing we did for them. I had more than one chance to meet the

President Mikhell Saakashville and one time the Secretary of State Colin Powell who came to see the Ambassador Richard M Miles. I did not know that they were going to present me with a Joint Service Achievement Medal and they took three pictures for the local newspaper. As I write this book I want to make it very clear that in all my time in the Republic of Georgia I had nothing to do with the fighting end of anything. I was only there as an adviser and not boots on the ground. I worked with LTC Rick Barr on the many different things that we could do for their country.

საქართველოს ეროვნული გვარდიის სარდალი

COMMANDER IN CHIEF OF NATIONAL GUARD OF GEORGIA

№------- "--------" --------------- 2004

Dear General,

The President of Georgia and our Government highly appreciates the friendly cooperation established between the National Guard of the State of Georgia and the National Guard of the Country of Georgia, as this promotes our National Guard to come closer to the modern military standards.

At present, reserve training and re-training centers are being formed, with the National Guard being tasked by the President to train 6000 reservists step by step in field conditions. Their main task will be to support the civilian government in case of emergency situations and at the same time serve as the military strategic reserve for the Supreme Commander-in-Chief.

For the implementation of this plan we need highly skilled instructors that have worked with reservists before.

I would like to tell you that two American military service-members and current State of Georgia National Guard members working at the Ministry of Defense, LTC Richard Barr and SFC Michael Conley, have expressed their desire to support the National Guard of Georgia's efforts and assist in field exercise preparation for our reservists. The military background especially of SFC Conley will facilitate great deal in our efforts to establish Western type practical military exercises. I cordially ask you to let them help us in this activity at their free time.

Besides that I'd like to inform you that our Minister of Defense whom I'll accompany also, is planning to visit the state of Georgia in order to see your bases and get your recommendations which I'm sure will be very important and useful for us.

I'd like to thank you for all the support given by the National Guard of the State of Georgia in the past and look forward to your continued support as the Country of Georgia builds and trains its reserve force for the future.

Sincerely Yours,

Brigadier – General
S. Kutateladze

We helped get a well dug for a very small village that had been hand carrying water from a small river that was totally polluted. We also helped get medical supplies into a village and towns when they were sickness over there. My job was to work with their Army and making up training for their military.

Not to be as all hell broke loose again just north of the border. School started across the Soviet Union and the third day of school some Ossetia rebels had been working on a school and as the students were brought into their class rooms and held for ransom and to have four of their men released from prison. Three days later a daring plan was put under way by the unidentified militant men and police but it failed and they as in the militants blew up this small school and over two hundred and twenty small children had been badly burned and some killed on the initial explosion. Oh God how can these crazy people in the world use children and school teachers to get what they want? It stands to reason that children are the innocent ones in all of this violence and they seem to suffer the worst of all.

American sent over burned units from Fort Gordon, Georgian and from Fort Sam Huston over there to help with the small children. The Minister of Defense and the President Mikhell Saakashville of the Republic of Georgia said they were trying to help in any way possible and helped take food and medical supplies over the mountains with the same helicopters we had used one month earlier up in South Ossetia conflict. Before leaving Tbilisi I went to two children's hospital and saw some of the children and I also went to an orphanage to see little children that had lost their parents and had nowhere else to go. I met a very small girl who had escaped and helped her seven year old brother and even carried him on her back for part of the way cross the mountain's and came through the snow and freezing weather to make it to safety. In this book I hope that some of the people who have a chance to read this understand what we have here in America and how blessed we really are. I have never been more humbled or felt as small as when I worked and gave a helping hand in the small little country as the Republican Georgia. So on a very cool morning and with sad good byes to my friends who I had spent days and nights with in the Ministry of Defense and I also stopped by the American embassy and spoke to the American Ambassador and also the Deputy Chief of Missions and the Community Liaison Officer and said my good byes. I picked up little spotty and put her in a small dog handling cage and headed for the airport. The last person I saw there before I left was my interpreter Paata and Maumka we quietly said our good byes. This was not about fighting a battle or war this was about friendship and freedom. I loved that job more than any job the military ever sent me on. I truly believe that and working for the Ministry of Defense was one of the best jobs I ever had. I was able to walk into churches over there that had been sealed up for almost two hundred years old and saw pictures of Jesus on their walls and I believed in these people. They wanted to be free.

One year later I was in Iraq and ten of the men who had fought with me or I fought with them. Those men that I had advised and worked with in the republic of Georgia and had been up in Rocki Pass walked into my tent in Iraq while I was at Camp Striker and gave me a big hug and we talked our night away for at least four or five hours as they were serving only ten kilometers from our mitt team that we were putting together and they had heard I was there and they came to see me. Much later I wondered how they found out I was there. I never got to talk to them again. I do not know to this day how they knew I was there but it was a very big surprise. Now in a military career when the men you have trained or worked with in your life comes to see you it is a very great feeling and we have a common bond together especially if one has been under fire together. One of the men before leave ask me about the little dog I had taken home with me to Georgia. He laughed and he cried and said to me" big Sarge you can take me home with you" to Georgia yes. I went on to work in Iraq for a little over three more months but I never saw these men again. I hope and pray they all made it back home alive.

It has now been a year since I wrote about my tour and mission in the Republic of Georgia. I had been hired by the Ministry of Defense, and the Special Operations for Special Forces out of Stuttgart, Germany. I had been working with a Lieutenant Colonial Rick Barr a good friend since the North Georgia College days in Dahlonega, Georgia.

In a telephone call yesterday, Russian Defense Minister Sergei Shoygu had reportedly assured Defense Secretary Chuck Hagel that the Russian forces will not invade Ukraine. Well I had been talking to a man who works here at Chattahoochee Technical College and he told me I needed to tell the real story about working in the Republic of Georgia. This call that was made public news on the world news. The news call was an attempt to get Russia to clarify the intentions of the 40,000 Russian front line troops that were being were amassed at the Ukrainian border. His promise that they will not invaded Ukraine isn't worth much. I have the experience while working in the Republic of Georgia to see how far the Russian army will go unless someone with real weapons and the guts to back it up will go.

While working in the Ministry of Defense as the Senior Operations Non Commissioned Officer in 2004 I was there to witness when the Russian troops and armor unites tried to invade the little country of Georgia. The Russian forces invaded South Ossetia and Abkhazia, who were two breakaway provinces of Russia. They wanted to be a part of the Republic of Georgia. Or so they told the world. This is the truth. The Russians did not come there to settle anything they came there to force the people of these provinces under their boots again. The Russians in their underhanded way had sent troops into these areas to cause trouble and had more than one mass killing of the free Georgians to stir things up. Then when Putin formed his large mass of troops and armor to invade Georgia. The Georgians stood up to them to protect their people and freedom, and their way of life.

I was there. Here is the truth and maybe this is not the place or the book to tell the truth. Russian troops massed along the Russian border and then using and ancient road that led them across the Caucasus mountains and through the Rocki pass they again were on their way to as far south as Gori. It did not happen. In a matter of three days and the brave heart and soul of the Georgia republic troops stood up to the Russian Army and with a little trickery the Russian turn their vehicles and did not attempt to cross the mountain pass.

For three days there were battles s and skirmish up in the mountains of Georgia and along a major road leading into the Georgian heartland. On the fifth morning as the Armor units were moving south they had to go along a very narrow and winding mountain road but on the very border of Georgia there was pass known as Rocki pass and before you could cross it there was a steel framed bridge almost two and a half miles down in a deep ravine with a river flowing and moving a very fast pass down the mountains. This was the only bridge that would hold up the Russians medium size tanks and their equipment. The Russians were using old time radios and their equipment was not able to talk to their commanders behind them. So the front line men used their cell phones and their messages were intercepted by the Georgian soldiers on relay stations along the way.

Cossack soldiers arrive in S. Ossetia

Georgian government detains supposed 'humanitarian aid' from Russia

By Nino Kopaleishvili

Cossack military formations help a demonstration of their force inside territory of South Ossetia on Tuesday. The well-equipped fighters, who arrived to South Ossetia following a decision of the Cossack Council, showed their skills and demonstrated weapons in training in territory controlled by the *de facto* government.

A Cossack leader interviewed by *Rustavi-2* stated that the fighters had arrived in South Ossetia to help their "brother Ossetians" and this was an official decision as 949 delegates of the Cossack Council voted for it.

"Here are our Cossack volunteers who want to take part in this," the Cossack *ottoman* told a *Rustavi 2* journalist. "90 percent of the population of South Ossetia are citizens of the Russian Federation. That is why we are obliged to support our citizens. We represent the voice of Russia. If it is necessary, all Russians will come to help our brothers."

While the Cossacks demonstrated their force, Georgian law-enforcers detained cargo trucks escorted by Russian peacekeepers at the Ergneti checkpoint.

According to the representative of the President of Georgia in Shida Kartli Micheil Kareli, Russian peacekeepers, who claimed they were carrying flour to Ossetian and mixed villages in Big Liakhvi as a present from President Putin, could not provide any documents that it was humanitarian aid.

See Shipments to S. Ossetia on p.5

315

After a small battle along the rocky gorge right before dark the night before the Republic of Georgian army of three companies with light weapons and light machine guns and small mortars were pulled back to a pass that was overlooking the bridge and more than seven hundred feet above the bridge and river below. In the early morning light, shortly after day light the tanks and trucks started again to advance into the sovereign state of the Republic of Georgia. As the first tanks put treads up on the steel bridge three American Helicopters came out of the early morning hills and the pass above them and hovered there for a lest twenty to thirty seconds and then turned and dropped out of sight. Again the first tank started forward and this time when it was almost half way across the bridge three American Helicopters came into sight just above them and this time it looked like they had missiles strapped on the under bellies of each choppers and they all had a red nose in front of each missile.

For over three or four minutes the choppers swung back and forth across the pass but they always kept the nose of the Hueys and the missiles pointed at the Russian tanks. The Russian's did stop. They stayed there for the next twenty or thirty minutes and then slowly they begin to reverse their big tanks and each truck in the convoy had to back more than a half mile down the winding road before there was enough room to turn them around. The Hueys then over the next hour would appear in pairs over the pass and would make small swoops down toward the river before going back up the mountain ad dropping out of sight on the other side.

Newspaper Clippings

I do know that before I left the Republic of Georgia that Colin Powell did come to meet the president of the Republic of Georgia and they did have a very big parade in the streets of Tbilisi, I also have photographs of this and the young men were so proud of everything they had done. I would meet these men later in the sands of Iraq. What a reunion it really was. I just wished that spotty could have been there to shake hands with each of these soldiers. They were also like my brothers that I trusted and depended on in the night of battle but we stopped the Russians. My opinion is that the Russian army is much out dated and they have very poor leadership at the ground level to lead their troops. My personal feeling if we and the Ukrainians would stand up to the Russian they would not dare cross that line and come across anyone border much less the Ukrainians. If they do take the country who will be next? How far would the Russian boots go before someone decided that is far enough? Maybe it's a military might and then again in might be a mouse who wants to think it is lion.

THE UNITED STATES OF AMERICA

TO ALL WHO SHALL SEE THESE PRESENTS, GREETING:

THIS IS TO CERTIFY THAT
THE SECRETARY OF DEFENSE
HAS AWARDED

THE JOINT SERVICE ACHIEVEMENT MEDAL

TO

SFC Michael J. Conley, GARNG

FOR
MERITORIOUS SERVICE
FOR THE ARMED FORCES OF THE UNITED STATES

GIVEN UNDER MY HAND THIS   9ᵀᴴ   DAY OF   NOVEMBER 2004

UNITED STATES EUROPEAN COMMAND
COMMAND OR OFFICE

SECRETARY OF DEFENSE
EDWARD L. LAFOUNTAINE
Major General, USAF
Director of Logistics and
Security Assistance

DD FORM 2414, MAY 1988

My last overseas mission

Heading for Iraq and running a Mitt team I was home only 14 days from the Republic of Georgia when notice was given that the 48th Infantry Brigade was being slotted to take a tour of Iraq. I received a phone call from my company commander Captain Michael Lipper commander of Company A 48th Infantry Brigade and was told they were being activated and they were going to nccd mc to help train and equip a Mitt team.

Another mission and I was leaving home again. I had been married for over twenty five years and now in the last two years I was on the move again. This was my fourth marriage and I had a very good wife who loved me and I loved her with all my heart and she didn't mind me being in the National Guard and being gone sometimes two or three weeks during summer. I thank sometimes she even enjoyed me being gone. Not in a bad way but so she could have a little space and I had all ways enjoyed going to summer camp but this was not going to be the same. I had had a very rough trip into the Republic of Georgia and I was more than wore out now. I was over there when the school house was blown up with over 240 little children had been burned and I was there when the Russians had attacked in North Osseta. Yes, I was there and I and Col Barr and Captain Phillips had worked very hard who was from the air force and was in charge of the American helicopters and teaching them how to use them. They were three violets and can't remember their names but have their pictures that were there with us. It had truly been a very hard tour and I had been gone six months and now with in eighteen days they had me back under orders again.

I loved my wife and I knew we needed some time together so I could get rested up. I loved her with all of my heart and knew this was going to very hard on her. Yes, all of you who are reading this book need to understand some things. I to the very bottom of my heart believe no one knows how hard these rotations are on a marriage and a family. I sometimes think the tours of duty are harder on our wife's than on us. I don't think those in Washington or Generals who live with their wives ever understand what these wives back home have to be and do while their husbands are gone. I was always back home in time to start school teaching in the fall and coaching basketball when I belonged to the National Guard or the Marines reserve's . I had been in the National Guard or Reserves almost every year since we had been married. I had belonged to the Marine Corp Reserve and the US Army Reserves and to the Georgia National Guard but after two or three weeks in the summer we always came home. I might at times be gone for six weeks but we were always stateside and near home. This was going to be different.

The year before I was teaching and coaching at Brandon Hall School in Dunwoody Georgia our basketball team had won the state championship and we had been undefeated. 28 and 0. My dream of being a head basketball coach had been a goal and now that I had achieved it I didn't want to lose it or my teaching job as a science teacher. I had belonged to the Georgia National Guard for almost ten years and had been training these same men. I been in an Infantry unit and then moved to Macon where I was a part of the training battalion there. I had been promoted again to Sgt. First Class and was sent to Winder with a Bradley Fighting unit.

I loved my teaching job and coaching and here I was in my mid-fifties and going on another mission. I would miss my wife and she would be alone again. Her father had not been well and her mother could hardly get around then and I was going to be gone again. We had a six month build up and training phase. We would all start down at Fort Stewart, Georgia and go out to California to do our desert training at Fort Irwin, California home of the Death Valley and then sometime in early or mid-April we would go to Iraq. There was a General Stewart Rodeheaver and I had known him for a long time. He had been a good soldier and he was the commander of the 48th Inf. Brigade. He called me in to talk to me about starting a Mitt team to train and equip the Iraqi army. I got the news and had already been warned by LT. Col Rick Barr before I left Georgia. I had not really thought it would happen and even if it did because of my age and a National Guard unit would really not be called to go over there. I had it figured out. We would train a few months and then they would tell us to go home.

Well our lives started as soldiers even before Christmas. I was down at Fort Stewart, Georgia and I even begin to thank this is actually going to happen. Right after the first of the year they called all the units up and we really started training. We trained hard in the middle of winter and did our rifle ranges and night marches and got to know our men. I was assigned to Charlie Company first foot of the 48th Inf. Brigade combat team with a First Sgt. Bobby Mayfield and a company commander by the name of Capt. Forneigh. They treated me very well and put me in charge of the headquarters platoon. It was there that Capt. Forneigh begin to call me a field First Sgt. I know in my heart that both First Sgt. Bobby Mayfield and the Capt. tried to get me promoted to a first Sergeants slot but it would take more than a year and twenty thousand miles before the promotion finally came down. It didn't matter to me I had a job to do. We all worked hard together and froze together. I was very proud of the men in Charlie Company and they were a very good unit, especially for a National Guard Unit. We had good platoon Sergeants and the men were by far above average for a National

Guard unit. We slept in tents when we did sleep and stayed out in the field for almost six weeks and then had four days to go home before shipping out to Fort Irwin, California. I slept most of my four days off and told my wife I would try to train the Mitt team out in California and see if I could be one of the men staying in the rear and not ship out over seas. I had become more and more tired. I wasn't sleeping well and I knew she needed me at home. I will be honest. I didn't think I could do a tour and do what was expected of a fifty-five year old man and I was really feeling old by then. I had a heart scan before I left the states and it told them that I was having a heart problem and it took over a year for the truth to come out about that. Ten months after shipping out to Iraq I got a letter at home from the military hospital down at Fort Gordon Georgia where they had detected something wrong with my heart and there was possibly a good reason for me being so tired all the time. The longer I went the worst I got to feeling. Oh, yes I ran the two mile run in time for the army standards and I did the pushups but my body was giving out on me and I could tell it. Our last twenty mile march down at Fort Stewart and I did not thank I was going to make it to the end and we marched all night and by day light the next morning we walked into the main post. I had made it. All I needed was some rest and I would be as good as new.

We flew out of Fort Stewart on the first week of April for Fort Irwin, California after a week out there living in tents and going to classes we started our desert preparations and training. We went to the field and it was so cold at night and the desert had received some rain right before we got there and it was absolutely beautiful and the flowers were blooming but the nights were cold, very cold. The drop in temperature as the sun set was almost a degree ever two minutes so it could drop 30 degrees in one hour. As it might be fifty degrees in the sun as the evening wore on and the sun set in one hour it could be twenty degrees. Three weeks of stuff to do and only two weeks to do it. After two weeks of desert training I had a call over the radio to report back to the rear where I met First Sgt Bobby Mayfield.

Battalion wanted us to practice filling sand bags.

Soldier returns to visit family

By MIKE LEWIS
Times-Mail Managing Editor

BEDFORD — Thanks to the American Red Cross, a soldier bound for Iraq got to visit his sick aunt and mother in Bedford.

Michael Conley, a 1966 graduate of Mitchell High School, is a science teacher and basketball coach in civilian life, working in Georgia. He's tasted some success. In 2002-2003, his Brandon Hall High School squad went 28-0 and won Georgia's Class AA state title.

A few weeks later, he was called into full-time duty with the Georgia Army National Guard.

"I've been on active duty since then," he said in a telephone interview from Bedford Regional Medical Center Monday.

Conley is a field first sergeant in the Guard. His mother, Laura Boone, 76, and his aunt, Alice Carter, 88, live in neighboring homes in Bedford.

"There's only about 12 feet between the houses," Conley said with a laugh.

But now both his aunt and his mother are ill. And that's where the American Red Cross steps in.

"I was able to get home because of Donna Eubank and the Red Cross here in Bedford," Conley said.

When people in the military face family emergencies, the Red Cross sends information to the commanding officer, who can send the soldier home.

"It's a 24/7 service for the Red Cross, anywhere in the world," said Betsy Henley of Bedford, the volunteer caseworker who handled Conley's paperwork.

"We have six volunteer caseworkers at the moment," Henley said. "We'd like to have more."

In Conley's case, he was able to come home for the weekend to visit Carter in the hospital. On Monday he was to meet with the physician handling his mother's heart condition.

It was a different world from where he had been, training for deployment to Iraq within 30 to 45 days.

Conley has been trained as a Green Beret and is a desert warfare specialist. His service has taken him to far-flung conflicts from Vietnam to Bosnia.

Now, at age 56, he has a command and is preparing troops for what they might face in Iraq.

"I've got my own command now, and they're good," he said. "My boys are good.

"I'm in charge of a company of 116 enlisted men and five officers. I'm in charge of all their training, their field training."

Getting back to those troops was

See **SOLDIER** back page

Come unto Me, all ye that labor and are eavy laden, and I will give you rest."
— Matthew 11:28

?-4405 • Phone (812) 275-3355

Article of News Paper going home and seeing my Aunt and mother (Bedford Times Mail)

324

On April the 12th I had received word that my Aunt Alice Carter had passed away back home in Indiana and I was sent word from the Red Cross for me to go home. I flew back to Fort Stewart, Georgia and picked up my car and went home. I called right after I got home and talked to Steve Robinson Aunt Alice's grandson and he informed me they had buried her the day before at Port Williams church. I was one day late in getting back. I never got to go to the funeral and it would be almost a year before I would be back home and stand beside of her grave and tell her I was sorry I had not made it home for the funeral. She had meant a lot to me and had helped shaped me into the man I would become. The last time I saw her she patted me on the cheek and told me to forgive my mother and that times were hard when I was a little boy. I thank she knew when I left there that day with my wife and that I would never see her alive again. She had been a blessing and taught me about God and loving Jesus and about Angels and God. When I go back home to Indiana I always try to go down to the little church on Kings ridge and when I walk into that church (Fairview Church of Christ) I always feel very close to her and Uncle Dutch for helping me out when I was a young man.

I was only home in Cherokee County for three days and then headed back for Fort Stewart, Georgia. As I drove down interstate 75 I did think about the years and miles and wondered in my own mind if I would ever see home or my wife again. The unit was on their way back from desert training from Fort Irwin, California. I went immediately to the company orderly room and found things in quiet the little mess. Men were not there and people just weren't doing their jobs. The sick and the lame and the lazy who had not went to desert phase training were having a ball in the rear .Oh they were doing nothing and some already knew they would not be going to Iraq.

It took two days to get the men lined up and have a formation and the barracks ready for the men coming back. I was very glad when first Sargent Bobby Mayfield came into the orderly room and the company commander was back in the next hour. The men had a lot to do and that night after a staff meeting when all the company was together we got out marching orders. Some were getting ready to be on leave and others were going to start by getting the Brady's ready for ship meant. Our whole unit and company stuff had to be packed and put into Conexus. We had three weeks of stuff to do and only two weeks to do it.

First Sergeant Bobby Mayfield called me into his office and we had a long talk about promotions and the men we had. We still had privates of E-2 status and we were going to war. My opinion and First Sergeant Mayfield agreed with me. No one should go to war as an E-2. Together we set down and put ever mans that was a private in for promotion to Private First Class or E-3. Next we promoted some of team leaders to E-4 and other we put in for promotion for Sargent Stripes. In our National Guard unit most of the people who got promoted were the rear detachments and those who worked in the main officers in the 48th Infantry brigade. We as line doggies called them clerks and jerks. No not all of them were bad or could not do their job but they always seem to get the best of everything. They sure did get a lot of promotions and medals were in their hands and on their uniforms before any line infantry soldier. This was a battle that was never ending. To this day I know for a fact the 48th had National Guard's men who had promotions after promotions that never for one reason or another where they were never promoted. I was pinned in front of the company by the first sergeant and the commanding officer and given the title as a field first sergeant before shipping out.

Charlie Company was a very good company and at the end of my book I will give all the names and rank of every man that served in this company. But here I want to thank First Sergeant Bobby Mayfield and the company commander Captain Fournier for running a very tight ship. We had one of the best if not the best company in the 48th Infantry Brigade. I was ordered two days before shipment to go to a promotion board where the Commander Captain Fournier had put me in for a promotion for my First Sargent stripe. On the day before we left Fort Stewart, Georgia and before we marched over to the parade ground with the 48th Infantry they brought me forward in front of the whole company and pined me with my new first Sergeant stripes and gave me the title of Field First Sargent. This was in the middle of our going to Iraq and I never received any orders as a first sergeant until August 23, 2005 signed then by a Lieutenant Colonel Lynn S Alsup and they put my date of rank as 1 June 2005. In other words I was never promoted by the 48th Infantry Brigade that I served with and only got my promotion while being held at the medical holding battalion after I came back from the war.

Three days before shipping out to Iraq my wife Dolores Little Conley drove down to Fort Stewart and we spent the last two nights together in a small motel not far from Savanna, Georgia. She came to a big parade where all the companies were lined up and the Governor of Georgia came down and talked to the parents and soldiers that were going off to war and told of how proud he was of us. General Stewart Rodeheaver spoke to the men and he too told us how proud he was of the 48th Infantry brigade and he would take us as our commander. I thought General Rodeheaver did a very good job of talking to us and I was also proud of the men and what we had accomplished in the last six months. This was as good a National Guard unit as I had ever seen and trained in my entire life. I still feel the same after all these years. The 48th Infantry of the Georgia National Guard had very good officers and some very good senior noncommissioned officer. We had other states like Illinois and Main National Guard units with us to help bring our numbers up and do truck driving and medical units to make us a fully deployable unit. We became known as the 48th Brigade Combat Team before shipping. Dee and I spent our last night together and in the early morning light I stood outside our company orderly room and kissed her good bye and told her how much I loved her and not to worry I would be home someday. I gave her a big hug and turned away so she could not see the tears on my face. I really did wonder if I would ever see her alive again I ask God to take care of her and her family until I could return.

I had questions about if we had trained long enough or if we had had trained for what was coming ahead of us. I was only one man in a command of more than four thousand men and I ask myself how many men here that had seen war and understood what was ahead. I said to long prayer and prayed to the angels and God above to watch over us and bring us home if it by thy will. Later we were loaded on buses and they took us over to Hunter Army Airfield and there is where we loaded the planes and headed for Iraq

We arrived in Iraq on May 20th 2005 after a 20 hour air trip over the Atlantic Ocean by the northern route and we landed in Kuwait and spent one week trying so very hard to get acclimatized. All I can tell you reading this book. I had never in my life been so hot in my whole life. We climbed off the air planes and the heat hit us square between the eyes. It was hot and every day I was there it got hotter. We lived in large tents and marched everywhere we went and as a company we picked up our Bradley's and started getting them ready for the road trip north. We went to the firing ranges and every one had a chance to zero our own weapons and also to fire the Bradley's and getting them ready for action. The days were so hot and in the evenings the sun would set but the heat would not go away.

After six days and five nights we headed north to Camp Striker as a unit. I and First Sergeant Bobby Mayfield along with some other men from our unit were to fly up there on a military C-130. What a ride it was. Right before we came into the Bagdad International Airport we did evasive maneuver in the air plane and dropped almost for ten to fifteen seconds and then came screaming across the at a very low altitude into the air field. Every person who was strapped in became a free falling person in that plane. That was mine and Frist Bobby Mayfield last plane ride together. We had gone to college together and had served in two different units together but I would come home early and he would spend the whole year as the Charlie Company First Sergeant. He ended up being one of best friends in life and we enjoyed our time together weather it w was at Fort Stewart, Georgia at below freezing in a tent or in the heat of the Iraqi sun into he Sunni desert it was always good to see his face and a smile on his lips as we met and he would say how is it going. One time he wrote me a e-mail and on it he said" Don't forget how bad things are you will always be a first Sergeant" Bobby Mayfield will always be my best friend and we had some of our best days in our life's together while wearing a uniform. Thank You First Sergeant Mayfield. When I needed something special done in the military while serving over in Iraq I could ask him and he would get it for me or tell me how to get things done. One of our big things before heading down rage with the second Mitt team was radios. Our up armored Humvees did not have radios and first Sergeant Mayfield helped me run some down and I had a chance to sign for them before we left camp Striker. I received the radios and had them put in the Humvees before we went south into the Indian Territory. Oh Ya over two years after coming back to the United States I received a letter from the Georgia National Guard saying I owed the unit for those radios and they sent me a IOU bill that I had signed before we left camp Striker for the radios and they wanted me to pay for them.

I found this Memorandum for orders a June 6th 2005

1st Sergeant Conley, 2nd Mitt team NCOIC, Dog Handler from Netherlands and his dog name Missile. A sniffer for bombs and booby traps.

Department of the Army

Headquarters 1st Battalion 108th Armor Bn

48th Brigade, 3rd Inf. Division

FOB St. Michael

Unit Mitt2   Number of PAX 20 Number of Vehicles 4 Destination   FOB Michael

Mission type: Train the Iraq Army Route: Jackson to 1a South Compound

Humv #1 Convoy Commander: OCIC LTC Joseph P Hoffman Call sign Stallion 6

Driver: Spies, William   Gunner: Morgan, John D Rifleman: Walton, Wave Radioman: Joniak

Rifleman: Shaw, Clinton

Humv #2 Convoy Co-commander: NCOIC 1SG Conley, MichelCall Sign Stallion 66 Charlie

Driver: Sgt. Gardner, Clifford J   Gunner: Douglas, James Rifleman: Mathewson, Lee Interpreter: Adam

Rifleman: Tidwell, RickySupply Sgt.: SSG Shaw, Clinton

Humv #3 Humv commander Dyer, Joe Call Sign Stallion 67 Delta

Driver: Epps, Billy Gunner: Allen, Michael   Rifleman Shaw, John Rifleman: Belisie, Danny

Radioman: Gross, Albert Platoon Sgt. SFC Teal

Michael J. Conley

" MITT-48th Aids Training for Transition   Atlanta Journal

By Spc 4 Tracy J. Smith

48th CBT Public Affairs

'MTT' – 48th Aids Training for Transition

by SPC Tracy J. Smith
48th CBT Public Affairs

CAMP STRIKER, Baghdad , Iraq , June 6, 2005 -- It promises to be a very dangerous job. But it is one of the 48th Brigade Combat Team's most important missions – the coalition team for training Iraqi forces. This, according to First Sergeant Mike Conley, a 2nd Battalion, 121st Infantry First Sergeant and veteran of the Vietnam War, is what he has trained his entire career to carry out. Now he's a member of a Military Training Team (MTT), a group of Georgia Guardsmen assigned to prepare Iraqi security forces to take on the job of protecting the fledgling republic.

"I've spent a lifetime training to do this mission," Conley said as he reviewed a convoy route with a MIT training team leader. "We are rolling out with some of the best from the 48th Brigade to give the Iraqi people a fighting chance at a new opportunity."

The six vehicle convoy was slated to head south to Mahmudiyah , Iraq to marry-up with Soldiers of the 270th Armor Battalion who had been training Iraqi forces for the past year.

This mission has been described by military officials as the end-state of the transition process -- training Iraqis to handle

Clarifying the route to transition - 1SG Mike Conley (l), military training team (MTT) NCOIC and MTT team leader MAJ Raymond Bossert confirm the route and battle tactics for a convoy to Al Mahmudiyah, south of Baghdad . They are two of several soldiers handpicked to train Iraqis for transition of force protection responsibility. (U.S. Army photo by SPC Tracy J. Smith)

their own country and security. The training team maintains a heightened alert, admits Conley, because they face the same urban warfare tactics as do other forces -- roadside bombings, rocket-propelled grenades and mortar attacks.

"Make no mistake the mission is dangerous," states Master sergeant Tony Winters of Headquarters and Headquarters Company, 2nd Battalion, 121st Infantry. "We are ready to handle any situation that may come our way and we will give the Iraqi's the same advantage."

"The IED (Improvised Explosive Device) threat is the main threat on this convoy," cautioned Major Raymond D. Bossert, the training team leader and a business owner from Douglasville , GA. Bossert did not underestimate the potential for danger as he continuously emphasized safety in his mission briefing. "We shoot and roll, no stopping! There is no change in that battle drill. It's all amber terrain, (meaning threatening activity has occurred within the last 24 hours). So stay alert. Any medical evacuations will be pushed forward to Mahmudiyah."

A one year mission awaits this motivated team of fighters once safely in their training area. "We are not here to train an army," said Conley, "we are here to build a nation."

Camp Striker, Baghdad. Iraq June 6, 2005

It promises to be a very dangerous job. But it is one of the 48th Brigade Combat Team's most important missions-the coalition team for training Iraqi forces. This, according to First Sergeant Mike Conley, a 2nd Battalion, 121st Infantry First Sargent and veteran of the Vietnam War, is what he has trained his entire career to carry out. Now he is a member of a Military Training Team (Mitt), a group of Georgian Guardsmen assigned to prepare Iraqi security forces to take on the job of protecting the fledgling republic.

I've spent a lifetime training to do this mission" Conley said as he reviewed a convoy route with a Mitt training team leader. "We are rolling out with some of the best men from the 48th Brigade to give the Iraqi people a fighting chance at a new opportunity. The four vehicle convoy was slated to head south to Mahmudiyah, Iraq to merry up with Soldiers of the 270th Armor Battalion who had been training Iraqi forces for the past year.

The mission has been described by military officials as the end state of the transition process—training Iraqis to handle their own country and security. The training team maintains a heightened alert admits Conley, because they face the same urban warfare tactics as do other forces—roadside bombings, rocket propelled grenades and mortar attacks.

" Make no mistakes the mission is dangerous," states Master sergeant Tony Winters of Headquarters and Headquarters Company, 2nd Battalion, 121st Infantry, "We are ready to handle any situation that may come our way and we will give the Iraqi's the same advantage.

"The IED (Improvised Explosive Device) threat is the main threat on this convoy." Cautioned Major Raymond D. Bossert. The training team leader and a business owner from Douglasville, Georgia. Bossert did not underestimate the potential for danger as he continuously emphasized safety in his mission briefing. "We shoot and roll, no stopping! There is no change in that battle drill. It's all amber terrain (meaning threatening activity has occurred within the last 24 hours). So stay alert. Any medical evacuations will be pushed forward to Mahmudiyah."

A one year mission awaits this motivated team of fighters once safely in their training area. "We are not hear to train an army," said 1Sg Conley, "we are here to build a nation."

That day before heading down range we had a good dinner at a dinning faculty and I heard soldiers in there complain about not having the kind of ice cream they wanted. I almost laughed out loud. These people in the rear in the Green Zone had a life. They lived in houses and had air conditions running twenty four hours a day and they walked around complained about their jobs, the heat and the dust. What a joke they were.

I had my driver Sgt. Clifford Gardner to take us over to Charlie Company and looked up the First Sergeant and asked him about the mail. It was the first mail we had received since getting to Iraq. We had been in country three weeks and the snail mail had finally caught up with us.

Not Alone

Thank You

Thank you for serveing our country. I hope that your doing well. We are praying for you. When I grow up I want to be in the army like you.

from: Sydney 8

Here is one of the letters I received from the great young people back at Antioch Christian Church. I want to thank Christopher Phillips, Sarah Rohland, Wendy Oliver, Lindy Smith, Katy Thomas, Selena Maddox, Jessica Phillips, Joseph Hulen, Austin Torcotte, Brandi L., Kelsey Byrd, Noah Smith, Cody Berrong, John Thomas Moezzi, Matt Bath, Andrea Swindell, Haley Barden, Sophie Turcotte, Caroline Schulte, Julia Ragsdale, and their teachers Angela Barden, Peggy Freeman, and Rinae Edmonds. I took this mail to our tent and had over 20 pieces of mail and that many prayers from those little people back home.

This is how I see our job over there. We were all volunteers. We all knew this was going to be a dangerous job but it's one we wanted to do. It was not for the president of the United States nor the Flag of America. IT WAS FOR FREEDOM we all believed that a man ought to have the right to choose his freedom and we thought it was worth fighting for. Maybe that why the American men and women who serve this great country feels the way they do about our country. Little did I know that the first week of July 2005 things would go to hell in a handbag? In two incidents separated by only six days, eight soldiers from Alpha Company 2nd Platoon 121st Infantry regiment had been killed.

We (2nd Mitt team) had just moved into Mahmudiyah south of Baghdad about 30 kilometers south of Baghdad. We were busy training the second Battalion of fourth Brigade of the sixth Iraqi Arm. We had been shot at and a couple of times and they had sent mortar rounds into our base camp but nothing bad yet had happened to us. A couple of soldiers and a very good friend of mine from Canton Georgia had been wounded at Mahmudiyah but nothing like these men. We came in from training and Bear (LTC Joe Hoffman) told me they had been some soldiers killed from Alpha Company second foot. A bomb under a Humvee killed four men in a roadside IED. The initial report that was told to us was that they had rolled over a massive bombs hidden in the roads of a local supply line that we used every day. Their life was gone in an instant in brutal swiftness.

These were the first to die. The Alpha Company soldiers were the first to die from the 48th Brigade in blast generated by the IED. They were the weapons of choice used by the insurgents. Did I thank about it. Every time we got ready to lead a patrol and we left the wire to go down the road I thought about it. I made up the roster and tried to rotate the first Humvees every day that we go out. Also the second in a convoy is a very dangerous position. LC Hoffman and I would talk about that and we had to live with these decisions every day. We started going into Mahmudiyah and then we received word that General Steward Rodeheaver was coming down to our FOB (Forward Operations Base) Oh yes, he did show up and we even went into the town of Mahmudiyah and walked down their streets with the new Iraqi army we were training to show the people that we were not afraid. What a day that was. I was very nervous but our training was coming along and then we heard another report coming down the pipe line. Six days later Alpha Company second platoon was hit again and again lost four more men. It could have been anyone in the platoon or the same company but eight men in six days from one platoon. It's a cliché' some of us may not make it back "Then all of a sudden it had happened again. Oh my God help us.

That night in our little FOB **(Forward Operations Base) Named St. Michael** we got mortar again and the rockets came raining down on us and the Chicken house had caught on fire and it begin to burn. It was the biggest and best place we had there. It was very large brick building and where all of our supplies and ammunition was in there plus a lot of the men from the rear detachment lived there. All of the mitt team members lived in tents with sandbags around them. There was nothing we could do to stop the fire. There was nothing we could do about it. Men had been wounded and we were training the Iraqi army and getting ready for our first mission. We were taking the men we had been training and going to Yusufiyah to help open up a hospitals part of a joint mission with the Iraq Army. This was going to be our first major mission of operations involving the 48th Brigade Combat team. Yes, so you as readers would understand in those three weeks of training we had been on operation like road patrols and searching for IED's with these men and house searching and looking for the enemy. We had captured some of the enemy and had turned them over to the Iraqi army. We also had the men on the rifle ranges and taught them how to make formations for battle drills and how to react in case of an attack or caught out in the open. One of my jobs over there in a Mitt team was to teach. I have never saw such a mess. There was no discipline. No one was really in charge nor did they train. I wanted to get back to the basics and tech. Their weapons on the first day I inspected them were beyond being bad. They really did look like they had never been cleaned. Most of their guns M-16's or the AR-15 had two places to change the sight settings and the weapons I looked at had never been changed since the day they were manufactured. The men really did not know how to sight a weapon or they never even heard of zeroing a weapon. Special Equipment was brought in by Col Sartain and was given to LTC Hoffman. LTC Hoffman went with me to the firing ranges and we begin by giving classes in tents when it was well over 120 degrees F. We had no fans nor electricity there for cooling. The men we were training thought it was a joke until I took a cleaning rod and slapped the top of a wooded table to wake up half of the student's. I made them stand up while I gave a block of instructions. Three times in one day we gave classes and then went to the firing range and let them fire. Bring them back into the tents and then give the next lesson. They were really slow to catch on. Most had not ever really fired a weapon. I was asked to eat and go over to the Iraqi unit where we had some long talks with our counter partners and taught them how to properly to fire their rifles and zero their weapons now we were going to the next step.

Three days out I know I was very nervous. We had been training the Iraqi Army and they were beyond being good they were bad to awful. No safety considerations and their tactics were beyond being bad. In this book I can actually tell the readers that the first real blood I saw in Iraq was when men were loading the back of their own pickup trucks Toyota and a man had his finger on a trigger and shot and wounded three men getting into the back of a truck before a mission. It was not that his finger was on the trigger the first mistake was there was around in the chamber. Not Good. We had been on patrols and had even been on night patrols but we always stayed very close to our FOB now this was going to be different. We had fixed up a shooting range and had worked on marksmanship. I had taught knife throwing and patrolling techniques. SFC (SERGEANT First Class) Dyer had taught them about stacking to search a building and we had practiced all kinds of very basic training stuff but they were very slow to catch on. I became very tense and did very little sleeping at night. Each day I was getting less and less sleep and more and more work load. Loading up our Humvees and getting everything just right or perfect where ever man knew his job. Our 2nd Mitt team was coming together and we were getting better every day but the rest of the men we were training for the Iraqi army became quiet an alarm in our heads. I was having dreams and found it very hard to get to sleep and the heat was relent-less. Every day it was hotter than the day be-fore. Getting ready for the mission we had to make two runs back to the Green Zone and one was to pick up the money to pay the Iraqi Army on pay day. We drove back and I had at least twenty minutes to see and talk to First Sargent Mayfield. He said I had a lateral Appointment from MSG (Master Sargent) to 1sg (First Sargent active on the 1 June 2005. I told him I did not really believe any of that until I got the paper work. We both laughed at that. Our promotion in the 48th Infantry Brigade was beyond being bad. Paper work got lost and only the rear detachment people got any promotions. Any way we said our good byes and he handed my mail that had come to Charlie Company addressed as Field First Sargent and I took the money that we picked up and headed back down main supply route where the men had been killed two times in less than eight days. I knew then I was not feeling well. I was totally exhausted and beyond being tired. All I really wanted to do was get some sleep for maybe 20 hours. I dosed off going back to our base camp. Nothing happened on the way back and the next day we prepared to pay the Iraqi Army before heading out for Yusufiyah. We had traveled over the

same supply route as the men of Alpha Company had traveled
and had been killed but we saw donkeys and small carts and only
a very few vehicles along the way. I think to this day we stopped
and looked at the road about five kilometers from camp Liberty
where they had painted the road and there had been a very large
hole had blown up something but we did not see anything or hear
anything out of the ordinary. For two days going up and coming
back I had been more than nervous and had been on heightened
alert now we were back and I felt much better. On July 2nd we
had the men we had been training to line up in company
formation and roll call was made and I had asked LTC Hoffman
if each man could carry their own weapon with them when they
got paid. I was in the receiving line and I checked of every
weapon that came through and had three men to escort them out
the back door with their weapon and not allow them to
intermingle with those that had not been paid. In the end we had
over 520 named but there was only 280 names and rifle numbers
that had cleared. We found some men's name on leave and
others that were in the infirmary and others in the hospitals but
OH NO they did not have near as many men as we had drawn
monthly for to be paid. The story is this Official's in charge
wanted us to give him the money and he was going to pay the
soldiers. I don't really know what happened after I left there but
I do know that LTC Joe Hoffman was a police officer and a
detective back in the states and I am sure there was much more
to this story than I will ever know. I did go talk to a Colonel Ben
Sartain and we had a long talk about how they received their
money and why we as was much more to this story than I will
ever know. I did go talk to a Colonel Ben Sartain and we had a
long talk about how they received their money and why we as
Americans were paying the Ira my life I wo my life I would like
to tell and some things I would like to clear up and maybe before
I pass on to the great beyond some of these things might be made

a little clearer in my mind and I could make it much cleaner with myself. In this book I have on purpose lift some things out and others I did not even mention because this was just not he time to clear all of this up I have many questions in my own mind and would love to have as some clear answers. I would like to tell the whole story about things I saw and the great waste, and some things I would like to clear up and maybe before I pass on to the great beyond some of these things might be made a little clearer in my mind and I could make it much cleaner with myself. In this book I have on purpose lift some things out and others I did not even mention because this was just not he time to clear all of this up I have many questions in my own mind and would love have as some clear answers. qi army without any accountability. There is a lot in my life I would like to tell and some things I would like to clear up and maybe before I pass on to the great beyond some of these things might be made a little clearer in my mind and I could make it much cleaner with myself. In this book I have on purpose lift some things out and others I did not even mention because this was just not he time to clear all of this up I have many questions in my own mind and would love have as some clear answers.

July 4th 2005 in Iraq was a very hot day. I had been asked to serve the men meals at the kitchen and we as the top NCO's on this FOB (forward operating base) fed the men. In just three days we were heading for Indian country. The cooks and the rear detachments did all they could do to serve us a very good Fourth of July dinner. That afternoon we had rumors and the Company B 108th Armor from Canton, Georgia my home town and where I had started teaching and coaching back in 1982 brought their tanks down to our FOB St, Michael and I saw some of my friends that I would not see again for the rest of my life.

After a three hour convoy and over roads that we knew we were being watched every kilometer along the way until we pulled into Yusufiyah.

There were some concert building and lots of trash and a dirtier place I had never seen in my whole life. They said there was a hospital there. Right after we moved into this place we as the U.S. Army doctoring asked the people and the little boy who lived into the house to leave and the last I ever saw of him was his mother and dad and little sister was walking down a dirt road in Iraq with tears on their faces. Maybe I feel like after reading the new

spaper clippings and their story would have been more to the point if they had told what happened to this family. I never knew what ever happened to them except they were told to get out of their home and they did. I am not sure it was their home but anyway they were living there when we got there. I would not have taken my little dog Boo Boo into this place. It was beyond being awful. Poor people were trying to make mud into bricks from the same water they were drinking out of. We were very near the Euphrates River and there were some fig trees and other green shrubs but the cattle and goats were starving to death. We had out dated maps and no one we could trust. I did not trust and the longer I was there the less trust I had in the Iraqi army and their interpreters. Working in a Mitt team is a very dangerous job but when the men you work with begins to not trust the other side that we were trying to train things really get beyond strained. I for one did not want them to hear our briefing or our missions before we left the wire and then they all seem to have cell phones and they could talk in different dialect so we could not understand them.

1st Sergeant Michael Conley and his driver Sgt. Clifford Gardner

We ran our first mission and we left the wire and went into enemy territory and then within two hours we were near a farm and watching men swap money and things being loaded into the back of a Toyota pickup truck. The next day we were able to take a unit of army infantry and with the helicopters overhead we went back and checked this area out and they ended up arresting three men and a lot of electrical wiring and some very old mortar rounds and maybe some 105 that were terrible rusty but would be used to make road side bombs. These men we also turned over to the Iraqi army and took away to a prison someplace. On the way back to our base camp with three other Humvees we became lost on unmarked roads and I stopped the convoy and after much talking and deliberating we decided to stay there for the day light. I was so afraid of hitting a IED's with every mile we traveled and every time the tires took a round turn it was that much closer to getting blown up. In the day light we traveled very slowly and our look out man is on the top and everyone is watching and looking at the road for any kind of a disturbance. We also had to keep our eyes on the people we passed along the road or near a bridge. A small boy or even young girls would be along the side of the road or watching a bridge and have a phone in their hand. They would make a phone call and be sitting there watching us as we rolled up onto the bridge or to a certain place in the road and would give the signal to blow us up. Sometimes they received some kind of composition for this and other times they received goods or gifts from the enemy.

We stayed at Yusufiyah from the 7th of July until the 18th of July. We did a lot of good and captured some of the enemy and a lots of supplies. Maybe we did some good and in some small way I hope we did. I know that before we left there to go back to Mahmudiyah I was feeling so tired and had a horrible pain in my chest and in my left shoulder the last three days we were there. My last 24 hours of duty in the field I never left a small room in our building even though it was over 130 degrees inside that building and I drank water and eat saltine crackers. I could not go to sleep and my mind would not shut itself off. I felt awful. I did not go out on the last two road recon or the last two missions because I was feeling very sick at my stomach and my left shoulder was hurting now twenty four hours a day. I was not even able to talk very coherently and was more than aggravated at the way things were going. I had so little sleep the last three days before we finally got back to our little FOB St Michael I went immediately to see the Doctors when I could.

The Rest is History:
Medevac to Baghdad

The rest is history. I started to tell the medics and doctors' what was happening to me and they had me to sit down and started taking my vitals' signs. Within a very few minutes I heard them calling a medevac chopper from Baghdad. I had already had a heart attack and they called it a myocardial infraction. The chopper was coming into our compound when the rockets begin to fall on the landing zone and they rushed me over r to a bunker beneath the ground and there they gave me my very first nitro glycerin. Within a very few seconds I felt like the pressure was off my chest and I cold actually breath again.

On the helicopter ride back to Baghdad I looked our over the desert and I thanked God for given me a heart attack. My body was old. My mind had grown older and I did not want to go on with this. It was just much more than I could take. To me the heat was the most horrible thing in my whole life. It was relentless Day after bloody day the heat into the 130 degrees F or even if you said it in degrees Celsius at 54 degrees "that is hot". On July the 4th back at a base camp I helped served the meal in the mess tent that was mostly underground and at noon on that day it was 136 degrees F. That evening during the one hour before darkness the temperature dropped almost 60 degrees in under one hour. That will put a chill into your old bones.

I was more than ready to go home. I left the Baghdad hospital two days later and they flew me down to Ali Ali Salem and then on down to Kuwait where they kept be for two days. I weighed a little over 136 lbs and body was tired beyond being tired. I asked or even in this book I begged not to go. I did not want to be sent over there and I knew my energy and enthusiasm that I had had for so many years was all gone. I had talked to the angels and they had sent me cards and sent me messages through the roughest of times and now they were signing and I was happy when I found out I was going back to the states. I had by now pulled more than forty years in the military and there was not anything I had left to prove to anyone especially myself. My angels had traveled with me and looked after me now I was going home to my wife to our family and our little home in the North Georgia Mountains where I wanted to live in peace and quiet for the rest of my life.

After a stopover in Stuttgart, Germany they sent me to Bethesda in Washington D.C. and then to Walter Reed where they finally got my orders and was going to send me to fort Gordon, Georgia. I flew into Fort Gordon, Georgia on a not so hot Aug.11th 2005. There to meet me was the whole world to me. This is what I had been hoping and fighting for was my beautiful wife. No horns. No drums No my children lived less than one hundred miles away but they did not show up. No parades and no one else around just me and her. This was more than great with me. I would be transferred to Fort Stewart to an army medical battalion and would spent the next five months there. My children never ever came to see me. I never received any cards or mail from them. I did receive some mail and letters from Antioch Christian Church (my little angels) not alone and from a small community not far from here called Bridge Mill.

I pulled another two years in the Army Reserve and all I did was train Army Reserves and go to post like camp Atterbury, Indiana, and work with National Guard and I also went over to Camp Shelby, Mississippi. One of my first duty stations I was given when I got to Fort Gillem was to be assigned as the NCOIC of a training team at Fort Polk, Louisiana. On, my a job it was in early March we hit the swamps and the bayou country off western Fort Polk, Louisiana. I had a blast as long as I received some rest each night and had been gaining a little weight. I was tired most of the time and had lost my spirit to be the best I could be. My body in the morning was older and felt stiff and I always very tired. As each day went by I grew more tired and more exhausted. I had no strength. What was once a easy movement phase or crossing became almost and impossibility to do any more. I just knew my days were over. My unit at Fort Gillem gave me a pat on my back and a Sergeant Major Big John that had served with me in Company B, 3d Battalion 11th Special Forces Group back in the 1970's gave me a gift as I walked out the door on my last day. I believe they just kept me around to give classes and to help some of the younger soldiers but I never really felt like I was worth it. My last walk I came out the door and there in front of me was most of my unit in the Army Reserve and they were lined up on both sides of the walk and as I walked in front of them some called me top dog or commandant Sgt. Major and there in the last team was a captain as he shook my hand he told me they were putting in the paper work for one last medal. Pryor to this I had told the Sargent Major Big John Callaway I did not want any more medals as the one's I was wearing most of them was because when my buddies and brothers were dying around me and men were getting killed I had been awarded a medal. He said he would not put me in for a parade or a medal. I received on the following year on my birthday a Meritorious Service medal and it said on the citation for 42 plus years of service as Regular Army, Paratrooper, Ranger and a Green Beret.

My dreams of jumping out of an airplane and going off to war had been real and now I had seen and done all a body could ever do. I had served with some of the finest fighting men in the world and had worn a Black Beret of the army Rangers and a

Green Beret as a Special Forces. Most of all we had the one fine thread that held us all together. I had been a paratrooper and a jump master. My dreams had come true the angels had been with me.

Team 2nd Mitt team (Stallions)
Col. Ben Sartain Comanding Officier in Charge
LtC Joe Hoffman in charge of the second Mitt team
1SG NCOIC Michael J. Conley   2nd Mitt Team 1st Sgt
Platoon Sgt. SFC Teal, 1st Squad Leader SSG Belisle   Team leader SSG Morgan   SSG Ruffenn Driver, SSG Rueffen gunner Sgt Jonier Sgt Gross, Sgt Spies, Sp4 Spies, Sp4 Epps,

2nd Squad Leader SSG Douglas   team leader SSG Gardner Sgt Tidwell gunner   Sp4 Allen driver PFC Bernardi rifleman SSG Matherson weapons specialist SFC King Rear detachment CO commander Lt. Walton   Supply/ TOC SSG Shaw

	NCO EVALUATION REPORT		SEE PRIVACY ACT STATEMENT
✛	For use of this form, see AR 623-205; the proponent agency is ODCSPER		IN AR 623-205, APPENDIX C

PART I – ADMINISTRATIVE DATA

a. NAME (Last, First, Middle Initial)	b. SSN	c. RANK	d. DATE OF RANK	e. PMO
CONLEY, MICHAEL		SFC	030111	11B

f. UNIT, ORG, STATION, ZIP CODE OR APO, MAJOR COMMAND		g. REASON FOR SUBMISSION	
Co C 1st Battalion 121st Infantry, Camp Liberty, Iraq APO AE 09372 48th BCT		2	ANNUAL

h. PERIOD COVERED		i. RATED MONTHS	j. NON-RATED CODES	k. NO. OF ENCL	l. RATED NCO COPY (Check one and Date)			m. PSC Initials	n. CMD Code
FROM YYYY MM	THRU YYYY MM						Date		
2004 10	2005 09	12			1. Given to NCO				
				X	2. Forwarded to NCO				NG

PART II – AUTHENTICATION

a. NAME OF RATER (Last, First, Middle Initial)	SSN	SIGNATURE	
MAYFIELD, BOBBY	264-53-6041		

RANK, PMOSC/BRANCH, ORGANIZATION, DUTY ASSIGNMENT		DATE
1SG, 11Z5H, Co C 1st Battalion 121st Infantry, Camp Liberty, Iraq APO AE 09372, First Sergeant		050816

c. NAME OF SENIOR RATER (Last, First, Middle Initial)	SSN	SIGNATURE	
FOURNIER, ANTHONY D.	255-37-6362		

RANK, PMOSC/BRANCH, ORGANIZATION, DUTY ASSIGNMENT		DATE
CPT, 11A00, Co C 1st Battalion 121st Infantry, Camp Liberty, Iraq APO AE 09372, Co Commander		050816

c. NAME OF REVIEWER (Last, First, Middle Initial)	SSN	SIGNATURE	DATE
		SIGNATURE	DATE
JACKSON, MARK C.	321-68-1328		

RANK, PMOSC/BRANCH, ORGANIZATION, DUTY ASSIGNMENT		DATE
LTC, 11A00, HHC 2nd Battalion 130th Infantry, Camp Liberty, Iraq APO AE 09372, BN Commander		050816

e. ☐ CONCUR WITH RATER AND SENIOR RATER EVALUATIONS	☐ NONCONCUR WITH RATER AND/OR SENIOR RATER EVAL (See attached)

PART III – DUTY DESCRIPTION (Rated)

a. PRINCIPLE DUTY TITLE	b. DUTY MOSC
PLATOON SERGEANT	11M40

c. DAILY DUTIES AND SCOPE (To include as appropriate people, equipment, facilities and dollars)

Serves as the principal noncommissioned officer; provides tactical and technical guidance to subordinates and professional to superiors in the accomplishment of their duties; leads, supervises, and trains subordinate personnel; plans, coordinates, supervises, and participates in activities pertaining to organization, training, combat operations, intelligence gathering, and communications; supervises proper operation, maintenance, and accountability of all equipment and weapons assigned to the unit; ensures the constant physical fitness and mental readiness of the unit; monitors the morale and general welfare of the unit.

d. AREAS OF SPECIAL EMPHASIS
Field logistic support

e. APPOINTED DUTIES
Family Readiness Group Liaison

f. COUNSELING DATES	INITIAL	LATER	LATER	LATER
	041115	050222	050502	050828

PART IV – ARMY VALUES/ATTRIBUTES/SKILLS/ACTIONS (Rated)

a. ARMY VALUES   Check either "YES" or "NO". Comments are mandatory for "No" entries, optional for "Yes" entries.

			YES
V A L U E S	Loyalty Duty Respect Selfless Service	1. LOYALTY: Bears true faith and allegiance to the U.S. Constitution, the Army, the unit, and other soldiers	X
		2. DUTY: Fulfills their obligations	X
		3. RESPECT/EO: Treats people as they should be treated	X
		4. SELFLESS-SERVICE: Puts the welfare of the nation, the Army, and subordinates before their own	X
		5. HONOR: Lives up to all the Army values	X
		6. INTEGRITY: Does what is right – legally and morally	X
	Honor Integrity Personal Courage	7. PERSONAL COURAGE: Faces fear, danger, or adversity (physical and moral)	X
		Bullet comments:	
		o treats all soldiers fairly and equally	
		o does the right thing when no one is watching	
		o places the good of the unit ahead of his own	

DA FORM 2166-8, OCT 2001	REPLACES DA FORM 2166-7, SEPT 87, WHICH IS OBSOLETE

Michael J. Conley

RATED NCO'S NAME (Last, First, Middle Initial)	SSN	THRU DATE 2003 09	
CONLEY, MICHAEL			

PART IV - ... VALUES/NCO RESPONSIBILITIES

COMPETENCE	o successfully mobilized his platoon for Operation Iraqi Freedom
	o personally remediated soldiers who performed poorly, resulting in 100% pass rate for all rated tasks during mobilization
EXCELLENCE SUCCESS NEEDS IMPROVEMENT	o promoted 22% of the soldiers in his platoon at least once

PHYSICAL FITNESS & MILITARY BEARING	APFT PASS 0605 HEIGHT/WEIGHT 72 176 YES
	o set the standard for the platoon by scoring 241 or better on APFT
	o consistently scores among the highest in the company for his age group
EXCELLENCE SUCCESS NEEDS IMPROVEMENT	o doubled the number of soldiers in the platoon passing the APFT the first time

LEADERSHIP	o acted as Company First Sergeant on numerous occasions
	o was the Senior NCO for the MET's team during OIF III
EXCELLENCE SUCCESS NEEDS IMPROVEMENT	o personally involved in helping soldiers with family problems find solutions

TRAINING	o qualified over 70% of platoon on multiple weapon systems
	o platoon had the highest marksmanship scores in the company
EXCELLENCE SUCCESS NEEDS IMPROVEMENT	o platoon was extremely well organized and set the example

RESPONSIBILITY & ACCOUNTABILITY	o platoon consistently set the standard on all inspections of barracks and of sensitive items
	o completed mobilization with no injuries due to unsafe acts
EXCELLENCE SUCCESS NEEDS IMPROVEMENT	o enrolled 40% of soldiers in online courses to further their military education

PART V - OVERALL PERFORMANCE AND POTENTIAL

	SENIOR RATER BULLET COMMENTS
	o soldier is the best NCO I have ever worked with
SUCCESS MARGINAL	o the success of our deployment is largely due to his management and leadership skills
	o soldier never shys from a challenge and encourages others to seek opportunities to challenge themselves

Company First Sergeant

Commander's Sergeant

Tnpcnurdnys Sergeant

RATER Overall performance	X		1 2 4 5 Successful Fair Poor	SENIOR RATER Overall potential for promotion and/or service in positions of greater responsibility	X		1 2 3 4 5 Superior Fair Poor

DA FORM 2166-8 OCT 2001

Mostly Special Forces go to other countries in teams to train their armies and most of the time this is done undercover, very quietly, you just do your job and then come home.

Fast striking, take a lick, make a snatch and get out of there.

I have served in the elite Special Forces, the Army Rangers and the time in Vietnam was with the famed 101st Airborne Division, 2nd Bn. 506th Airborne Infantry. I was a Currahee. This is an Indian word for "stand alone "There training goes back to World war 2 where they trained on Currahee Mountain in North Georgia and would become a famed and much highly decorated unit of the One Hundred and first Airborne Division. Their background and rich traditions go back to World War 2 where they fought against the Germans at the battle of the Bulge. I also served with the 82nd Airborne Division and Company D Rangers, Muncie Indiana, and Company H Long Range Surveillance Unit in Newnan, Georgia the Georgia National guard. I also served in the United States Marine Corp Reserve and the United States Army Reserve. My tour of duty has lasted from the summer of 1966 to the end of the road in October, 2008. My last three years were with the Army Reserve at Fort Gillem, Georgia where I served as an Instructor in small unit tactics, urban warfare and Mount training and a lane instructors training the Army National guard and the Army Reserve getting ready for their turn in Iraq or Afghanistan. I also spent a lot of my time training men how to fire different kinds of weapons on different kind of rifle ranges such as the M-16 , M-4 and three different types of machine guns from the M-60's to , 240 Bravos and the 240 Charlie, on our last trip to Iraq my men would carry the SAW(squad automatic weapon) which fired a 5.56mm round the same as the M-4 and AR 15 rifle better known as the M-16 we had carried so many years earlier in Vietnam. Our unit also worked on the firing ranges with the Bradley Fighting Vehicles where we used the twenty millimeter guns and the co-axel 240Bravo. I have served as a Bradley commander in a mechanized unit with the 48th Infantry Brigade and found it to be very fast, very loud and very hard to camouflage it at night. No really that's a joke on my part. I found getting the men out of the back of a Bradley was not much different than going in by helicopter and a lot of the same tactic tics were also employed against the enemy. The last unit I served with overseas during my final tour in Iraq was the Georgia National Guards. These men made me so very proud and the officer corps here in the state and they did a very good job from the very top man to the lowest private in the field. I loved the men I trained with and those I served in the field with and the men I fought with. I had a lot of admiration for the whole unit. General Stewart Rodeheaver was the commander of the 48th Infantry Brigade down though the platoon leaders on the ground in getting the 48th Infantry Brigade up and ready to go do a very dangerous mission in a very short amount of time. I also thought and have told people my commander in Charlie Company from Gainesville, Georgia Captain Anthony Fournier` was as good a captain as I ever served with in my 42 years. I had also served with a Captain Michael Lipper in Alpha Company and I thought both of these men were very good officers. I also served under a very good friend for many years and had worked with the first Sargent Bobby Mayfield and he did a most wonderful job of letting me as a MITT team leader take the ball and run with it as I saw fit. First Sargent Mayfield double slotted me and put me in for a first Sargent slot and gave me the title of Field First Sgt serving in a double slot with him as a first Sargent.

First Sergeant Mayfield and Capt. Fournier giving me my last promotion May 8th, 2005

Both of these men did all they could do to run a great company but we truly enjoyed working hard and getting ready to go to war was a fun time for most of us. Together these two men had the very best company in the forty eight infantry brigade and ran their company's even though there were some very difficult times they gave inspiration and compassion to their company and to their men. One of the biggest problems had in the National Guard was trying to get any one promoted. In the line company's we could not get hardly anyone promoted. Yes, the rear detachments and the rear echelon were able to get promoted and they also made sure the clerks did receive medals for going overseas and they also go their promotions I for one never received my promotions papers in my hand or got paid as an E-8 over seas until I was back here in the states in a Medical Hold Battalion down at Fort Stewart, Georgia. They did back date it and made it retroactive but I thank it was ashamed that some of our boys and young men were killed over in Iraq and they were still wearing PFC (Private First Class) and they had been in the National Guard for over two years and one man who had been in for almost five years and he was still a private.. A big thing in the Georgia National Guard. As soon as we left Fort Stewart Georgia and headed out to Fort Irwin, California they begin to build the Mitt teams with Colonial Ben Sartain and Lieutenant Joe Hoffman and they selected me to help head up what would become known as the Mitt Teams. We would go about training the Iraqi army and teaching them about tactics and weapons qualifications and how to run patrols and supervise these men and help them to take over the army once we were gone. The National Guard and Army Reserves are fighting in a new kind of war. They are serving in war on terrorism in faraway countries and in a new environment of the highlands and mountains in Afghanistan and the Sands of Iraq.

THE UNITED STATES OF AMERICA

TO ALL WHO SHALL SEE THESE PRESENTS, GREETING: THIS IS TO CERTIFY THAT THE PRESIDENT
OF THE UNITED STATES OF AMERICA AUTHORIZED BY EXECUTIVE ORDER, 16 JANUARY 1969 HAS AWARDED

THE MERITORIOUS SERVICE MEDAL

TO   SERGEANT FIRST CLASS MICHAEL J. CONLEY
              1ST BATTALION, 347TH REGIMENT

FOR EXCEPTIONALLY MERITORIOUS SERVICE FOR OVER FORTY YEARS AS A LEADER IN THE ARMY.
SERGEANT FIRST CLASS CONLEY MAINTAINED HIS FOCUS ON THE SOLDIER AS THE MILITARY'S MOST
IMPORTANT ASSET. ULTIMATELY, HE SET THE EXAMPLE OF THE WARRIOR ETHOS BEFORE ITS CONCEPTION
TO LEAD THE ARMY RESERVE INTO THE NEXT CENTURY AND HAS LEFT A MARK ON ALL SERVICE MEMBERS
WITH WHOM HE SERVED. SERGEANT FIRST CLASS CONLEY'S PERFORMANCE REFLECTS GREAT CREDIT UPON
HIM, THE 188TH INFANTRY BRIGADE, FIRST ARMY DIVISION EAST AND THE UNITED STATES ARMY.

FROM 21 OCTOBER 1998 – 20 OCTOBER 2008

GIVEN THIS 1ST DAY OF DECEMBER 2009

PERMANENT ORDER #341-01
HEADQUARTERS
FIRST ARMY DIVISION EAST
FORT MEADE, MARYLAND

MICHAEL BEDNAREK
MAJOR GENERAL, US ARMY
COMMANDING

DA FORM 4980-13, NOV 97

This is a true story and after 42 years of Military History it encompasses much of my life as a soldier, a Green Beret, a Ranger and a Ranger Instructor. I have served as a team leader, a squad leader, a platoon Sargent, a Field First Sergeant in Iraq and served as the Senior Operations Non Commissioned Officer in the Republic of Georgia and as First Sergeant and a NCOIC of a Mitt team in Iraq. I must surely tell the truth that all of my dreams have come true and some way on beyond what I could ever have hoped for. I did actually get to fly in an airplane and later I found I had at least 286 parachute jumps and I have no idea how many times I did Jump Master Duties. Sometimes at the Mountain Ranger Camp in Dahlonega we would do Jump Master duties and then after all the students had jumped and we checked the helicopter to make sure all were gone we would jump in behind them and take over the grading stage of the movement phase. I have trained some of America's bravest fighting men and took them into battles.

I have been blessed with a long life and many friends. I have a wonderful wife who has stayed with me for more than thirty years. I do know some parts of it was very rough on her because I was gone some times for a year at time with only maybe a short week or two at home and then would leave again. As we now have been married for over thirty years and in those years I belonged to one kind of the military or another for at least twenty seven of those years. Now I live in peace and enjoy my time working on a small farm and working in the garden in Cherokee County Georgia lying at the foothills of the Blue Ridge Mountains.

Before I had a chance to finish my book I was invited to Camp Frank D. Merrill and there I learned that I had been nominated for the Ranger Hall of Fame in June, 2014 and the board accepted my packet on July 3, 2014. It really does not matter to me if I ever get this award but the fact that others believed that I deserve this very prestigious award makes me feel great. The Selection for this will be next July 6th. 20115 at Fort Benning, Georgia at the Infantry Museum

Following is a summary of 1st Sgt. Michael J. Conley's 42 years of military history. It encompasses much of his life as a soldier, a Green Beret, a Ranger and a Ranger Instructor. He has served as a team leader, a squad leader, a platoon Sergeant, a Field First Sergeant in Iraq, as the Senior Operations Non-Commissioned Officer in the Republic of Georgia and Afghanistan, and as a First Sergeant and a NCOIC as a Mitt team in Iraq. Over these 42 years he accumulated 41 medals and awards.

LOCAL | HOOSIER TIMES | SUNDAY, AUGUST 24, 2014 | A5

COMMENTARY

Military service leads to prestigious nomination

Former Mitchell resident First Sgt. Michael J. Conley described his nomination for the U.S. Army Mountain Ranger Hall of Fame as being "beyond my wildest dreams."

He added, "I had never even thought about ever getting anything like this."

"I feel more than anything that I have been humbled by the situation, for the men I've worked with and have trained."

Conley is one of five men who were chosen by the U.S. Mountain Ranger Association Nominating Committee. (One of the five died last week.) The final selection for the 2015 inductee into the hall of fame won't be known until July 6.

Conley is the son of the late Robert H. Conley, who was a postal carrier in Bedford, and Laura Ellen Conley Boone, who lived in Lawrence County. Conley will be 66 in October. He is a graduate of Mitchell High School and returned to his hometown to ride in the Mitchell Persimmon Festival Parade

Roger Moon
T/M COLUMNIST

with other veterans in 2008. At the time, he was less than a month away from retiring after having served in the Army for 42 years.

The hall of fame nominee boasts impressive military and civilian accomplishments that factored into his nomina-

tion. His resume and a list of his service-time medals are outlined in a summary prepared for Conley as part of the nomination process. Conley boasts a long list of connections to Lawrence County residents with military credentials.

After his high school graduation, Conley joined the Army in 1966 with his brother William Conley as part of the "buddy" system. Both went to Fort Knox, Ky, for basic training and went to airborne jump school together in May 1967. William broke his leg, but Michael continued, made his final

jumps and graduated on June 10, 1967.

He arrived in Vietnam in November 1967 and became part of the TET Offensive in 1968. He was in the Hobo Woods during the early days of the TET Offensive. Three times in one night, his platoon was overrun by the enemy. By sunrise the following morning, Conley was one of only eight men still alive.

Among highlights of Conley's career, as presented in the hall of fame nomination summary, were his receiving his first Air Medal (for 50 combat assaults into an enemy-held landing zone) and receiving the Bronze Star for saving the life of the company commander in September 1968 during the battle on Bloody Ridge.

Conley returned to the United States, but later returned to Vietnam for another six-month tour. He attended the Army Ranger School beginning in October 1973. He worked out of Camp Atterbury in 1974 and then, for 30 years, served with Company H Long Range Surveillance Unit in Newman, Ga. And, in more recent years, served

in Iraq.

The Ranger nominating committee was impressed with Conley's activities as a civilian since his retirement. Among those activities is his role as a teacher and tutor at Chattahoochee Technical College in Canton, Ga. As a civilian, he has taught general science, biology, chemistry and physics and U.S. history in public schools. He also has coached football and basketball, with one of his teams having won a state championship.

Conley belongs to a local VFW post and works with veterans as their service officer. He also rides with the Patriot Guards and sometimes is asked to speak at the national cemetery where heroes of yesteryear are laid to rest.

Even if Conley isn't ultimately chosen as next year's non-commissioned inductee into the Ranger Hall of Fame, he considers it a great honor to have been nominated.

"I am blessed," Conley said. "I have two legs, two arms, I have been burned — second- and third-degree burns. I've been wounded, but I'm still alive."

**To the U.S. Mountain Ranger Association Nominating
Committee
Ranger Hall of Fame
July 3, 2014**

1st Sgt. Michael J. Conley (Retired) joined the U.S. Army in the summer of 1966 at the age of 17. He entered the Army Reserve Program under a 90 Day Delayed Entry Program with a waiting period until he turned 18 years old. On November 20, 1966 he enlisted in the Army with his brother, William H. Conley, (Bill) on the buddy program. They went through basic training together at Fort Knox, Ky, where Michael won the Company Shooting Award for being the best shot in his basic training company. He finished second on the Rifle Range Shoot Out in his training battalion. After completing advanced individual training at Aberdeen Proving Ground in Maryland, his brother finished at the top of their class and he was promoted to PFC (Private First Class) then they were off to Fort Benning, Ga. Or Airborne Jump School. On their third jump, Michael's brother broke his leg, but Michael continued, made his final two jumps and graduated from Airborne Jump School as a PFC on 10 June 1967.

PFC Conley's first assignment was at Fort Bragg, NC, with Alpha Company 594th Infantry, 82nd Airborne Division. The 82nd Airborne Division was called in to help the police in the race riots in Detroit. Mi. Two months later the call came down the 101st Airborne Division out of Fort Campbell, Ky. They were looking for volunteers to help fill out their ranks as they were headed for Vietnam. On the 9 September 1967, PFC Michael J. Conley reported to Alpha Company, 2nd Bn 506th Infantry, 101st Airborne Division. The company spent two months training and preparing for war. On 2 December 1967 they flew out of Fort Campbell, Ky headed for Vietnam. After landing at the Bien Hoa Airbase, they moved north to Phuc Vinh, a small village on the northern end of the Iron triangle. ON 19 December 1967, PFC Michael J. Conley won his first Soldier's Medal for saving another's soldier's life. PFC Conley pulled this soldier out of a burning, exploding helicopter after it had been shot down.

Corporal Conley was in the Hobo Woods during the early days of the TET Offensive; three times in one night his platoon was overrun by the enemy. By sunrise the following morning, he was one of only eight men still alive. He received a field grade promotion on 17 May 1967 to Sgt. E-5, as well as taking over as the Platoon Sgt, for Alpha Company. Sgt Conley was wounded on 20 August 1968 where he won his Purple Heart, and was medevac's out. By the early days of September, Sgt. Conley had reunited with his unit as they were preparing for the A-Shau Valley. On 16 September 1967 members of Alpha Company completed an air assault into the northern end of the A-Shau Valley. Sgt Conley and ten members of the original Alpha Company were on helicopters as they came in to the LZ. There he won his Air Medal for 50 combat assaults into enemy-held landing zone (LZ). During the same operation, Sgt Conley killed a team of 8 NVA trying to shoot up the command post and was awarded his Bronze Star with Valor where many wounded and dying men lay on the ground waiting on a medevac helicopter.

Upon returning to the United States Sgt. Conley was sent back to Fort Bragg, NC. Assigned to the 47th Combat Eng. 12th Support Brigade. On April 1st 1969 he then returned to Vietnam for another six month tour. There he was awarded his 1st Silver Star for fighting on Hamburger Hill in May 1969. Given credit for saving a medic and three wounded soldiers by rescuing them in the dark. After the second tour in Vietnam, Sgt Conley attended the Army Ranger School beginning in October 1973, He graduated after winning the Merrill's Marauders Award upon graduation in February 1974. In the summer of 1974 after being promoted to SSgt. E-6 he worked out of Camp Atterberry, Indiana. There he taught the Indiana National Guard helicopter assault techniques and also taught airborne tactics to Company D Rangers and survival training to other National Guardsmen. In the winter of 1974 he received his marching orders to return to Camp Frank D. Merrill as a Mountain Ranger Instructor. He spent the next two years as a Mountain Ranger Instructor where he first worked as a mountaineering instructor and later as a member of the Mountain Patrolling Committee. Teaching cross country navigation, mountain climbing, and parachuting into very small drop zones in the mountainous terrain along with actions at objective and many different kinds of ambushes.

Over the next 30 plus years Staff Sergeant Conley would serve three years with Company H LRSU (Long Range Surveillance Unit) out of Newnan, Ga. He spent three years with the 4th Marine Division, of the United States Marine Corp in training for desert warfare; they also trained in Alaska with the Alaskan National Guard and one summer in the mountains of Southern Germany. Later he joined the Georgia National Guard and continued his military career as a field Instructor with the Georgia National Guard where he worked with the RTI (Regional Training Instructors) out of Macon, Ga for four years. In the early spring 2004 he was sent from here to the republic of Georgia to work with the American Embassy personnel under HQ USEUCOM Special Forces Command to the Far East. He was serving as an advisor to the Republic of Georgia Army when they were attacked by the Russian Army in the area of northern Ossetia, on the northern border. The Russians were turned back after some very heavy fighting. Next SFC Conley went with the Georgian Army to the mountains of Afghanistan. He did not see any fighting in Afghanistan, but did go on patrols and into villages and saw some very, very poor people. Maybe these were the poorest people I ever saw in my life. The mountains were so steep and some even had snow on the top of them in September. I returned to Georgia and then was getting ready to come home and bring my little dog Spotty with me. I thought I was going to be finished with the military and I sure needed a rest very bad I really had thought at this time I would be getting out of the army. I was beyond being tired and my body and mind was worn out.

I returned home, only to be reactivated after 18 days at home to serve as the 2nd Mitt team NCOIC where he became a field first

Sergeant with the 48th Infantry, Brigade, Georgia National Guard and was sent to Iraq. He was promoted to First Sergeant on 5tm May, 2005 before shipping out to Iraq. He became the NCOIC of the second Mitt Team along with the OIC Lt. Col Joe Hoffman. Their team was sent into one of the worst places in Iraq known as the "Triangle of Death" to teach and work and live with the 2nd Bn. 4th Brigade, 6th Iraqi Army. After a heart attack in mid-July, he was sent home to a medical hold battalion Fort Stewart, Ga. There is where he received his orders for his First Sergeant stripes in late October 2005 but back dated to time he served in Iraq. He would spend the next three years of his long career with the 1st Battalion, 347th Infantry Regiment training national guardsmen and Army Reservists all over the eastern United States. He retired with a letter in 2008 that said he had spent 42 years plus or minus in his military career in the defense of the United States of America.

As a civilian, Conley has taught and coached in public schools, He taught general science, biology, chemistry, and physics. His best subject was U.S. history and World History. He coached varsity basketball and football. When he was the head coach at Brandon Hall Preparatory School, his team had an undefeated year with the record of 29 wins, 0 losses, concluding with the team winning the State championship. In another year he was working as an assistant varsity coach when their team went to the State Finals and lost by one point, As the Varsity Football Coach in Bulloch County, Ga. His team was the best team they had had in years. He won the All Star Defensive Coach of the Year award in 1989 while working in Greenville, Ga. That team the patriots, finished fourth in the state triple A.

Michael has always demonstrated a desire to help others. He has been given very high marks where his superiors wrote, "Treats all soldiers fairly and equally, does the right thing when no is watching, places the good of the unit ahead of his own, and gave of his own personnel money to help others. Two different times in his long career he was given a soldiers medal for saving the life of another soldier under very high and stressful situations. He provided tactical and technical guidance to his subordinates. He has been an outstanding Ranger and has always kept the ranger's oath. He has always maintained a professional attitude and demeanor to his superiors regarding his accomplishments." Conley is now teaching and tutoring at Chattahoochee Technical College, in Canton, Ga. He also belongs to the local VFW- 2553 where he works with veterans, as their service officer. He also rides with the Patriot Guards and sometimes is asked to speak at the National Cemetery where these heroes of yesteryear are being laid to rest. He is a member of the Antioch Christian Church and helps others in every way possible, keeping the Rangers Oath.

The years have been long and some of the nights were even longer but my life as I have seen it has past so quickly it is really hard to believe. I would not ever have done anything different in my life and I have met and worked with some of the bravest men in our country. I have fought in three different wars and each one was different than the other two. I just know I left Vietnam with a wish that I would never fight or be alone again in my life. Now I know one is never alone, nor ever forgotten as long as we have memories of their smiles, the sound of the laughter, or see a sitting of the sun that those faces and all of those faces we have met with and fought with will be with me until the day or night I am gone. Thanks to all the angels and God for helping me get to this place in life. I am so lucky to have had friends and families that has helped me down the road of life.

I have now been working on this book for more than 6 years. I am 66 years old, I ride my motor cycle with the Patriot Riders. We often go to the National Cemetery in Cherokee County and help bury our fallen comrade. I also belong to the local VFW in Canton, Ga and serve them as a service officer. I have many good friends and even my old buddies still call me on my birthday. As a member of a Special Forces Association and also the Mountain Ranger Association, I get to see and talk to my friends and buddies from yesteryear. I have a great wife who loves me and I love her with all my heart. I am trying so hard to live in peace and quiet. I thank God for all of His blessings and a free country to live in. May all of my buddies get some kind of benefit out of this book as they read it and enjoy the rest of their lives.

The National Cemetery in Cherokee County Georgia, Memorial Day 2014

Walking across the Mountains of the Republic of Georgia 2005

I am looking forward to owning a home in the mountains where I can feel the spring breeze and watch the fall colors paint the great Blue Ridge Mountains. I look forward to the rest of my life in living in peace. I now know for sure I am a very blessed man and I will never be alone in this world because the angels have always been with me.

All the money above and beyond the cost to print this book will be given to the wounded warrior project. Michael J. Conley

Michael J. Conley

CAUTION: NOT TO BE USED FOR IDENTIFICATION PURPOSES
THIS IS AN IMPORTANT RECORD SAFEGUARD IT.
ANY ALTERATIONS IN SHADED AREAS RENDER FORM VOID

CERTIFICATE OF RELEASE OR DISCHARGE FROM ACTIVE DUTY

1. NAME (Last, First, Middle)	2. DEPARTMENT, COMPONENT AND BRANCH	3. SOCIAL SECURITY NUMBER
CONLEY, MICHAEL JOSEPH	ARMY/ARNGUS	

4a. GRADE, RATE OR RANK	b. PAY GRADE	5. DATE OF BIRTH (YYYYMMDD)	6. RESERVE OBLIGATION TERMINATION DATE (YYYYMMDD)
SFC	E07	19481020	00000000

7a. PLACE OF ENTRY INTO ACTIVE DUTY	b. HOME OF RECORD AT TIME OF ENTRY (City and state, or complete address if known)
WINDER, GEORGIA	350 BUFORD WEST WAY CANTON GEORGIA 30115

8a. LAST DUTY ASSIGNMENT AND MAJOR COMMAND	b. STATION WHERE SEPARATED
010121INBN HHC FWD NT	FORT STEWART, GA 31314-5019

9. COMMAND TO WHICH TRANSFERRED	10. SGLI COVERAGE	NONE
CO A 1ST BN 121ST IN (WPDAA0) 261E CROGAN ST LAWRENCEVILLE GA 30045	AMOUNT: $400,000.00	

11. PRIMARY SPECIALTY (List number, title and years and months in specialty. List additional specialty numbers and titles involving periods of one or more years.)	12. RECORD OF SERVICE	YEAR(S)	MONTH(S)	DAY(S)
63H4S H8 TRACKED VEHICLE MECH - 24 YRS 1 MOS //11B4P INFANTRYMAN - 24 YRS 1 MOS//NOTHING FOLLOWS	a. DATE ENTERED AD THIS PERIOD	2005		
	b. SEPARATION DATE THIS PERIOD	2005		
	c. NET ACTIVE SERVICE THIS PERIOD	0000	11	12
	d. TOTAL PRIOR ACTIVE SERVICE	0006	10	11
	e. TOTAL PRIOR INACTIVE SERVICE	0016	05	26
	f. FOREIGN SERVICE	0000	07	27
	g. SEA SERVICE	0000	00	00
	h. EFFECTIVE DATE OF PAY GRADE	2003	01	09

13. DECORATIONS, MEDALS, BADGES, CITATIONS AND CAMPAIGN RIBBONS AWARDED OR AUTHORIZED (All periods of service)	14. MILITARY EDUCATION (Course title, number of weeks, and month and year completed)
SILVER STAR (USA/USAF) (2ND AWARD)//SOLDIERS MEDAL (2ND AWARD)//BRONZE STAR MEDAL W/COMBAT DISTINGUISHING DEVISE "V"//BRONZE STAR//PURPLE HEART//MERITORIOUS SERVICE MEDAL//JOINT SERVICE ACHIEVEMENT MEDAL//ARMY GOOD CONDUCT MEDAL (2ND AWARD)//NATIONAL DEFENSE SERVICE MEDAL (3RD AWARD)//VIETNAM//CONT IN BLOCK 18	NONE//NOTHING FOLLOWS

15a. MEMBER CONTRIBUTED TO POST-VIETNAM ERA VETERANS' EDUCATIONAL ASSISTANCE PROGRAM		YES	X	NO
b. HIGH SCHOOL GRADUATE OR EQUIVALENT	X	YES		NO

16. DAYS ACCRUED LEAVE PAID 0.5	17. MEMBER WAS PROVIDED COMPLETE DENTAL EXAMINATION AND ALL APPROPRIATE DENTAL SERVICES AND TREATMENT WITHIN 90 DAYS PRIOR TO SEPARATION	YES	NO X

18. REMARKS
ITEM 12D ABOVE DOES NOT ACCOUNT FOR ANNUAL AND/OR WEEKEND TRAINING THIS SOLDIER MAY HAVE ACCOMPLISHED PRIOR TO DATE ENTERED IN ITEM 12A //INDIVIDUAL COMPLETED PERIOD FOR WHICH ORDERED TO ACTIVE DUTY FOR PURPOSE OF POST SERVICE BENEFITS AND ENTITLEMENTS //ORDERED TO ACTIVE DUTY IN SUPPORT OF OPERATION IRAQI FREEDOM IAW 10 USC 12302//MEMBER HAS COMPLETED FIRST FULL TERM OF SERVICE//SOLDIER SERVED IN SUPPORT OF OPERATION IRAQI FREEDOM WHILE SERVING IN KUWAIT AND IRAQ FROM 20050516 THRU 20051 //SOLDIER SERVED IN A DESIGNATED IMMINENT DANGER PAY AREA// //CONTINUED FROM BLK 13 : ARMY LAPEL BUTTON//CONT FROM BLOCK 13: SERVICE MEDAL//NON COMMISSIONED OFFICER PROFESSIONAL DEVELOPMENT RIBBON (3RD AWARD)//ARMY SERVICE RIBBON// OVERSEAS SERVICE RIBBON (3RD AWARD)//ARMED FORCES RESERVE MEDAL W M DEVICE (3RD AWARD)//RVN GALLOR UGIT (2ND AWARD) //REPUBLIC OF VIETNAM CAMPAIGN MEDAL (4TH AWARD)//SPECIAL FORCES TAB B//COMBAT INFANTRY BADGE (2ND AWARD)//PARACHUTIST (BASIC)//MASTER//SEE ATTACHED CONTINUATION SHEET

19a. MAILING ADDRESS AFTER SEPARATION (Include ZIP Code)	b. NEAREST RELATIVE (Name and address - Include ZIP Code)
350 BUFORD WEST WAY CANTON GEORGIA 30115	DOLORES L CONLEY 350 BUFORD WEST WAY CANTON GEORGIA 30115

20. MEMBER REQUESTS COPY 6 BE SENT TO	GA	DIRECTOR OF VETERANS AFFAIRS	X	YES	NO

21. SIGNATURE OF MEMBER BEING SEPARATED	22. OFFICIAL AUTHORIZED TO SIGN (Type name, grade, title and signature)
Michael J Conley	VIRGINIA GAMMONS, , HUMAN RESOURCES ASST

SPECIAL ADDITIONAL INFORMATION (For use by authorized agencies only)

23. TYPE OF SEPARATION	24. CHARACTER OF SERVICE (Include upgrades)
RELEASE FROM ACTIVE DUTY	HONORABLE

25. SEPARATION AUTHORITY	26. SEPARATION CODE	27. REENTRY CODE
AR 635-200, CHAP 4	LBK	NA

28. NARRATIVE REASON FOR SEPARATION
COMPLETION OF REQUIRED ACTIVE SERVICE

29. DATES OF TIME LOST DURING THIS PERIOD (YYYYMMDD)	30. MEMBER REQUESTS COPY 4 (Initials) M JC
NONE	

DD FORM 214-AUTOMATED FEB 2000   PREVIOUS EDITION IS OBSOLETE   MEMBER - 4

DD FORM 214 CONTINUATION PAGE

NAME: CONLEY, MICHAEL JOSEPH
SSN: 306-54-0863

CONT FROM BLOCK 18: PRCHT BADGE//PARACHUTIST BADGE//GLOBAL WAR ON TERRORISM SERVICE
MEDAL//IRAQ CAMPAIGN MEDAL//NOTHING FOLLOWS

SIGNATURE OF MEMBER BEING SEPARATED   OFFICIAL AUTHORIZED TO SIGN

ASST   VIRGINIA G AMMONS, GS07, HUMAN RESOURCES

4*A DD-214

AREAS RENDER FORM VOID

CERTIFICATE OF RELEASE OR DISCHARGE FROM ACTIVE DUTY

1. NAME (Last, First, Middle)	2. DEPARTMENT, COMPONENT AND BRANCH	3. SOCIAL SECURITY NO.
CONLEY, MICHAEL JOSEPH	ARNG	

4.a. GRADE, RATE OR RANK	4.b. PAY GRADE	5. DATE OF BIRTH (YYMMDD)	6. RESERVE OBLIG. TERM. DATE
SFC	E7	19481020	Year 0000 Month 00 Day 00

7.a. PLACE OF ENTRY INTO ACTIVE DUTY	7.b. HOME OF RECORD AT TIME OF ENTRY (City and state, or complete
STUTTGART, GERMANY	350 BUFORD WEST WAY CANTON, GA 30115

8.a. LAST DUTY ASSIGNMENT AND MAJOR COMMAND	8.b. STATION WHERE SEPARATED
HQ EUCOM ECJ4 (N092AA) APO AE 09131 E1	TRANSITION CENTER, STUTTGART GERMANY

9. COMMAND TO WHICH TRANSFERRED	10. SGLI COVERAGE	None
A COMPANY, 1/121ST IN BN 95 MAYNARD STREET WINDER, GA 30680	Amount: $ 250,000.00	

11. PRIMARY SPECIALTY (List number, title and years and months in specialty, list additional specialty numbers and titles involving periods of one or more years.)	12. RECORD OF SERVICE	Year(s)	Month(s)	Day(s)
11B4P INFANTRYMAN--00 YRS-05 MOS//NOTHING FOLLOWS	a. Date Entered AD This Period	2004	04	23
	b. Separation Date This Period	2004	10	18
	c. Net Active Service This Period	0000	05	26
	d. Total Prior Active Service	SEE BLOCK 18//		
	e. Total Prior Inactive Service	SEE BLOCK 18//		
	f. Foreign Service	0000	05	26
	g. Sea Service	0000	00	00
	h. Effective Date of Pay Grade	2003	01	10

13. DECORATIONS, MEDALS, BADGES, CITATIONS AND CAMPAIGN RIBBONS AWARDED OR AUTHORIZED (All periods of service)
SILVER STAR (2ND AWARD)//BRONZE STAR MEDAL (W/V DEVICE)//BRONZE STAR MEDAL//PURPLE HEART// MERITORIOUS SERVICE MEDAL//GOOD CONDUCT MEDAL//NATIONAL DEFENSE SERVICE MEDAL (2ND AWARD)// VIETNAM SERVICE MEDAL//NCO PROFESSIONAL DEVELOPMENT RIBBON (W/NUM 3)//ARMY SERVICE RIBBON// OVERSEAS SERVICE RIBBON (W/NUM 3)//COMBAT INFANTRY BADGE//MASTER//CON'T IN BLOCK 18

14. MILITARY EDUCATION (Course title, number of weeks, and month and year completed)
NONE.

15.a. MEMBER CONTRIBUTED TO POST-VIETNAM ERA VETERANS' EDUCATIONAL ASSISTANCE PROGRAM	Yes	No X	15.b. HIGH SCHOOL GRADUATE OR EQUIVALENT	Yes X	No	16. DAYS ACCRUED LEAVE PAID 7.5

17. MEMBER WAS PROVIDED COMPLETE DENTAL EXAMINATION AND ALL APPROPRIATE DENTAL SERVICES AND TREATMENT WITHIN 90 DAYS PRIOR TO SEPARATION	Yes	No X

18. REMARKS
DATA HEREIN SUBJECT TO COMPUTER MATCHING WITHIN DOD OR WITH OTHER AGENCIES FOR VERIFICATION PURPOSES AND DETERMINING ELIGIBILITY OR COMPLIANCE FOR FEDERAL BENEFITS//INDIVIDUAL COMPLETED PERIOD FOR WHICH ORDERED TO ACTIVE DUTY FOR PURPOSE OF POST-SERVICE BENEFITS AND ENTITLEMENTS//MEMBER HAS COMPLETED FIRST FULL TERM OF SERVICE//SUBJECT TO ACTIVE DUTY RECALL AND/OR ANNUAL SCREENING//SEPARATED FROM SERVICE ON TEMPORARY RECORDS AND SOLDIERS AFFIDAVIT. A DD FORM 215 WILL BE ISSUED TO PROVIDE MISSING INFORMATION OR TO CORRECT ANY INFO//CON'T FROM BLOCK 13: PARACHUTIST BADGE//PARACHUTIST BADGE//PATHFINDER BADGE//EXPERT MARKSMANSHIP BADGE (RIFLE M-16)//SPECIAL FORCES TAB//RANGER TAB//SOLDIERS MEDAL (2ND AWARD)//VIETNAM CROSS OF GALLANTRY UNIT CITATION W/BRONZE STAR//ARMY LAPEL BUTTON//GLOBAL WAR ON TERRORISM SERVICE MEDAL//AIR MEDAL//NOTHING Follows

19.a. MAILING ADDRESS AFTER SEPARATION (Include Zip Code)	19.b. NEAREST RELATIVE (Name and address - Include Zip Code)
350 BURFORD WEST WAY CANTON, GA 30115	MRS. DOLORES L. CONLEY (SPOUSE) SAME AS ITEM 19A

20. MEMBER REQUESTS COPY 6 BE SENT TO	GA	DIR. OF VET AFFAIRS X Yes	No	22. OFFICIAL AUTHORIZED TO SIGN (Typed name, grade, title and signature)
21. SIGNATURE OF MEMBER BEING SEPARATED SOLDIER NOT AVAILABLE FOR SIGNATURE				JERRY L. ANDERSON, TRANSITION SPECIALIST

SPECIAL ADDITIONAL INFORMATION (For use by authorized agencies only)

23. TYPE OF SEPARATION RELEASE FROM ACTIVE DUTY	24. CHARACTER OF SERVICE (Include upgrades) HONORABLE

25. SEPARATION AUTHORITY AR 635-200, CHAP 4	26. SEPARATION CODE LBK	27. REENTRY CODE NA

28. NARRATIVE REASON FOR SEPARATION COMPLETION OF REQUIRED ACTIVE SERVICE

29. DATES OF TIME LOST DURING THIS PERIOD NONE	30. MEMBER REQUESTS COPY 4 Initials

DD Form 214, NOV 88   Previous editions are obsolete.

MEMBER - 4

371

3AD DD-214   DEC. 30 2003

AREAS RENDER FORM VOI

CERTIFICATE F RELEASE OR DISCHARGE ..ROM ACTIVE DUTY

1. NAME (Last, First, Middle)	2. DEPARTMENT, COMPONENT AND BRANCH	3. SOCIAL SECURITY
CONLEY, MICHAEL JOSEPH	ARMY/ARNG	

4.a GRADE, RATE, OR RANK	4.b PAY GRADE	5. DATE OF BIRTH (YYYYMMDD)	6. RESERVE OBLIG. TERM. DA
SFC	E7	19481020	Year 2005 Month 01 Day

7.a PLACE OF ENTRY INTO ACTIVE DUTY	7.b HOME OF RECORD AT TIME OF ENTRY (City and state, or comple address if known)
CANTON, GA	350 BUFORD WEST WAY CANTON, GA 30115

8.a LAST DUTY ASSIGNMENT AND MAJOR COMMAND	8.b STATION WHERE SEPARATED
A CO 1/121ST INFANTRY TC	FORT GORDON, GA 30905-5000

9. COMMAND TO WHICH TRANSFERRED	10. SGLI COVERAGE	No
A CO -I/121ST INF (WPDAAO) WINDER, GA 30043	Amount: $ 250,000.00	

11. PRIMARY SPECIALTY (List number, title and years and months in specialty. List additional specialty numbers and titles involving periods of one or more years.)	12. RECORD OF SERVICE	Year(s)	Month(s)	Day(s)
11B5P INFANTRYMAN--37 YRS-7 MOS//63H5O TRACK VEH REPAIRER--37 YRS-0 MOS//NOTHING FOLLOWS	a. Date entered AD This Period	2003	06	16
	b. Separation Date This Period	2003	12	30
	c. Net Active Service This Period	0000	06	15
	d. Total Prior Active Service	0005	10	1.0
	e. Total Prior Inactive Service	0031	00	18
	f. Foreign Service	0000	00	00
	g. Sea Service	0000	00	00
	h. Effective Date of Pay Grade	2003	01	02

13. DECORATIONS, MEDALS, BADGES, CITATIONS AND CAMPAIGN RIBBONS AWARDED OR AUTHORIZED *(All periods of service)*
SILVER STAR (2ND AWARD)//SOLDIER'S MEDAL (2ND AWARD)//BRONZE STAR MEDAL WITH COMBAT DISTINGUISHED DEVICE "V"//BRONZE STAR MEDAL (2ND AWARD)//PURPLE HEART//MERITORIOUS SERVICE MEDAL//AIR MEDAL//ARMY COMMENDATION MEDAL//OVERSEAS SERVICE BAR (2ND AWARD)//ARMY GOOD CONDUCT MEDAL//NATIONAL DEFENSE SERVICE MEDAL (2ND AWARD)//VIETNAM SERVICE//CONT IN BLOCK 1

14. MILITARY EDUCATION *(Course title, number of weeks and month and year completed)*
NONE//NOTHING FOLLOWS

15.a MEMBER CONTRIBUTED TO POST-VIETNAM ERA VETERAN'S EDUCATIONAL ASSISTANCE PROGRAM	Yes	No X	15.b HIGH SCHOOL GRADUATE OR EQUIVALENT	Yes X	No	16. DAYS ACCRUED LEAVE PAID NONE

17. MEMBER WAS PROVIDED A COMPLETE DENTAL EXAM AND ALL APPROPRIATE DENTAL SERVICES AND TREATMENT WITHIN 90 DAYS PRIOR TO SEPARATION	Yes	X N

18. REMARKS
DATA HEREIN SUBJECT TO COMPUTER MATCHING WITHIN DOD OR WITH OTHER AGENCIES FOR VERIFICATION PURPOSES AND DETERMINING ELIGIBILITY OR COMPLIANCE FOR FEDERAL BENEFITS//CONT FROM BLOCK 1 MEDAL//REPUBLIC OF VIETNAM GALLANTRY CROSS UNIT CITATION WITH BRONZE STAR//COMBAT INFANTRYMA BADGE//MASTER PARACHUTIST BADGE//PARACHUTIST BADGE//PATHFINDER BADGE//RANGER TAB//SPECIAL FORCES TAB//NOTHING FOLLOWS

19.a. MAILING ADDRESS AFTER SEPARATION (Include Zip Code)	19.b NEAREST RELATIVE (Name and address - include Zip Code)
350 BUFORD WEST WAY CANTON, GA 10115	DOLORES E. CONLEY 350 BUFORD WEST WAY CANTON, GA 30115

20. MEMBER REQUESTS COPY 6 BE SENT TO (A) OR OR VET. AFFAIRS X Yes No	22. OFFICIAL AUTHORIZED TO SIGN (Typed name, grade, title and signature)
21. SIGNATURE OF MEMBER BEING SEPARATED	HILLARY E. BOYCE, CHIEF, TRANSITION CENTER

SPECIAL ADDITIONAL INFORMATION *(For use by authorized agencies only)*	
23. TYPE OF SEPARATION	24. CHARACTER OF SERVICE(Include upgrades)
RELEASE FROM ACTIVE DUTY	HONORABLE
25. SEPARATION AUTHORITY	26. SEPARATION CODE	27. REENTRY CODE
AR 635-200	MBK	1
28. NARRATIVE REASON FOR SEPARATION		
COMPLETION OF REQUIRED ACTIVE DUTY		
29. DATES OF TIME LOST DURING THIS PERIOD		30. MEMBER REQUESTS COPY 4
NONE		Initials

DD Form 214 AUTOMATED, NOV 88   *Previous editions are obsolete.*   MEMBER - 4

2nd DD-214

THIS IS AN IMPORTANT RECORD
SAFEGUARD IT

1. LAST NAME-FIRST NAME-MIDDLE NAME		2. SEX	3. SOCIAL SECURITY NUMBER		4. DATE OF BIRTH	YEAR	MONTH	DAY
CONLEY, MICHAEL JOSEPH		M	███ ██ ████			48	10	20
5. DEPARTMENT, COMPONENT AND BRANCH OR CLASS			6a. GRADE, RATE OR RANK	6b. PAY GRADE	7. DATE OF RANK	YEAR	MONTH	DAY
U.S. Army National Guard			SGT	E-5		75	08	21

8a. SELECTIVE SERVICE NUMBER	8b. SELECTIVE SERVICE LOCAL BOARD NUMBER, CITY, STATE AND ZIP CODE	8c. HOME OF RECORD AT TIME OF ENTRY INTO ACTIVE SERVICE (Street, RFD, City, County, State and ZIP Code)
INA	LB #47 Bedford, IN	2317 30th St Bedford, IN 47421

9a. TYPE OF SEPARATION	9b. STATION OR INSTALLATION AT WHICH EFFECTED
Released to ARNG State of IN	Fort Benning, Georgia 31905

10. AUTHORITY AND REASON		EFFECTIVE DATE	YEAR	MONTH	DAY
REFRAD			77	01	30

	9c. TYPE OF CERTIFICATE ISSUED	10. REENLISTMENT CODE
	INA	- RA

11. CHARACTER OF SERVICE	12. COMMAND TO WHICH TRANSFERRED
Honorable	

13. LAST DUTY ASSIGNMENT AND MAJOR COMMAND		
2nd Ranger Company TNG	Fifth USA	

14a. TERMINAL DATE OF RESERVE/MSO OBLIGATION	14. PLACE OF ENTRY INTO CURRENT ACTIVE SERVICE (City, State and ZIP Code)	15. DATE ENTERED ACTIVE DUTY THIS PERIOD	YEAR	MONTH	DAY
YEAR MONTH DAY	Fort Leonard Wood, MO 65473		75	01	30

16a. PRIMARY SPECIALTY NUMBER AND TITLE	3. RELATED CIVILIAN OCCUPATION AND D.O.T. NUMBER	19. RECORD OF SERVICE	YEARS	MONTHS	DAYS
11B2V Infantryman NCO 85 (7462)	INA	(a) NET ACTIVE SERVICE THIS PERIOD	02	00	00
		(b) PRIOR ACTIVE SERVICE	03	10	09
16b. SECONDARY SPECIALTY NUMBER AND TITLE	3. RELATED CIVILIAN OCCUPATION AND D.O.T. NUMBER	(c) TOTAL ACTIVE SERVICE (a+b)	05	10	09
		(d) PRIOR INACTIVE SERVICE	05	11	20
INA	INA	(e) TOTAL SERVICE FOR PAY (c+d)	11	09	29
		(f) FOREIGN AND/OR SEA SERVICE THIS PERIOD	00	00	00

18. INDOCHINA OR KOREA SERVICE SINCE AUGUST 5, 1964 ☐ YES ☒ NO

20. HIGHEST EDUCATION LEVEL SUCCESSFULLY COMPLETED (In Years)
SECONDARY/HIGH SCHOOL ___ YRS (1-12 years) COLLEGE ___ YRS

21. TIME LOST (Preceding Two Years)	22. DAYS ACCRUED LEAVE PAID	23. SERVICEMEN'S GROUP LIFE INSURANCE COVERAGE	24. DISABILITY SEVERANCE PAY	25. PERSONNEL SECURITY INVESTIGATION
1 Day	None	$20,000.00 ☐$15,000 ☐$5,000 ☐$10,000 ☐NONE	☒ NO ☐ YES	a. TYPE: INA b. DATE COMPLETED: INA

AMOUNT ☐ NOT AUTHORIZED

26. DECORATIONS, MEDALS, BADGES, COMMENDATIONS, CITATIONS AND CAMPAIGN RIBBONS AWARDED OR AUTHORIZED
NDSM/GCM/VSM VietSvcMdl/AM/PH/VCM w 60 Device/ARCOM/EM/FRCMT Bdg/Ranger Tab/
2 OS Svc Bars/VN CstRef 60

27. REMARKS

28. MAILING ADDRESS AFTER SEPARATION (Street, RFD, City, County, State and ZIP Code)	29. SIGNATURE OF PERSON BEING SEPARATED
2317 30th St Bedford, IN 47421	

30. TYPED NAME, GRADE AND TITLE OF AUTHORIZING OFFICER	31. SIGNATURE OF OFFICER AUTHORIZED TO SIGN
JOHN D. HUSS Army Assistant Adjutant General	

REPORT OF SEPARATION FROM ACTIVE DUTY

1ST DD-214

THIS IS AN IMPORTANT RECORD
SAFEGUARD IT.

CONLEY, MICHAEL JOSEPH		RA 16 946 808				17	MAY	68
ARMY RA ORD		SGT (P)	E-5			20	OCT	48
BEDFORD, INDIANA								
N/A LSO		N/A					N/A	
TRANSFERRED TO USAR (1-16)		FORT BRAGG, NORTH CAROLINA 28307				20	NOV	69
AR 635-200 SPN 201 ETS		HONORABLE				NONE		
CO. A 47TH ENGR BN (CBT ARM) TUSA								
TRANSFERRED TO USAR CON GP (REINF) USAAC, ST. LOUIS, MISSOURI						RE- 1		
						3	21 NOV 66
20 NOV 72	PVT E-1 (P)	AFEES, INDIANAPOLIS, INDIANA			3	0	0
NONE					0	0	0
RURAL ROUTE 1, WILLIAMS, LAWRENCE, INDIANA					3	0	0
63B2P					3	0	0
AUTOREPRMN	N/A		USARPAC		1	0	0

NATIONAL DEFENSE SERVICE MEDAL , VIETNAM SERVICE MEDAL, COMBAT INFANTRYMANS BADGE
PARACHUTE BADGE , BRONZE STAR MEDAL, AIR MEDAL, PURPLE HEART
VIETNAM CAMPAIGN MEDAL W/60 DEVICE, ARMY COMMENDATION MEDAL, SOLDIERS MEDAL

BASIC TRAINING
CODE OF CONDUCT
MILITARY JUSTICE
BASIC AIRBORNE
CBR TRAINING
GENEVA CONVENTION

NON JUDICIAL PUNISHMENT
AUTO REPAIRMAN

NONE	0		☐ YES ☐ NO	$ N/A	N/A
	NONE		☒ $10,000 ☐ $5,000 ☐ NONE		

BLOOD TYPE: O
HIGH SCHOOL (4 YEARS) GENERAL

RURAL ROUTE 1, WILLIAMS,
LAWRENCE, INDIANA

DAVID C. MUELLER 2LT AGC ASST ADJ

ARMED FORCES OF THE UNITED STATES
REPORT OF TRANSFER OR DISCHARGE

National Personnel Record Center
US Decorations and Badges

Silver Stars w (one oak leaf cluster)	2
Soldier Medal (w one oak leaf cluster)	2
Bronze Star w Valor	1
Bronze Star (w oak leaf cluster)	2
Purple Heart	1
Air Medal	1
Meritorious Service Medal (w oak leaf cluster)	2
2 Army Commendation Medal	2
Joint Service Achievement Medal	2
Good Conduct Medal (w two knots)	3
National Defense Service Medal (w 2 bronze stars)	3
Vietnam Service Medal (w 1 silver service star)	2
Global War on Terrorism Service Medal	1
3 Armed Forces Reserve Medal (w M device)	4
NCO Professional Development Ribbon (w 3 affixed)	4
Overseas Service Bar w two stars	3
Army Service Ribbon	1
Republic of Vietnam Campaign (w/Device 1960)	1
Combat Infantry Badge (w 2 stars)	3
Master Parachute Badge	1
Senior Parachute Badge	1

Parachute Badge	1
Jungle Expert Badge	1
Path Finder Badge	1
Special Forces Tab	1
Ranger Tab	1
Presidential Unit Citation on (rt. side)	1
Meritorious Unit Citation on (rt. side)	1
Expert Badge w Auto Rifle and M-60 Machine Gun	2

Total=51 Medals and Badges

Michael J. Conley

CANTON ∎ VETERANS

Man nominated for the U.S. Ranger Hall of Fame

By Michelle Babcock
mbabcock@cherokeetribune.com

After more than 40 years of military service, Canton resident and retired 1st Sgt. Michael Conley said he's honored to be nominated for the U.S. Mountain Ranger Hall of Fame.

Conley, 66, of Canton, joined the U.S. Army when he was 17 years old, in 1966, and retired 42 years later with 41 medals and awards.

"I am so humbled," Conley said. "I was a solider and just tried to do a good job."

In Vietnam in 1967, Conley was said to have pulled a solider from an exploding helicopter, earning him his first Soldier's Medal, according to the nomination letter.

In 1968, he won a Bronze Medal for saving another life during what was called the "Battle on Bloody Ridge."

Later, Conley would travel to the mountains of Afghanistan and Iraq and spent time in one of the most dangerous areas of the Sunni triangle, known as the "Triangle of Death."

Conley retired five years ago, and is now being considered for the 2015 Ranger Hall of Fame induction, he said, which is set to happen around July 2015.

LUCKY TO BE ALIVE

Conley said he was nominated for the U.S. Army Ranger Hall of Fame by a fellow member of the U.S. Mountain Ranger Association, but he just felt lucky to have come home from war alive and with all his limbs.

"I'm humbled that the men I fought with in wars ... these people are the ones that nominated me," he said.

Only two rangers will be inducted next year, Conley explained, and even being nominated was a great honor.

Conley said he just wanted to help people, and that's what he felt like he did by becoming a ranger. He now teaches chemistry at Chattahoochee Technical College, and is glad to be able to keep helping people "down the road of life."

In his teaching career, Conley said he had been named an All Star Coach of the Year and was nominated for a Teacher of the Year award, but neither of those honors impacted him quite like being nominated for the Ranger Hall of Fame.

"This one here was enough to make me look up into the sky one day and thank God that I was blessed to be able to come home alive," he said.

CONTINUED SERVICE

Conley now acts as a service officer for the Canton Veterans of Foreign Wars, continuing his service.

He said helping people is "what it's all about."

To young people who are thinking about following in Conley's footsteps by joining the armed services, he said, "solider, you're going to sacrifice."

"You're going to sacrifice a family. You're going to sacrifice being away from your children. Your country is going to ask you to do things and go places that sometimes you don't really want to go," he said. "You're going to spend a lot of your life away from home in the far reaches of the world where sometimes men and women don't know who you are, much less care who you are. And your closest friends will be the buddies you trained with and fight with."

CPSIA information can be obtained at www.ICGtesting.com
Printed in the USA
LVOW05s1544131214

417948LV00001BA/1/P